Travels
In North America
From Modern Writers

by

William Bingley

Double 9
BOOKS

Travels In North America
From Modern Writers
by William Bingley

Copyright © 2023

All Rights reserved.

ISBN: 978-93-59955-57-5

Published by

DOUBLE 9 BOOKS

2/13-B, Ansari Road
Daryaganj, New Delhi – 110002
info@double9books.com
www.double9books.com
Tel. 011-40042856

This book is under public domain

ABOUT THE AUTHOR

William Bingley was a British creator, naturalist, and clergyman who lived at some stage in the past due 18th and early 19th centuries. He is exceptional known for his extensive travels and natural records writings. One of his excellent works is "Travels in North America,". "Travels in North America" is a detailed travelogue chronicling Bingley's adventure through the United States and Canada throughout the early 19th century. In the book, Bingley gives a complete and insightful account of the landscapes, people, and natural history of North America. His observations embody a wide range of subjects, which includes the indigenous flowers and fauna, geology, weather, and the cultural diversity of the areas he visited. Bingley's paintings reflects his eager hobby in natural history and his fascination with the unexplored and untamed desolate tract of North America. He gives precious descriptions of the natural world and vegetation he encountered, contributing to the wider information of the continent's biodiversity at some point of that era. Additionally, "Travels in North America" is historically sizeable because it gives a window into the early interactions among European tourists and indigenous peoples, capturing the cultural and social landscapes of North America as they were at the start of the 19th century.

CONTENTS

First Day's Instruction

NORTH AMERICA.

This division of the great western continent is more than five thousand miles in length; and, in some latitudes, is four thousand miles wide. It was originally discovered by Europeans, about the conclusion of the fifteenth century; and, a few years afterwards, a party of Spanish adventurers obtained possession of some of the southern districts. The inhabitants of these they treated like wild animals, who had no property in the woods through which they roamed. They expelled them from their habitations, established settlements; and, taking possession of the country in the name of their sovereign, they appropriated to themselves the choicest and most valuable provinces. Numerous other settlements have since been established in different parts of the country; and the native tribes have nearly been exterminated, while the European population and the descendants of Europeans, have so much increased that, in the United States only, there are now more than ten millions of white inhabitants.

The *surface* of the country is extremely varied. A double range of mountains extends through the United States, in a direction, from south-west to north-east; and another range traverses nearly the whole western regions, from north to south. No part of the world is so well watered with rivulets, rivers, and lakes, as this. Some of the *lakes* resemble inland seas. Lake Superior is nearly 300 miles long, and is more than 150 miles wide; and lakes Huron, Michigan, Erie, Ontario, and Champlain, are all of great size. The principal navigable *rivers* of America are the Mississippi, the Ohio, the Missouri, and the Illinois. Of these the *Mississippi* flows from the north, and falls into the Gulf of Mexico. The *Ohio* flows into the Mississippi: it extends in a north-easterly direction, and receives fifteen large streams, all of which are navigable. The *Missouri* and the *Illinois* also flow into the Mississippi: and, by means of these several rivers, a commercial intercourse is effected, from the ocean to vast distances into the interior of the country. Other important rivers are the *Delaware* and the *Hudson*, in the United States, and the *St. Lawrence*, in Canada. The *bays* and harbours of North America are numerous, and many of them are well adapted for the reception and protection of ships. *Hudson's Bay* is of greater extent than the whole Baltic sea. *Delaware Bay* is 60 miles long; and, in some parts, is so wide, that a vessel in the middle of it cannot be seen from either bank. *Chesapeak Bay* extends 270 miles inland. The *Bay of Honduras* is on the south-eastern side of New Spain, and is noted for the trade in logwood and mahogany, which is carried on upon its banks.

The *natural productions* of North America are, in many respects, important. The forests abound in valuable timber-trees; among which are enumerated no fewer than forty-two different species of oaks. Fruit-trees of various kinds are abundant; and, in many places, grapes grow wild: the other vegetable productions are numerous and important. Among the quadrupeds are enumerated some small species of tigers, deer, elks of immense size, bisons, bears, wolves, foxes, beavers, porcupines, and opossums. The American forests abound in birds; and in those of districts that are distant from the settlements of men, wild turkeys, and several species of grouse are very numerous. In some of the forests of Canada, passenger-pigeons breed in myriads; and, during their periodical flight, from one part of the country to another, their numbers darken the air. The coasts, bays, and rivers, abound in fish; and various species of reptiles and serpents are known to inhabit the interior of the southern districts. Among the mountains most of the important metals are found: iron, lead, and copper, are all abundant; and coals are not uncommon.

THE UNITED STATES.

That part of North America which is under the government of the United States, now constitutes one of the most powerful and most enlightened nations in the world. The inhabitants enjoy the advantage of a vast extent of territory, over which the daily increasing population is able, with facility, to expand itself; and much of this territory, though covered with forests, is capable of being cleared, and many parts of it are every day cleared, for the purposes of cultivation.

The origin of the United States may be dated from the time of the formation of an English colony in Virginia, about the year 1606. Other English colonies were subsequently formed; and, during one hundred and fifty years, these gradually increased in strength and prosperity, till, at length, the inhabitants threw off their dependance upon England, and established an independent republican government. This, after a long and expensive war, was acknowledged by Great Britain, in a treaty signed at Paris on the 30th of November, 1782.

The *boundaries* of the States were determined by this treaty; but, some important acquisitions of territory have since been made. In April, 1803,

Louisiana was ceded to them by France; and this district, in its most limited extent, includes a surface of country, which, with the exception of Russia, is equal to the whole of Europe. *Florida*, by its local position, is connected with the United States: it belonged to Spain, but, in the year 1820, it was annexed to the territories of the republic.

Geographical writers have divided the United States into three regions: the *lowlands* or flat country; the highlands, and the mountains. Of these, the first extend from the Atlantic ocean to the falls of the great rivers. The *highlands* reach from the falls to the foot of the mountains; and the *mountains* stretch nearly through the whole country, in a direction from south-west to north-east. Their length is about 900 miles, and their breadth from 60 to 200. They may be considered as separated into two distinct chains; of which the eastern chain has the name of *Blue Mountains,* and the western is known, at its southern extremity, by the name of *Cumberland* and *Gauley Mountains,* and afterwards by that of the *Alleghany Mountains.* The Alleghanies are about 250 miles distant from the shore of the Atlantic. Towards the north there are other eminences, called the *Green Mountains* and the *White Mountains.* The loftiest summits of the whole are said to be about 7000 feet in perpendicular height above the level of the sea.

Few countries can boast a greater general fertility of *soil* than North America. The soil of the higher lands consists, for the most part, of a brown loamy earth, and a yellowish sandy clay. Marine shells, and other substances, in a fossil state, are found at the depth of eighteen or twenty feet below the surface of the ground. Some of these are of very extraordinary description. In the year 1712, several bones and teeth of a vast nondescript quadruped, were dug up at Albany in the state of New York. By the ignorant inhabitants these were considered to be the remains of gigantic human bodies. In 1799 the bones of other individuals of this animal, which has since been denominated the *Mastodon* or *American Mammoth,* were discovered beneath the surface of the ground, in the vicinity of Newburgh, on the river Hudson. Induced by the hope of being able to obtain a perfect skeleton, a Mr. Peale, of Philadelphia, purchased these bones, with the right of digging for others. He was indefatigable in his exertions, but was unable, for some time, to procure any more. He made an attempt in a morass about twelve miles distant from Newburgh, where an entire set of ribs was found, but unaccompanied by any other remains. In another morass, in Ulster county, he found several bones; among the rest a complete under jaw, and upper part of the head. From the whole of the fragments that he obtained, he was enabled to form two skeletons. One of these, under the name of mammoth, was exhibited in London, about a year afterwards. Its height at the shoulder was eleven feet; its whole length was fifteen feet; and its weight about one thousand pounds. This skeleton was furnished with large and curved ivory tusks, different in shape from those of an elephant, but similar in quality. In 1817 another skeleton was dug up, from the depth of only four feet, in the town of *Goshen*, near Chester. The tusks of this were more than nine feet in length.

In a region so extensive as the United States, there must necessarily be a great variety of *climate*. In general, the heat of summer and the cold of winter are more intense, and the transitions, from the one to the other, are more sudden than in the old continent. The predominant winds are from the west; and the severest cold is felt from the north-west. Between the forty-second and forty-fifth degrees of latitude, the same parallel as the south of France, the winters are very severe. During winter, the ice of the rivers is sufficiently strong to bear the passage of horses and waggons; and snow is so abundant, as to admit the use of sledges. In Georgia the winters are mild. South Carolina is subject to immoderate heat, to tremendous hurricanes, and to terrific storms of thunder and lightning.

The United States are usually classed in three divisions: the northern, the middle, and the southern. The *northern states* have the general appellation of *New England*: they are Massachusetts, New Hampshire, Vermont, Connecticut, and Rhode Island. The *middle states* are New York, New Jersey, Delaware, Pennsylvania, Ohio, and Indiana. The *southern states* are Maryland, Virginia, Kentucky, North Carolina, South Carolina, Tenessee, and Louisiana.

Besides these, the United States claim the government of the *territories* of the Illinois, Alabama, and Mississippi. By a public ordinance, passed in the year 1787, a territory cannot be admitted into the American Union, until its population amounts to 60,000 free inhabitants. In the mean time, however, it is subject to a regular provisional form of government. The administration of this is entrusted to a governor, who is appointed by the president and congress of the United States; and who is invested with extensive powers, for protection of the interests of the States, and the observance of a strict faith towards the Indians, in the exchange of commodities, and the purchase of lands.

The *government* of the United States is denominated a "Federal Republic." Each state has a constitution for the management of its own internal affairs; and, by the federal constitution, they are all formed into one united body. The legislative power is vested in a *congress* of delegates from the several states; this congress is divided into two distinct bodies, the *senate* and the *house of representatives*. The members of the latter are elected every two years, by the people; and the senators are elected every six years, by the state legislatures. A senator must be thirty years of age, an inhabitant of the state in which he is elected, and must have been nine years a citizen of the United States: the present number of senators is thirty-eight. The executive power is vested in a *president*, who is chosen every four years. In the election both of members of congress, and of the president of the United States, it is asserted, that there is much manœuvering, and much corrupt influence exerted. In the electioneering addresses of the defeated parties, these are, perhaps, as often made a subject of complaint and reproach, as they are in those of defeated candidates for the representation of counties or boroughs in the British House of Commons.

Washington is the seat of government; and the president, when there, lives in a house destined for his use, and furnished at the expense of the nation. His annual salary is 25,000 dollars, about £.5600 sterling. The president, in virtue of his office, is commander-in-chief of the army and navy of the United States, and also of the militia, whenever it is called into actual service. He is empowered to make treaties, to appoint ambassadors, ministers, consuls, judges of the supreme court, and all military and other officers whose appointments are not otherwise provided for by the law.

The *national council* is composed of the President and Vice President; and the heads of the treasury, war, navy, and post-office establishment.

The *inhabitants* of the United States (says Mr. Warden [1]) have not that uniform character which belongs to ancient nations, upon whom, time and the stability of institutions, have imprinted a particular and individual character. The general physiognomy is as varied as its origin is different. English, Irish, Germans, Scotch, French, and Swiss, all retain some characteristic of their ancient country.

The account given by Mr. Birkbeck is somewhat different from this. He asserts that, as far as he had an opportunity of judging, the native inhabitants of the towns are much alike; nine out of ten (he says) are tall and long limbed, approaching or even exceeding six feet. They are seen in pantaloons and Wellington boots; either marching up and down, with their hands in their pockets, or seated in chairs poised on the hind feet, and the backs rested against the walls. If a hundred Americans, of any class, were to seat themselves, ninety-nine (observes this gentleman) would shuffle their chairs to the true distance, and then throw themselves back against the nearest prop. The women exhibit a great similarity of tall, relaxed forms, with consistent dress and demeanour; and are not remarkable for sprightliness of manners. Intellectual culture has not yet made much progress among the generality of either sex; but the men, from their habit of travelling, and their consequent intercourse with strangers, have greatly the advantage, in the means of acquiring information. Mr. Birkbeck says that, in every village and town, as he passed along, he observed groups of young able-bodied men, who seemed to be as perfectly at leisure as the loungers of Europe. This love of indolence, where labour is so profitable, is a strange affection. If these people be asked why they so much indulge in it, they answer, that "they live in freedom; and need not work, like the English."

In the interior of the United States, and in the back settlements, *land* may be purchased, both of individuals and of the government, at very low rates. The price of uncleared land, or of land covered with trees, and not yet in a state fit for cultivation, is, in many instances, as low as two dollars an acre. The public lands are divided into townships of six miles square; each of which is subdivided into thirty-six sections, of one mile square, or 640 acres; and these are usually offered for sale, in quarter sections, of 160 acres. The purchase money may be paid by four equal instalments; the first within forty days, and the others within two, three, and four years after the completion of the purchase.

Mr. Birkbeck thus describes the mode in which *towns are formed* in America. On any spot, (says he,) where a few settlers cluster together, attracted by ancient neighbourhood, or by the goodness of the soil, or vicinity to a mill, or by whatever other cause, some enterprising proprietor perhaps finds, in his section, what he deems a good site for a town: he has it surveyed, and laid out in lots, which he sells, or offers to sale by auction. When these are disposed of, the new town assumes the name of its founder: a store-keeper builds a little framed store, and sends for a few cases of goods; and then a tavern starts up, which becomes the residence of a doctor and a lawyer, and the boarding house of the store-keeper, as well as the resort of the traveller. Soon follow a blacksmith, and other handicraftsmen, in useful succession. A school-master, who is also the minister of religion, becomes an important acquisition to this rising community. Thus the town proceeds, if it proceed at all, with accumulating force, until it becomes the metropolis of the neighbourhood. Hundreds of these speculations may have failed, but hundreds prosper; and thus trade begins and thrives, as population increases around favourite spots. The town being established, a cluster of inhabitants, however small it may be, acts as a stimulus on the cultivation of the neighbourhood: redundancy of supply is the consequence, and this demands a vent. Water-mills rise on the nearest navigable streams, and thus an effectual and constant market is secured for the increasing surplus of produce. Such are the elements of that accumulating mass of commerce which may, hereafter, render this one of the most important and most powerful countries in the world.

Though the Americans boast of the freedom which they personally enjoy, they, most inconsistently, allow the importation and employment of *slaves*; and, with such unjust detestation are these unhappy beings treated, that a negro is not permitted to eat at the same table, nor even to frequent the same place of worship, as a white person. The white *servants*, on the contrary, esteem themselves on an equality with their masters. They style themselves "helps," and will not suffer themselves to be called "servants." When they speak to their masters or mistresses, they either call them by their names; or they substitute the term "boss," for that of master. All this, however, is a difference merely of words; for the Americans exhibit no greater degree of feeling, nor are they at all more considerate in their conduct towards this class of society, than the inhabitants of other nations. Indeed the contrary is very often the case. Most persons, in America, engage their servants by the week, and no enquiry is ever made relative to character, as is customary with us.

The *constitution* of the United States guarantees freedom of speech and liberty of the press. By law all the inhabitants are esteemed equal. The chief military strength of the country is in the militia; and, whenever this is embodied, every male inhabitant beyond a certain age, is compellable either to bear arms, or to pay an equivalent to be excused from this service. Trial by jury is to be preserved inviolate. A republican form of government is guaranteed to all the states, and hereditary titles and distinctions are prohibited by the law. With regard to religion, it is stipulated that no law shall ever be passed to establish any particular form of religion, or to prevent the free exercise of it; and, in the United States, no religious test is required as a qualification to any office of public trust.

In *commerce* and *navigation* the progress of the States has been rapid beyond example. Besides the natural advantages of excellent harbours, extensive inland bays, and navigable rivers, the Americans assert that their trade is not fettered by monopolies, nor by exclusive privileges of any description. Goods or merchandise circulate through the whole country free of duty; and a full drawback, or restitution of the duties of importation, is granted upon articles exported to a foreign port, in the course of the year in which they have been imported. Commerce is here considered a highly honourable employment; and, in the sea-port towns, all the wealthiest members of the community are merchants. Nearly all the materials for manufactures are produced in this country. Fuel is inexhaustible; and the high wages of the manufacturers, and the want of an extensive capital, alone prevent the Americans from rivalling the English in trade. The produce of cultivation in America is of almost every variety that can be named: wheat, maize, rye, oats, barley, rice, and other grain; apples, pears, cherries, peaches, grapes, currants, gooseberries, plums, and other fruit, and a vast variety of vegetables. Lemons, oranges, and tropical fruits are raised in the southern States. Hops, flax, and hemp are abundant. Tobacco is an article of extensive cultivation in Virginia, Maryland, and some other districts. Cotton and sugar are staple commodities in several of the states. The northern and eastern states are well adapted for grazing, and furnish a great number of valuable horses, and of cattle and sheep; and an abundance of butter and cheese.

It will be possible to describe nearly all the most important places within the limits of the United States, by reciting, in succession, the narratives of different travellers through this interesting country. In so doing, however, it may perhaps be found requisite, in a few instances, to separate the parts of their narrations, for the purpose of more methodical illustration; but this alteration of arrangement will not often occur.

FOOTNOTES:

[1] Statistical, political, and historical account of the United States.

Second Day's Instruction

UNITED STATES CONTINUED.

An account of New York and its vicinity. From Sketches of America by Henry Bradshaw Fearon.

Mr. Fearon was deputed by several friends in England, to visit the United States, for the purpose of obtaining information, by which they should regulate their conduct, in emigrating from their native country, to settle in America. He arrived in the bay of New York, about the beginning of August, 1817.

Here every object was interesting to him. The pilot brought on board the ship the newspapers of the morning. In these, many of the advertisements had, to Mr. Fearon, the character of singularity. One of them, announcing a play, terminated thus: "gentlemen are informed that no smoking is allowed in the theatre." Several sailing boats passed, with respectable persons in them, many of whom wore enormously large straw hats, turned up behind. At one o'clock, the vessel was anchored close to the city; and a great number of persons were collected on the wharf to witness her arrival. Many of these belonged to the labouring class; others were of the mercantile and genteeler orders. Large straw hats prevailed, and trowsers were universal. The general costume of these persons was inferior to that of men in the same rank of life in England: their whole appearance was loose, slovenly, careless, and not remarkable for cleanliness. The wholesale stores, which front the river, had not the most attractive appearance imaginable. The carts were long and narrow, and each was drawn by one horse. The hackney-coaches were open at the sides, an arrangement well suited to this warm climate; and the charge was about one fourth higher than in London.

This city, when approached from the sea, presents an appearance that is truly beautiful. It stands at the extreme point of Manhattan, or York island, which is thirteen miles long, and from one to two miles wide; and the houses are built from shore to shore. Vessels of any burden can come close up to the town, and lie there in perfect safety, in a natural harbour formed by the *East* and *Hudson's rivers*. New York contains 120,000 inhabitants, and is, indisputably, the most important commercial city in America.

The *streets* through which Mr. Fearon passed, to a boarding-house in State-street, were narrow and dirty. The *Battery*, however, is a delightful walk, at the edge of the bay; and several of the houses in State-street are as large as those in Bridge-street, Blackfriars, London. At the house in which Mr. Fearon resided, the hours of eating were, breakfast, eight o'clock; dinner half-past three, tea seven, and supper ten; and the whole expence of living amounted to about eighteen dollars per week.

The *street population* of New York has an aspect very different from that of London, or the large towns in England. One striking feature of it is formed by the number of blacks, many of whom are finely dressed: the females are ludicrously so, generally in white muslin, with artificial flowers and pink shoes. Mr. Fearon saw very few well-dressed white ladies; but this was a time of the year when most of them were absent at the springs of Balston and Saratoga, places of fashionable resort, about 200 miles from New York.

All the native inhabitants of this city have sallow complexions. To have colour in the cheeks is here considered a criterion by which a person is known to be an Englishman. The young men are tall, thin, and solemn: they all wear trowsers, and most of them walk about in loose great coats.

There are, in New York, many *hotels*; some of which are on an extensive scale. The City Hotel is as large as the London Tavern. The dining-room and some of the private apartments seem to have been fitted up regardless of expense. The *shops*, or stores, as they are here called, have nothing in their exterior to recommend them to notice: there is not even an attempt at tasteful display. In this city the linen and woollen-drapers expose great quantities of their goods, loose on boxes, in the street, without any precaution against theft. This practice, a proof of their carelessness, is at the same time an evidence as to the political state of society which is worthy of attention. Great masses of the population cannot be unemployed, or robbery would be inevitable.

There are, in New York, many excellent private dwellings, built of red painted brick, which gives them a peculiarly neat and clean appearance. In Broadway and Wall-street, trees are planted along the side of the pavement. The City Hall is a large and elegant building, in which the courts of law are held. Most of the *streets* are dirty: in many of them sawyers prepare their wood for sale, and all are infested with pigs.

On the whole, a walk through New York will disappoint an Englishman: there is an apparent carelessness, a laziness, an unsocial indifference, which freezes the blood and disgusts the judgment. An evening stroll along Broadway, when the lamps are lighted, will please more than one at noonday. The shops will look rather better, but the manners of the proprietors will not greatly please an Englishman: their cold indifference may be mistaken, by themselves, for independence, but no person of thought and observation will ever concede to them that they have selected a wise mode of exhibiting that dignified feeling.

[There is, in New York, a seminary for education, called *Columbia College*. This institution was originally named "King's College," and was founded in the year 1754. Its annual revenue is about 4000 dollars. A botanic garden, situated about four miles from the city, was, not long ago, purchased by the state, of Dr. Hosach, for 73,000 dollars, and given to the college. The faculty of medicine, belonging to this institution, has been incorporated under the title of "The College of Physicians and Surgeons of the University of New York."]

The *Town Hall* of this city is a noble building, of white marble; and the space around it is planted and railed off. The interior appears to be well arranged. In the rooms of the mayor and corporation, are portraits of several governors of this state, and of some distinguished officers. The state rooms and courts of justice are on the first floor. In the immediate vicinity of the hall is an extensive building, appropriated to the "New York Institution," the "Academy of fine Arts," and the "American Museum." There are also a state prison, an hospital, and many splendid churches.

When a traveller surveys this city, and recollects that, but two centuries since, the spot on which it stands was a wilderness, he cannot but be surprised at its present comparative extent and opulence.

With regard to *trades* in New York, Mr. Fearon remarks that building appeared to be carried on to a considerable extent, and was generally performed by contract. There were many timber, or lumber-yards, (as they are here called,) but not on the same large and compact scale as in England. Cabinet-work was neatly executed, and at a reasonable price. Chair-making was an extensive business. Professional men, he says, literally swarm in the United States; and lawyers are as common in New York as paupers are in England. A gentleman, walking in the Broadway, seeing a friend pass, called out to him, "Doctor!" and immediately sixteen persons turned round, to answer the call. It is estimated that there are, in New York, no fewer than 1500 spirit shops, yet the Americans have not the character of being drunkards. There are several large carvers' and gilders' shops; and glass-mirrors and picture-frames are executed with taste and elegance. Plate-glass is imported from France, Holland, and England. Booksellers' shops are extensive; but English novels and poetry are the primary articles of a bookseller's business. Many of the popular English books are here reprinted, but in a smaller size, and on worse paper than the original. There are, in this city, a few boarding-schools for ladies; but, in general, males and females, of all ages, are educated at the same establishment. No species of correction is allowed. Children, even at home, are perfectly independent; subordination being foreign to the comprehension of all persons in the United States.

The *rents of houses* are here extremely high. Very small houses, in situations not convenient for business, and containing, in the whole, only six rooms, are worth from £.75 to £.80 per annum; and for similar houses, in first-rate situations, the rents as high as from £.160 to £.200 are paid. Houses like those in Oxford-street and the best part of Holborn, are let for £.500 or £.600 pounds per annum.

Provisions are somewhat cheaper than in London; but most of the articles of clothing are dear, being chiefly of British manufacture. With regard to *religion* in the United States, there is legally the most unlimited liberty. There is no established religion; but the professors of the presbyterian and the episcopalian, or church of England tenets, take the precedence, both in numbers and respectability. Their ministers receive each from two to eight thousand dollars per annum. All the churches are said to be well filled. The episcopalians, though they do not form any part of the state, have their bishops and other orders, as in England.

Mr. Fearon remarks, generally, respecting the United States, that every industrious man may obtain a living; but that America is not the political elysium which it has been so floridly described, and which the imaginations of many have fondly anticipated.

In the *courts of law* there appears to be a perfect equality between the judge, the counsel, the jury, the tipstaff, and the auditors; and Mr. Fearon was informed that great corruption exists in the minor courts.

New York is called a "free state;" and it may perhaps be so termed theoretically, or in comparison with its southern neighbours; but, even here, there are multitudes of negroes in a state of slavery, and who are bought and sold as cattle would be in England. And so degrading do the white inhabitants consider it, to associate with blacks, that the latter are absolutely excluded from all places of public worship, which the whites attend. Even the most degraded white person will neither eat nor walk with a negro.

Long Island is a part of the state of New York, one hundred and twenty miles in length, and twelve in breadth. It is chiefly occupied by farmers; and is divided into two counties.

Mr. Fearon made several excursions into the state of *New Jersey*, situated opposite to that of New York, and on the southern side of the river *Hudson*. The valleys abound in black oaks, ash, palms, and poplar trees.

Oak and hickory-nut trees grow in situations which are overflowed. The soil is not considered prolific. *Newark* is a manufacturing town, in this province, of considerable importance, and delightfully situated. It contains many excellent houses, and a population of about eight thousand persons, including slaves. Carriages and chairs are here made in great numbers, chiefly for sale in the southern markets.

For the purpose of visiting the property of a gentleman who resided in the vicinity of *Fishkill*, a creek somewhat more than sixty miles from New York, Mr. Fearon took his passage in a steam-boat. He paid for his fare three dollars and a half, and the voyage occupied somewhat more than eight hours. The vessel was of the most splendid description. It contained one hundred and sixty beds; and the ladies had a distinct cabin. On the deck were numerous conveniences, such as baggage-rooms, smoking-rooms, &c. The general occupation, during the voyage, was card-playing. In the houses of two gentlemen whom Mr. Fearon visited near Fishkill, he was much gratified by the style of living, the substantial elegance of the furniture, and the mental talents of the company. Here he found both comfort and cleanliness, requisites which are scarcely known in America.

In a general summary of his opinion respecting persons desirous of emigrating from England to America, Mr. Fearon says, that the capitalist may obtain, for his money, seven per cent. with good security. The lawyer and the doctor will not succeed. An orthodox minister would do so. The proficient in the fine arts will find little encouragement. The literary man must starve. The tutor's posts are all occupied. The shopkeeper may do as well, but not better than in London, unless he be a man of superior talent, and have a large capital: for such requisites there is a fine opening. The farmer must labour hard, and be but scantily remunerated. The clerk and shopman will get but little more than their board and lodging. Mechanics, whose trades are of the *first necessity*, will do well: but men who are not mechanics, and who understand only the cotton, linen, woollen, glass, earthenware, silk, or stocking manufactories, cannot obtain employment. The labouring man will do well; particularly if he have a wife and children who are capable of contributing, not merely to the consuming, but also to the earning of the common stock.

Narrative of Mr. Fearon's *Journey from New York to Boston.*

ON the 8th of September this gentleman left New York for Boston. After a passage of twelve hours, the vessel in which he sailed arrived at *New Haven*, a city in Connecticut, distant from New York, by water, about ninety miles. This place has a population of about five thousand persons, and has the reputation of ranking among the most beautiful towns in the United

States. [It is situated at the head of a bay, between two rivers, and contains about five hundred houses, which are chiefly built of wood, but on a regular plan: it has also several public edifices, and about four thousand inhabitants. The harbour is spacious, well protected, and has good anchorage. There is at New Haven a college, superintended by a president, a professor in divinity, and three tutors.]

From this place Mr. Fearon proceeded to *New London*, a small town on the west side of the river Thames. Here he took a place in the coach for Providence. American stages are a species of vehicles with which none in England can be compared. They carry twelve passengers: none outside. The coachman, or driver, sits inside with the company. In length they are nearly equal to two English stages. Few of them go on springs. The sides are open; the roof being supported by six small posts. The luggage is carried behind, and in the inside. The seats are pieces of plain board; and there are leathers which can be let down from the top, and which, though useful as a protection against wet, are of little service in cold weather.

The passengers breakfasted at *Norwich*, a manufacturing and trading town, about fourteen miles from New London; and, at six o'clock in the evening, they arrived at *New Providence*, the capital of Rhode Island, having occupied thirteen hours in travelling only fifty miles. In the general appearance of the country, Mr. Fearon had been somewhat disappointed. All the houses within sight from the road were farm-houses. He remarks that, in Connecticut and Rhode Island, the land was stony, and the price of produce was not commensurate to that of labour.

On entering Providence, Mr. Fearon was much pleased with the beauty of the place. In appearance, it combined the attractions of Southampton and Doncaster, in England. There are, in this town, an excellent market-house, a workhouse, four or five public schools, an university with a tolerable library, and an hospital. Several of the churches are handsome, but they, as well as many private houses, are built of wood painted white, and have green Venetian shutters. Mr. Fearon had not seen a town either in America or Europe which bore the appearance of general prosperity, equal to Providence. Ship and house-builders were fully occupied, as indeed were all classes of mechanics. The residents of this place are chiefly native Americans; for foreign emigrants seem never to think of New England. Rent and provisions are here much lower than in New York.

At *Pawtucket*, four miles from Providence, are thirteen cotton manufactories; six of which are on a large scale. Mr. Fearon visited three of them. They had excellent machinery; but not more than one half of this was in operation, and the persons employed in all the manufactories combined, were not equal in number to those at one of moderate size in Lancashire.

The road from Providence to Boston is much better than that which Mr. Fearon had already passed from New London. The aspect of the country also was improved; but there was nothing in either, as to mere appearance, which would be inviting to an inhabitant of England.

From its irregularity, and from other circumstances, *Boston* is much more like an English town than New York. The names are English, and the inhabitants are by no means so uniformly sallow, as they are in many other parts of America. This town is considered the head quarters of Federalism in politics, and of Unitarianism in religion. It contains many rich families. The Bostonians are also the most enlightened, and the most hospitable people whom Mr. Fearon had yet seen in America: they, however, in common with all New Englanders, have the character of being greater sharpers, and more generally dishonourable, than the natives of other sections of the Union.

The *Athæneum public library*, under the management of Mr. Shaw, is a valuable establishment. It contained, at this time, 18,000 volumes, four thousand of which were the property of the secretary of state.

The society in Boston is considered better than that in New York. Many of the richer families live in great splendour, and in houses little inferior to those of Russell-square, London. Distinctions here exist to an extent rather ludicrous under a free and popular government: there are the first class, second class, third class, and the "old families." Titles, too, are diffusely distributed.

Boston is not a thriving, that is, not an increasing town. It wants a fertile back country; and it is too far removed from the western states to have much trade.

On an eminence, in the Mall, (a fine public walk,) is built the *State House,* in which the legislature holds its meetings. The view from the top of this building is peculiarly fine. The islands, the shipping, the town, the hill and dale scenery, for a distance of thirty miles, present an assemblage of objects which are beautifully picturesque. Boston was the birth-place of Dr. Franklin, and in this town the first dawnings of the American revolution broke forth. The heights of Dorchester and Bunker's Hill are in its immediate vicinity.

On the 20th of September Mr. Fearon walked to *Bunker's Hill.* It is of moderate height. The monument, placed here in commemoration of the victory obtained by the English over the Americans, on the 17th of June, 1776, is of brick and wood, and without inscription.

[At *Cambridge*, four miles from Boston, is a college, called *Harvard College*, in honour of the Rev. John Harvard of Charleston, who left to it his library, and a considerable sum of money. This college is upon a scale so large and liberal, as to consist of seven spacious buildings, and to contain two hundred and fifty apartments for officers and students. It has an excellent library of about 17,000 volumes, a philosophical apparatus, and a museum of natural history. The average number of students is about two hundred and sixty. Admission into this college requires a previous knowledge of mathematics, Latin, and Greek. All the students have equal rights; and each class has peculiar instructors. Degrees are here conferred, as in the English universities; and the period of study requisite for the degree of bachelor of arts is four years. The professorships are numerous. Harvard College furnishes instructors and teachers to the most distant parts of the union; and, in general, for the extent of its funds, the richness of its library, the number and character of its establishments, and the means it affords of acquiring, not only an academical, but a professional education, it is considered to be without an equal in the country. It is, however, remarked, that this college is somewhat heretical in matters of religion; as most of the theological students leave it disaffected towards the doctrine of the Trinity.]

From this place we must return to New York, for the purpose of accompanying Mr. Weld on a voyage up the river Hudson to Lake Champlain.

Third Day's Instruction

UNITED STATES, and PART OF CANADA.

Narrative of a Voyage up the River Hudson, from New York to Lake Champlain.
By Isaac Weld, Esq.

Mr. Weld, having taken his passage in one of the sloops which trade on the North or Hudson's river, betwixt New York and Albany, embarked on the second of July. Scarcely a breath of air was stirring, and the tide carried the vessel along at the rate of about two miles and a half an hour. The prospects that were presented to his view, in passing up this magnificent stream, were peculiarly grand and beautiful. In some places the river expands to the breadth of five or six miles, in others it narrows to that of a few hundred yards; and, in various parts, it is interspersed with islands. From several points of view its course can be traced to a great distance up the Hudson, whilst in others it is suddenly lost to the sight, as it winds between its lofty banks. Here mountains, covered with rocks and trees, rise almost perpendicularly out of the water; there a fine champaign country presents itself, cultivated to the very margin of the river, whilst neat farm-houses and distant towns embellish the charming landscapes.

After sunset a brisk wind sprang up, which carried the vessel at the rate of six or seven miles an hour for a considerable part of the night; but for some hours it was requisite for her to lie at anchor, in a place where the navigation of the river was intricate.

Early the next morning the voyagers found themselves opposite to *West Point*, a place rendered remarkable in the history of the American war, by the desertion of General Arnold, and the consequent death of the unfortunate Major André. The fort stands about one hundred and fifty feet above the level of the water, and on the side of a barren hill. It had, at this time, a most melancholy aspect. Near West Point the Highlands, as they are called, commence, and extend along the river, on each side, for several miles.

About four o'clock in the morning of the 4th of July, the vessel reached *Albany*, the place of its destination, one hundred and sixty miles distant from New York. Albany is a city which, at this time, contained about eleven hundred houses; and the number was fast increasing. In the old part of the town, the streets were very narrow, and the houses bad. The latter were all in the old Dutch taste, with the gable ends towards the street, and ornamented at the top with large iron weather-cocks; but in that part of the town which had been lately erected, the streets were commodious, and many of the houses were handsome. Great pains had been taken to have the streets well paved and lighted. In summer time Albany is a disagreeable place; for it stands in a low situation on the margin of the river, which here runs very slowly, and which, towards the evening, often exhales clouds of vapour.

[In 1817, Albany is described, by Mr. Hall, to have had a gay and thriving appearance, and nothing Dutch about it, except the names of some of its inhabitants. Being the seat of government for New York, it has a parliament-house, dignified with the name of Capitol. This stands upon an eminence, and has a lofty columnar porch; but, as the building is small, it seems to be all porch. There is a miserable little museum here, which contains a group of waxen figures brought from France, representing the execution of Louis the Sixteenth. Albany is now a place of considerable trade; and, if a canal be completed betwixt this town and Lake Erie, it will become a town of great importance.]

The 4th of July, the day of Mr. Weld's arrival at Albany, was the anniversary of the declaration of American independence. About noon a drum and trumpet gave notice that the rejoicings would immediately commence; and, on walking to a hill, about a quarter of a mile from the town, Mr. Weld saw sixty men drawn up, partly militia, partly volunteers, partly infantry, partly cavalry. The last were clothed in scarlet, and were mounted on horses of various descriptions. About three hundred spectators attended. A few rounds from a three-pounder were fired, and some volleys of small-arms. When the firing ceased, the troops returned to the town, a party of militia officers, in uniform, marching in the rear, under the shade of umbrellas, as the day was excessively hot. Having reached the town, the whole body dispersed. The volunteers and militia officers afterwards dined together, and thus ended the rejoicings of the day.

Mr. Weld remained in Albany for a few days, and then set off for Skenesborough, upon Lake Champlain, in a carriage hired for the purpose. In about two hours he arrived at the small village of *Cohoz*, close to which is a remarkable cataract in the *Mohawk River*. This river takes its rise to the north-east of Lake Oneida, and, after a course of one hundred and forty miles, joins the Hudson about ten miles above Albany. The *Cohoz fall* is about three miles from the mouth of this river, and at a place where its width is about three hundred yards: a ledge of rocks extends quite across the stream, and from the top of these the water falls about fifty feet perpendicular: the line of the fall, from one side of the river to the other, is nearly straight. The appearance of this cataract varies much, according to the quantity of water: when the river is full, the water descends in an unbroken sheet from one bank to the other; but, at other times, the greater part of the rocks is left uncovered.

From this place Mr. Weld proceeded along the banks of the *Hudson River*, and, late in the evening, reached *Saratoga*, thirty-five miles from Albany. This place contained about forty houses; but they were so scattered, that it had not the least appearance of a town.

Near Saratoga, on the borders of a marsh, are several remarkable mineral springs: one of these, in the crater of a rock, of pyramidical form, and about five feet in height, is particularly curious. This rock seems to have been formed by the petrifaction of the water; and all the other springs are surrounded by similar petrifactions.

Of the works thrown up at Saratoga, during the war, by the British and American armies, there were now scarcely any remains. The country around was well cultivated, and most of the trenches had been levelled by the plough. Mr. Weld here crossed the Hudson River, and proceeded, for some distance, along its eastern shore. After this the road was most wretched, particularly over a long causeway, which had been formed originally for the transporting of cannon. This causeway consisted of large, trees laid side by side. Some of them being decayed, great intervals were left, in which the wheels of the carriage were sometimes locked so fast, that the horses alone could not possibly extricate them. The woods on each side of the road had a much more majestic appearance than any that Mr. Weld had seen since he had left Philadelphia. This, however, was owing more to the great height than to the thickness of the trees, for he could not see one that appeared more than thirty inches in diameter. The trees here were chiefly oaks, hiccory, hemlock, and beech; intermixed with which appeared great numbers of smooth-barked, or Weymouth pines. A profusion of wild raspberries were growing in the woods.

After having experienced almost inconceivable difficulty, in consequence of the badness of the road; and having occupied five hours in travelling only twelve miles, Mr. Weld arrived at *Skenesborough*. This is a little town, which stands near the southern extremity of Lake Champlain. It consisted, at this time, of only twelve houses, and was dreadfully infested with musquitoes, a large kind of gnats, which abound in the swampy parts of all hot countries. Such myriads of these insects attacked Mr. Weld, the first night of his sleeping there, that, when he rose in the morning, his face and hands were covered with large pustules, like those of a person in the small-pox. The situation of Skenesborough, on the margin of a piece of water which is almost stagnant, and which is shaded by thick woods, is peculiarly favourable to the increase of these insects.

Shortly after their arrival in Skenesborough, Mr. Weld, and two gentlemen by whom he was accompanied, hired a boat of about ten tons burden, for the purpose of crossing *Lake Champlain*. The vessel sailed at one o'clock in the day; but, as the channel was narrow, and the wind adverse, they were only able to proceed about six miles before sunset. Having brought the vessel to an anchor, the party landed and walked to some adjacent farm-houses, in the hope of obtaining provisions; but they were not able to procure any thing except milk and cheese. The next day they reached *Ticonderoga*. Here the only dwelling was a tavern, a large house built of stone. On entering it, the party was shown into a spacious apartment, crowded with boatmen and other persons, who had just arrived from St. John's in Canada. The man of the house was a judge; a sullen, demure old gentleman, who sate by the fire, with tattered clothes and dishevelled locks, reading a book, and was totally regardless of every person in the house.

The old fort and barracks of Ticonderoga, are on the top of a rising ground, just behind the tavern: they were at this time in ruins, and it is not likely that they ever will be rebuilt; for the situation is a very insecure one, being commanded by a lofty hill, called Mount Defiance. During the great American war, the British troops obtained possession of this place, by dragging cannon and mortars up the hill, and firing down upon the fort.

Mr. Weld and his friends, on leaving Ticonderoga, pursued their voyage to *Crown Point*: Here they landed to inspect the old fort. Nothing, however, was to be seen but a heap of ruins; for, shortly before it was surrendered by the British troops, the powder-magazine blew up, and a great part of the works was destroyed; and, since the final evacuation of the place, the people of the neighbourhood have been continually digging in different parts, in the hope of procuring lead and iron shot. At the south side only the ditches remain perfect: they are wide and deep, and are cut through immense rocks of limestone; and, from being overgrown, towards the top, with different kinds of shrubs, they have a grand and picturesque appearance.

While the party were here, they were agreeably surprised with the sight of a large birch-canoe, upon the lake, navigated by two or three Indians, in the dresses of their nation. These made for the shore, and soon landed; and, shortly afterwards, another party arrived, that had come by land.

Lake Champlain is about one hundred and twenty miles in length, and is of various breadths: for the first thirty miles it is, in no place, more than two miles wide; beyond this, for the distance of twelve miles, it is five or six miles across; but it afterwards narrows, and again, at the end of a few miles, expands. That part called the *Broad Lake*, because broader than any other, is eighteen miles across. Here the lake is interspersed with a great number of islands. The soundings of Lake Champlain are, in general, very deep; in many places they are sixty and seventy, and in some even one hundred fathoms in depth.

The scenery, along the shores of the lake, is extremely grand and picturesque; particularly beyond Crown Point. Here they are beautifully ornamented with hanging woods and rocks; and the mountains, on the western side, rise in ranges one behind another, in the most magnificent manner possible.

Crossing from the head of Lake Champlain, westward to the river St. Lawrence, we shall describe the places adjacent to that river, and some of the north-western parts of the state of New York, in

A Narrative of Lieutenant Hall's *Journey from*
Canada to the Cataract of Niagara.

Mr. Hall had travelled from Montreal, in Canada, to Prescott, in a stage-waggon, which carried the mail; and he says that he can answer for its being one of the roughest conveyances on either side of the Atlantic.

The face of the country is invariably flat; and settlements have not, hitherto, spread far from the banks of the *St. Lawrence*.

Prescott is remarkable for nothing but a square redoubt, or fort, called Fort Wellington. The accommodations at this place were so bad that Mr. Hall, at midnight, seated himself in a light waggon, in which two gentlemen were proceeding to Brockville. These gentlemen afterwards offered him a passage to Kingston, in a boat belonging to the British navy, which was waiting for them at *Brockville*.

The banks of the river St. Lawrence, from the neighbourhood of Brockville, are of limestone, and from twenty to fifty feet in height. Immense masses of reddish granite are also scattered along the bed of the stream, and sometimes project from the shore. The numerous islands which crowd the approach to *Lake Ontario*, have all a granite basis: they are clothed with cedar and pine-trees, and with an abundance of raspberry plants. The bed of the *Gananoqua* is also of granite. This river is rising into importance, from the circumstance of a new settlement being formed, under the auspices of the British government, on the waters with which it communicates.

This settlement lies at the head of the lakes of the *Rideau*, and, in case of another American war, is meant to secure a communication betwixt Montreal and Kingston, by way of the Utawa. The settlers are chiefly disbanded soldiers, who clear and cultivate the land, under the superintendance of officers of the quarter-master-general's department. A canal has been cut to avoid the falls of the Rideau; and the communication, either by the Gananoqua, or Kingston, will be improved by locks. *Kingston*, which is within the Canadian dominions, is admirably situated for naval purposes.

The basis of the soil on which this town is situated is limestone, disposed in horizontal strata. Kingston contains some good houses and stores; a small theatre, built by the military, for private theatricals; a large wooden government house, and all the appendages of an extensive military and naval establishment; with as much society as can reasonably be expected, in a town but lately created from the "howling desert." The adjacent country is flat, stony, and barren. Mr. Hall says that fleets of ships occasionally lie off Kingston, several of which are as large as any on the ocean. Vessels of large dimensions were at this time building, on the spot where, a few months before, their frame-timbers had been growing.

Mr. Hall left Kingston, in a packet, for the American station of *Sackett's harbour*. This, after Kingston, has a mean appearance: its situation is low, its harbour is small, and its fortifications are of very different construction, both as to form and materials, from those of the former town. The navy-yard consists merely of a narrow tongue of land, the point of which affords just space sufficient for the construction of one first-rate vessel; with room for work-shops, and stores, on the remaining part of it. One of the largest vessels in the world, was at this time on the stocks. The town consists of a long street, in the direction of the river, with a few smaller streets crossing it at right angles: it covers less ground than Kingston, and has fewer good houses; but it has an advantage which Kingston does not possess, in a broad flagged footway.

The distance from Sackett's harbour to *Watertown* is about ten miles. This is an elegant village on the *Black River*. It contains about twelve hundred inhabitants, chiefly emigrants from New England. The houses are, for the most part, of wood, but tastefully finished; and a few are built of bricks.

At Watertown there was a good tavern, which afforded to Mr. Hall and his companions a luxury unusual in America, a private sitting-room, and dinner at an hour appointed by themselves. Within a few miles of Watertown the country rises boldly, and presents a refreshing contrast, of hill and valley, to the flat, heavy woods, through which they had been labouring from Sackett's harbour.

Utica, the town at which the travellers next arrived stands on the right bank of the *River Mohawk*, over which it is approached by a covered wooden bridge, of considerable length. The appearance of this town is highly prepossessing: the streets are spacious; the houses are large and well built; and the stores, the name given to shops throughout America, are as well supplied, and as handsomely fitted up, as those of New York or Philadelphia.

There are at Utica two hotels, on a large scale; one of which, the York House, was equal in arrangement and accommodation, to any hotel beyond the Atlantic: it was kept by an Englishman from Bath. The inhabitants, from three to four thousand in number, maintained four churches: one episcopal, one presbyterian, and two Welsh.

This town is laid out on a very extensive scale. A small part of it only is yet completed; but little doubt is entertained that ten years will accomplish the whole. Fifteen years had not passed since there was here no other trace of habitation than a solitary log-house, built for the occasional reception of merchandise, on its way down the Mohawk. The overflowing population of New England, fixing its exertions on a new and fertile soil, has, within a few years, effected this change.

Independently of its soil, Utica has great advantages of situation; for it is nearly at the point of junction betwixt the waters of the lakes and of the Atlantic.

With Utica commences a succession of flourishing villages and settlements, which renders this tract of country the astonishment of travellers. That so large a portion of the soil should, in less than twenty years, have been cleared, brought into cultivation, and have acquired a numerous population, is, in itself, sufficiently surprising; but the surprise is considerably increased, when we consider the character of elegant opulence with which it every where smiles on the eye. Each village teems, like a hive, with activity and employment. The houses, taken in the mass, are on a large scale; for (except the few primitive log-huts that still survive) there is scarcely one below the appearance of an opulent London tradesman's country box. They are, in general, of wood, painted white, with green doors and shutters; and with porches, or verandas, in front.

The travellers passed through *Skaneactas*, a village, pleasantly situated, at the head of the lake from which it is named. They then proceeded to *Cayuga*, which, besides its agreeable site, is remarkable for a bridge, nearly a mile in length, over the head of the Cayuga lake: it is built on piles, and level. Betwixt Cayuga and Geneva is the flourishing little village of *Waterloo*, formed since the battle so named. *Geneva* contains many elegant houses, beautifully placed, on the rising shore, at the head of the Geneva lake.

From Geneva to *Canandaigua*, a tract of hill and vale extends, for sixteen miles, and having (within that space) only two houses. Canandaigua is a town of villas, built on the rising shore of the *Canandaigua lake*. The lower part of the main street is occupied by stores and warehouses; but the upper part of it, to the length of nearly two miles, consists of ornamented cottages, tastefully finished with colonnades, porches, and verandas; and each within its own garden or pleasure-ground. The prospect, down this long vista, to the lake, is peculiarly elegant.

From Canandaigua the travellers turned from the main road, nine miles, south-west, to visit what is called *"the burning spring."* On arriving near the place, they entered a small but thick wood, of pine and maple-trees, enclosed within a narrow ravine. Down this glen, the width of which, at its entrance, may be about sixty yards, trickles a scanty streamlet. They had advanced on its course about fifty yards, when, close under the rocks of the right bank, they perceived a bright red flame, burning briskly on the water. Pieces of lighted wood were applied to different adjacent spots, and a space of several yards in extent was immediately in a blaze. Being informed by the guide that a repetition of this phenomenon might be seen higher up the glen, they scrambled on, for about a hundred yards, and, directed in some degree by a strong smell of sulphur, they applied their match to several places, with similar effect. These fires continue burning unceasingly, unless they are extinguished by accident. The phænomenon was originally discovered by the casual rolling of lighted embers, from the top of the bank, whilst some persons were clearing it for cultivation; and, in the intensity and duration of the flame, it probably exceeds any thing of the kind that is known.

Rochester stands immediately on the great falls of the Genesee, about eight miles above its entrance into lake Ontario. When Mr. Hall was here, this town had been built only four years, yet it contained a hundred good houses, furnished with all the conveniences of life; several comfortable taverns, a cotton-mill, and some large corn-mills. Its site is grand. The Genesee rushes through it, over a bed of limestone, and precipitates itself down three ledges of rock, ninety-three; thirty, and seventy-six feet in height, within the distance of a mile and a half from the town. The immediate vicinity of Rochester is still an unbroken forest, consisting of oak, hickory, ash, beech, bass, elm, and walnut-trees. The wild tenants of the woods have, naturally, retired before the sound of cultivation; but there are a few wolves and bears still in the neighbourhood. One of the latter had lately seized a pig close to the town. Racoons, porcupines, squirrels black and grey, and foxes, are still numerous. The hogs have done good service in destroying the rattlesnakes, which are already becoming rare. Pigeons, quails, and blackbirds abound. At Rochester, the line of settled country, in this direction, terminates; for, from this place to Lewistown, are eighty miles of wilderness.

The traveller, halting on the verge of these aboriginal shades, is inclined to pause in thought, and to consider the interesting scenes through which he has been passing. They are such as reason must admire, for they are the result of industry, temperance, and freedom. Five or ten, or, at the utmost, twenty years before Mr. Hall was in America, where there are now corn-fields, towns, and villages, the whole country was one mass of forest.

Notwithstanding the bad state of the roads, the stage-waggon runs from Rochester to Lewistown in two days. This journey is so heavy, that it is sometimes necessary to alight, and walk several miles, or to suffer almost a dislocation of limbs, in jolting over causeys or logged roads, formed of pine, or oak-trees, laid crossways. At different intervals, square patches seem cut out of the forest, in the centre of which low log-huts have been constructed, without the aid of saw or plane; and are surrounded by stumps of trees, black with the fires kindled for the purpose of clearing the land.

Lewistown was one of the frontier villages burnt during the last war, to retaliate upon the Americans for the destruction of Newark. It has, however, been since rebuilt, and all the marks of its devastation have been effaced. It is agreeably situated, at the foot of the limestone ridge, on the steep bank of the river St. Lawrence, which here rushes, with a boiling and eddying torrent, from the falls to Lake Ontario. Lewistown, notwithstanding its infancy, and its remote situation, contains several good stores.

Queenston, on the opposite side of the river, stands in the midst of corn-fields and farm-houses; a rare and interesting sight in Canada. It is built on the river's edge, at the foot of the heights. Before the late war it was embosomed in peach-orchards; but these were all felled, to aid the operations of the English troops. The heights are still crowned by a redoubt, and by the remains of batteries, raised to defend the passage of the river. It was near one of these that Sir Isaac Brocke was killed, on the 13th of October, 1812, while, with four hundred men, he gallantly opposed the landing of fifteen hundred Americans, the whole of whom were afterwards captured by g\ General Sheaffe.

From Queenston Mr. Hall proceeded to *York*, a town within the British territory, situated on the north-western bank of lake Ontario. The country through which he passed abounded in game of various kinds. From the head of the lake it was, however, less varied than on the Niagara frontiers; and, for many miles, it was an uniform tract of sandy barrens, unsusceptible of culture.

York, being the seat of government for Upper Canada, is a place of considerable importance in the eyes of its inhabitants. To a stranger, however, it presents little more than about one hundred wooden houses, several of them conveniently, and even elegantly built; one or two of brick. The public buildings were destroyed by the Americans.

From York, Mr. Hall went, through the little town of *Ancaster*, to visit a *Settlement of Mohawk Indians*, on the banks of the *Grand River*. In the American war the Mohawks were strongly attached to the British interest, and first followed Sir William Johnson in Canada, under their chieftain, a celebrated warrior, whose name was Brandt. This man accustomed his people to the arts of civilized life, and made farmers of them. He built a church, and himself translated one of the gospels into the Mohawk language. His grave is to be seen under the walls of his church. The son of this extraordinary Indian is now living, and is a fine young man, of gentlemanly manners and appearance: he both speaks and writes the English language with correctness; and he dresses nearly in the English fashion. Brandt left also a daughter, who is living, and who would not disgrace the fashionable circles of Europe. Her face and person are fine and graceful: she speaks English, not only correctly, but elegantly; and, both in her speech and manners, she has a softness approaching oriental languor. She retains so much of her national dress as to identify her with her people; over whom she affects no superiority, but with whom she seems pleased to preserve all the ties and duties of relationship. She held the infant of one of her relations at the font, on the Sunday that Mr. Hall visited the church at Ancaster. The usual church and baptismal service was performed by a Dr. Aaron, an Indian, and an assistant priest; the congregation consisted of sixty or seventy persons, male and female. Many of the young men were dressed in the English fashion, but several of the old warriors came with their blankets, folded over them; and, in this dress, with a step and mien of quiet energy, they forcibly reminded Mr. Hall of ancient Romans. Some of them wore large silver crosses, medals, and other trinkets, on their backs and breasts; and a few had bandeaus, ornamented with feathers. Dr. Aaron, a grey-headed Mohawk, had touched his cheeks and forehead with a few spots of vermilion, in honour of Sunday: he wore a surplice, and preached at considerable length; but his delivery was unimpassioned and monotonous.

The Mohawk village stands on a little plain, and looks down upon the Grand River. The houses of the inhabitants, built of logs, rudely put together, exhibit, externally, a great appearance of neglect and want of comfort: some few are in a better condition. The house belonging to Brandt's family resembled that of a petty English farmer: Dr. Aaron's was neat and clean. The doctor, who had been regularly ordained, and spoke very good English, told Mr. Hall that the village had been much injured by the wars, which had impeded its improvements, and had dispersed the inhabitants over the country.

Mr. Hall had little opportunity of observing the manners and character of these Indians. It may, however, be conjectured that European intercourse is fast obliterating the characteristic features of their former social system. Their increased knowledge of European arts and enjoyments, has been probably followed by a proportionate increase of wants and desires. Their manners seemed, to Mr. Hall, remarkable for nothing so much as for that quiet self-possession, which constitutes the reverse of vulgarity. Their women, before strangers, are extremely timid: most of those who lived at a distance from the church, came mounted, with their husbands walking by their sides; a symptom, perhaps, that the sex is rising among them into an European equality of rights and enjoyments. The whole of the settlements are reckoned to furnish about five hundred warriors to the British government.

Mr. Hall next describes the celebrated *Cataract* or *Falls of Niagara*. At the distance of about a mile from this cataract, a white cloud, hovering over the trees, indicates its situation: it is not, however, until the road emerges from a close country, into the space of open ground immediately in its vicinity, that white volumes of foam are seen, as if boiling up from a sulphureous gulph. Here a foot-path turns from the road, towards a wooded cliff. The rapids are beheld on the right, rushing for the space of a mile, like a tempestuous sea. A narrow tract descends about sixty feet down the cliff, and continues across a plashy meadow, through a copse, encumbered with masses of limestone. Beyond this, Mr. Hall found himself upon what is called the Table Rock, on the west side of the upper part of the cataract, at the very point where the river precipitates itself into the abyss. The rapid motion of the waters, the stunning noise, and the mounting clouds, almost persuade the startled senses, that the rock itself is tottering, and is on the point of being precipitated into the gulph, which swallows the mass of descending waters. He bent over it, to mark the clouds rolling white beneath him, as in an inverted sky, illuminated by a most brilliant rainbow; one of those features of softness which nature delights to pencil amid her wildest scenes, tempering her awfulness with beauty, and making even her terrors lovely.

There is a ladder about half a mile below the Table Rock; and, by this, Mr. Hall descended the cliff, to reach the foot of the fall. There was formerly much difficulty in the descent, but a few years have made a great change: the present dangers and difficulties may easily be enumerated. The first is, the ordinary hazard that every one runs who goes up or down a ladder: this ladder is a very good one, of thirty steps, or about forty feet; and, from it, the path is a rough one, over the fragments and masses of rock which have gradually crumbled, or have been forcibly riven, from the cliff, and which cover a broad declining space, from its foot to the brink of the river. The only risk, in this part of the pilgrimage, is that of a broken shin from a false step. The path gradually becomes smooth as it advances towards the cataract. Mr. Hall, as he drew near, says that he felt a sensation of awe, like that caused by the first cannon, on the morning of a battle. He passed, from sunshine, into gloom and tempest. The spray beat down in a heavy rain; a violent wind rushed from behind the sheet of water: it was difficult to respire, and, for a moment, it seemed temerity to encounter the convulsive workings of the elements, and to intrude into the dark dwellings of their power. But the danger is in appearance only: it is possible to penetrate only a few yards beyond the curtain, and, in these few, there is no hazard; the footing is good, and the space is sufficiently broad and free. There is even no necessity for a guide: the eyes amply suffice to point out all that is to be seen or avoided. During Mr. Hall's first visit, there were two young American ladies on the same errand; and they, as well as himself, were drenched in the cloud of spray.

The larger fall was formerly called the "Horse-shoe," but this name is no longer applicable; for its shape has become that of an acute angle. An officer, who had been stationed in the neighbourhood thirty years, pointed out to Mr. Hall the alteration which had taken place in the centre of the fall, and which he estimated at about eighteen feet in that time.

The lesser fall, on the American side, had the appearance of a considerable elevation, above the bed of the greater: on enquiry, Mr. Hall found that there was a difference between them, of about fifteen feet, caused, probably, by the greater weight of water descending down one than the other.

The island which divides the falls has, of late years, been frequently visited; nor is the visit to it an adventure of much hazard. At the point where the rapids commence, the current separates, and is drawn, on either side, towards the centre of the two falls, while the centre of the stream, being in the straight line of the island, descends towards it, without any violent attraction; and, down this still water, American boats, well manned, and furnished with poles to secure them from the action of the two currents, have frequently dropt to the island.

There is a whirlpool about half way betwixt Niagara and Queenston. The river, boiling and eddying from the falls, enters a circular basin, round which the lofty cliff sweeps, like an antique wall, overgrown with trees at its base, and amid its clefts and crevices. The cause of the whirlpool is perceptible to the spectator, who looks down, and observes that the stream, being compelled into this basin, by the direction of its channel, and unable to escape with celerity, is forced to gain time by revolving within its own circumference.

[Mr. Weld, who visited Niagara, about the year 1797, observes that, although the spray, and the noise of the cataract, are sometimes not observable so far as half a mile, yet, at other times, the noise has been heard at the distance of forty miles; and that he has himself seen the spray, like a cloud, at the distance of fifty-four miles. The river, as it approaches the falls, runs with astonishing impetuosity. Just at the precipice, down which it tumbles, it takes a considerable bend towards the right; and the line of the falls, instead of extending from bank to bank, in the shortest direction, runs obliquely across. The whole width of the fall is estimated to be about three quarters of a mile, including a rocky island, a quarter of a mile wide, by which the stream is divided. This cataract is divided, by islands, into three distinct falls, the loftiest of which is one hundred and sixty feet in perpendicular height.

Mr. Weld observes that it is possible not merely to pass to the very foot of the great fall; but even to proceed behind the tremendous sheet of water which comes pouring down from the top of the precipice; for the water falls from the edge of a projecting rock, and, by its violent ebullition, caverns of considerable size have been hollowed out of the rocks at the bottom, and extend some way beneath the bed of the upper part of the river. Mr. Weld advanced within about six yards of the edge of the sheet of water, just far enough for him to peep into the caverns behind it. But here his breath was nearly taken away by the violent whirlwind, that always rages at the bottom of the cataract, occasioned by the concussion of such a vast body of water against the rocks. Indeed Mr. Weld had no inclination either to go further, or to explore the dreary confines of these caverns, where death seemed to await any one who should be daring enough to enter their threatening jaws. No words, he says, can convey an adequate idea of the awful grandeur of the scene, at this place. The senses are appalled by the sight of the immense body of water that comes pouring from the top of the precipice; and by the thundering sound of the billows dashing against the rocky sides of the cavern below. He trembled with reverential fear, when he considered that a blast of the whirlwind might have swept him from off the slippery rocks on which he stood, and have precipitated him into the dreadful gulph beneath; whence all the power of man could not have extricated him. He here felt what an insignificant being man is in the creation; and his mind was forcibly impressed with an awful idea of the power of that mighty Existence, who commanded the waters to flow.]

Fourth Day's Instruction

UNITED STATES CONTINUED.

Narrative of Lieutenant Hall's *Journey from Niagara to Philadelphia.*

Mr. Hall crossed the river from *Fort Erie,* and proceeded to *Buffalo,* one of the frontier villages which had been burnt during the great American war. Not a house had been left standing; yet, when Mr. Hall was there, it was not merely a flourishing village, but a considerable town, with good shops and hotels. The celerity with which Buffalo had risen from its ashes, indicates the juvenile spirit of life and increase, which so eminently distinguishes the American population.

As Mr. Hall proceeded on his journey, he found the country thickly settled, but dull and uniform in feature; being an entire flat. The autumn had been dry, and water was, in many places, extremely scarce. This is an evil not uncommon in newly-settled districts. Draining follows clearing; the creeks, no longer fed by the swamps, disencumbered also of fallen trunks of trees, and other substances, by which their waters were, in a great degree, stayed, easily run dry in summer, and soon fail altogether.

The principal inn at *Batavia* is large, and yet constructed upon an economical principle; for one roof covers hotel, prison, court-house, and assembly-room. The inhabitants were, at this time, building, by subscription, an episcopal church, the cost of which was to be twenty thousand dollars.

Caledonia is a small, but flourishing village, which has a handsome inn, with very comfortable accommodations; and, close to the road, is a large sheet of water, from which a clear and rapid stream descends, through a pleasing valley, into Allen's Creek, before the latter unites with the *Genesee River.* The banks of this creek are adorned with natural groves and copses, in which Mr. Hall observed the candleberry myrtle in great abundance: but a more interesting sight was afforded by numerous organic remains, with which the blocks of limestone, scattered through the low ground around it, are encrusted, as if with rude sculpture. These blocks are mixed with nodules of granite, and present innumerable forms, both of shells and aquatic plants. This district had been settled fifteen years; and, when Mr. Hall was here, cleared land was worth fifty dollars, and uncleared land about fifteen dollars per acre. At *Avon* Mr. Hall quitted the main road, and followed the right bank of the Genesee. The scenery, in the vicinity of this place, began to improve, but the roads were proportionally deteriorated. Wild even to savageness, mountain heights branched thickly across the country, with no seeming order or direction. The only level ground was in the narrow valleys, along the course of the streams.

The woods in the vicinity of the Genesee abound in large black squirrels, some of which are as big as a small cat. They are destructive to grain, and are, therefore, keenly pursued by sportsmen, who frequently make parties to kill them, and who destroy several thousands at one chase: their flesh is considered a great delicacy. These animals migrate, at different seasons; and have the credit of ingeniously ferrying themselves over rivers, by using a piece of bark for a raft, and their tails for sails.

Bath is embosomed in wild mountains. The principal houses are constructed round the three sides of a square, or green; and, as most of them were at this time new, white, and tastefully finished, they had a lively appearance, and were agreeably contrasted with the dark adjacent mountain scenery.

The road from Bath to *Painted Post*, though stony, is tolerably level. The adjacent mountains have a slaty appearance, with horizontal strata. Mr. Hall was disappointed at Painted Post, to find the post gone, broken down or rotted, within the last few years. It had been an Indian memorial, either of triumph or death, or of both.

When he was at Ancaster, this gentleman had been shown the grave of an Indian, among the woods, near the head of the stream: it was covered with boards, and a pole was erected at each end, on which a kind of dance was rudely painted with vermilion. The relatives of the deceased brought offerings to it daily, during their stay in the neighbourhood.

After passing through some other villages, Mr. Hall reached the banks of the *Susquehanna*: these have no great variety of scenery, though they frequently present grand features. The space betwixt the mountains and the river is often so narrow, that it barely suffices for one carriage to pass; and, in many places, the road, for a mile or two, seems to have been hewn from the rock. Near the creeks there is tolerable land, and two or three pleasant villages. The face of the landscape is no where naked: mountain and vale are alike clothed with pine and dwarf oak-trees; the swamp lands are covered with hemlock-trees, and the bottoms of the woods with rhododendrons.

Wilksbarre is a neat town, regularly laid out, on the left bank of the Susquehanna. Its locality is determined by the direction of one of the Alleghany ridges, which recedes from the course of the river, a few miles above the town, and, curving south-west, encloses a semicircular plot of land, towards the centre of which the town is built. Its neighbourhood abounds in coal. The pits are about a mile distant. They lie under a stratum of soft clay slate, which contains impressions of ferns, oak-leaves, and other vegetables, usually found in such situations. The town itself, in consequence of the frequent separation of its streets and houses, by grass-fields and gardens, has a quiet and rural aspect. It contains a neat church, appropriated to the alternate use of episcopalians and presbyterians. Wilkesbarre is built on the site of *Wyoming*: a small mound, near the river, is pointed out, as that on which the fort stood; and the incursion of the Indians, when most of the inhabitants fell, in an unsuccessful battle, is still remembered. Some few escaped, by swimming across the stream, and fled, naked, through the woods, for several days, till they reached the nearest settlement; and this is all the record that exists of Albert and Gertrude, the foundation of Campbell's poem of Gertrude of Wyoming.

At Wilkesbarre the road quits the Susquehanna, and, ascending a ridge of the Alleghany Mountains, crosses through deep forests and hemlock swamps, sparingly interspersed with settlements. The Pokono Mountain, over which Mr. Hall passed, is famous with the sportsmen and epicures of Philadelphia, for its grouse. Mr. Hall crossed the *Blue Ridge*, at the stupendous fissure of the *Wind Gap*, where the mountain seems forcibly broken through, and is strewed with the ruin of rocks. There is a similar aperture, some miles north-east, called the Water Gap. This affords a passage to the Delaware; and all the principal rivers of the states, that rise in the Alleghanys, pass through similar apertures.

Betwixt the Blue Ridge and the Lehigh River, are two Moravian settlements, called *Bethlehem* and *Nazareth*. [The inhabitants of the former constitute a large society, and occupy several farms. They have a spacious apartment, in which they all daily assemble, for the purpose of public worship. The single men and women have each a separate dwelling. The women are occupied in various domestic employments; in fancy and ornamental works; and, occasionally, in musical practice, under the direction of a superintendant. The walls of the large hall, where the society dine, are adorned with paintings, chiefly Scripture pieces, executed by members. Various branches of trade and manufacture are carried on, the profits of which go to the general stock; and, from this, all are supplied with the necessaries of life. Their whole time is spent in labour, and in prayer; except an hour in the evening, which is allotted for a concert. Among the

Moravians marriage is contracted in a singular manner. If a young man has an inclination to marry, he makes application to the priest, who presents a young woman, designated by the superintendant as the next in rotation for marriage. Having left the parties together for an hour, the priest returns, and, if they consent to live together, they are married the next day; if otherwise, each is put at the bottom of the list, containing perhaps sixty or seventy names; and, on the part of the girl, there is no chance of marriage, unless the same young man should again feel disposed for matrimony. When united, a neat habitation, with a pleasant garden, is provided; and their children, at the age of six years, are placed in the seminary. If either of the parties die, the other returns to the apartment of the single people. In the Moravian establishment at Bethlehem, there is a tavern, with extensive and excellent accommodations.]

Madame de Stael, in describing the Moravians, says, "Their houses and streets are peculiarly neat. The women all dress in the same manner, conceal their hair, and surround their heads with a ribbon, the colour of which indicates whether they are single, married, or widows. The men dress in brown, somewhat like quakers. A mercantile industry occupies nearly the whole community; and all their labours are performed with peculiar regularity and tranquillity." Mr. Hall attended one of the meetings which the inhabitants of Bethlehem commonly hold every evening, for the joint purposes of amusement and devotion. The women were ranged at one end of the room, and the men at the other. Their bishop presided: he was an old man, dressed in the plainest manner, and possessed a countenance singularly mild and placid. He gave out a psalm, and led the choir; and the singing was alternately in German and English.

There is another Moravian settlement about a mile and a half from Nazareth. This, though small, exceeds both the others, in the calm and pensive beauty of its appearance. The houses are built of limestone: they are all on a similar plan, and have their window-frames, doors, and other wood-work, painted fawn-colour: before each house are planted weeping willows, whose luxuriant shade seems to shut out worldly glare, and throws an air of monastic repose over the whole village.

The *Lehigh Mountain* is the last of the Allegheny Ridges; the country is thenceforth level, fertile, and thickly inhabited, by steady Germans, who wear broad hats, and purple breeches; and whose houses and villages have the antique fashion of Flemish landscape. German is so generally spoken here, that the newspapers and public notices are all printed in that language.

The approach to Philadelphia is announced by a good turnpike road. *German Town* is a large suburb to the city, and the traveller here feels himself within the precincts of a populous and long-established capital.

A Description of Philadelphia.

The first impressions, on entering this city, are decidedly favourable. It possesses a character essentially different from that of New York. It has not so much business, nor so much animation; but there is, in Philadelphia, a freedom from mere display; an evidence of solidity, of which its more commercial rival is nearly destitute.

All the *streets* are spacious; the names of many of them, as Sassafras, Chesnut, and Locust, record their sylvan origin: rows of Lombardy poplars are planted in them. The private *houses* are characterized by elegant neatness; the steps and window-sills of many of them are of grey marble, and they have large mats placed before the doors. The streets are carefully swept, as well as the foot-paths, which are paved with brick. The *shops* do not yield, in display, to those of London. The principal street is one hundred feet wide; and the others vary from eighty to fifty. In the foot-paths a great inconvenience is experienced by the injudicious mode in which cellars are constructed, the openings of which project into the street; and also by the slovenly practice of the store or shopkeepers placing great quantities of loose goods on the outside of their doors.

Philadelphia stands on the bank of the river *Delaware*; and, in 1795, when Mr. Weld was there, its appearance, as approached from the water, was not very prepossessing. Nothing was visible but confused heaps of wooden store-houses, crowded upon each other, and wharfs, which projected a considerable way into the river. The wharfs were built of wood; they jutted out, in every direction, and were well adapted for the accommodation of shipping; the largest merchant vessels being able to lie close alongside of them. Behind the wharfs, and parallel to the river, runs a street called *Water-street*. This is the first street which the stranger in America usually enters, after landing; and (says Mr. Weld) it will not give him a very favourable opinion either of the neatness or commodiousness of the public ways of Philadelphia. Such stenches, at times, prevail in it, owing in part to the quantity of filth and dirt that is suffered to remain on the pavement, and in part to what is deposited in waste-houses, of which there are several in the street, that it is really dreadful to pass through it. It was here, in the year 1793, that the malignant yellow fever broke out, which made such terrible ravages among the inhabitants; and, in the summer season, in general, this street is extremely unhealthy.

Few of the *public buildings* in Philadelphia pretend to great architectural merit. The churches are neat, but plain. The Masonic Hall is an unsightly combination of brick and marble, in the Gothic style. The Philadelphia bank is in a similar style. The United States and Pennsylvania banks are the finest edifices in the city: the first has a handsome portico, with Corinthian columns of white marble, and the latter is a miniature representation of the temple of Minerva at Athens, and is the purest specimen of architecture in the states: the whole building is of marble.

The *State House* is a plain brick building, which was finished in 1735, at the cost of £.6000. The most interesting recollections of America are attached to this edifice. The Congress sat in it during the greatest part of the war; and the Declaration of Independence was read, from its steps, on the 4th of July, 1776. The Federal Convention also sat in it, in 1787. It is now occupied by the supreme and district courts below, and by Peale's Museum above. This museum, among other articles, contains an immense fossil skeleton of the great Mastodon, or American Mammoth, which, some years ago, was publicly exhibited in London.

The *University* of Pennsylvania was instituted several years ago, by some of the citizens of Philadelphia; among whom was Dr. Franklin, who drew up the original plan. It is governed by a provost and vice-provost. In 1811, the number of students amounted to five hundred. The lectures commence the first Monday in November, and end on the first day of March. Among others, are professors of anatomy, surgery, midwifery, chemistry, moral philosophy, mathematics, and natural philosophy, belles lettres, and languages.

The Philadelphia *prison* is a more interesting object to humanity than the most gorgeous palaces. Its exterior is simple, and has rather the air of an hospital than a gaol: a single grated door separates the interior from the street. On entering the court, Mr. Hall found it full of stone-cutters, employed in sawing and preparing large blocks of stone and marble; smiths' forges were at work on one side, and the whole court was surrounded by a gallery and a double tier of work-shops, in which were brush-makers, tailors, shoemakers, weavers, all at their several occupations, labouring, not only to defray, to the public, the expenses of their confinement, but to provide the means of their own honest subsistence for the future. It had none of the usual features of a prison; neither the hardened profligacy which scoffs down its own sense of guilt, nor the hollow-eyed sorrow which wastes away in a living death of unavailing expiation: there was neither the clank of chains, nor the yell of execration; but a hardworking body of men were seen, who, though separated by justice from society, were not supposed to have lost the distinctive attribute of human nature: they were treated as rational beings, were operated upon by rational motives; and they repaid this treatment by improved habits, by industry, and submission. They had been profligate, they were now sober and decent in their behaviour; they had been idle, they were now actively and usefully employed; they had disobeyed the laws, they now submitted (armed as they were with all kinds of utensils) to the government of a single turnkey, and the barrier of a single grating.

The *markets* of Philadelphia are well supplied; and the price of provisions is considerably lower than in London. No butchers are permitted to slaughter cattle within the city, nor are live cattle permitted to be driven to the city markets.

The *inhabitants* of this city are estimated at one hundred and twenty thousand, and many of them live in houses which would adorn any city in the world. They have, universally, a pallid and sallow countenance, except the younger females; and many of these, even quakers, adopt the disgusting practice of ornamenting their faces with rouge. In their dress, the gentlemen follow the fashions of England, and the ladies those of France. Mr. Fearon perceived here, what, he says, pervades the whole of the new world, an affectation of splendour, or, what may be called style, in those things that are intended to meet the public eye; with a lamentable want, even of cleanliness, in such matters as are removed from that ordeal. To this may be added an appearance of uncomfortable extravagance, and an ignorance of that kind of order and neatness, which, in the eyes of those who have once enjoyed it, constitute the principal charm of domestic life. The Philadelphians consist of English, Irish, Scotch, Germans, and French; and of American-born citizens, descended from people of those different nations. It is a remark very generally made, not only by foreigners, but also by persons from distant parts of the United States, that they are extremely deficient in hospitality and politeness towards strangers. Among the uppermost circles in Philadelphia, pride, haughtiness, and ostentation, are conspicuous; and, in the manners of the people in general, there is much coldness and reserve.

Philadelphia is the grand residence of the quakers in America, but their number does not now bear the same proportion to that of the other citizens, which it formerly did. This, however, is not occasioned by a diminution of quakers, so much as by the great influx, into the city, of persons of a different persuasion.

In this city *funerals* are uniformly attended by large walking processions. The newspapers frequently contain advertisements, stating the deaths of individuals, and inviting all friends to attend the burial. The dead are seldom kept more than two days. At the time appointed, intimate friends enter the house; others assemble on the outside, and fall into the procession when the body is brought out.

With regard to the *climate* of Philadelphia, it is observed that the heats of summer are excessive; and that the cold of winter is equally extreme.

During the few days which Mr. Weld spent at Philadelphia, in the month of June, 1795, the heat was almost intolerable. For two or three days the thermometer stood at 93°, and, during these days, no one stirred out of doors who was not compelled to do so. Light white hats were universally worn, and the young men appeared dressed in cotton or linen jackets and trowsers. The window-shutters of the houses were closed early in the mornings, so as to admit no more light than what was absolutely necessary for domestic business. Indeed, many of the houses were kept so dark, that, on going into them from the street, it was impossible, at first entrance, to perceive who was present. The best houses in the city are furnished with Venetian blinds, at the outside, to the windows and hall doors, which are made to fold together like common window-shutters. A very different scene was presented after sunset. Every house was then thrown open, and all the inhabitants crowded into the streets, to take their evening walks, and to visit their acquaintance. This usually lasted till about ten o'clock: at eleven all was quiet; and a person might have passed over half the town without seeing a single human being, except the watchmen. Heavy dews sometimes fall after the sun is down, and the nights are then very cold: at other times there are no dews, and the air continues hot all the night through. At this season of the year meat cannot be kept sweet, even for a single day, except in an icehouse or a remarkably cold cellar. Milk generally turns sour in an hour or two; and fish is never brought to market without being covered with lumps of ice. Poultry, intended for dinner, is never killed till about four hours before it is wanted, and even then it is kept immersed in water.

The *carriages* used in Philadelphia consist of coaches, chariots, chaises, coachees, and light waggons. The equipages of a few individuals are extremely ostentatious; but there does not appear, in any, that neatness and elegance which might be expected among people who are desirous of imitating the fashions of England, and who are continually procuring models from that country. The coachee is a carriage peculiar to America; the body of it is somewhat longer than that of a coach, but of the same shape. In front it is left quite open, down to the bottom, and the driver sits on a bench under the roof. It has two seats for the passengers, who sit with their faces towards the horses. The roof is supported by small props, which are placed at the corners. On each side of the doors, above the pannels, it is quite open; and, to guard against bad weather, there are curtains, which are made to let down from the roof, and which fasten to buttons, placed for the purpose, on the outside. There is also a leathern curtain, to hang occasionally between the driver and passengers.

The light waggons are on the same construction, but are calculated to accommodate from four to twelve people. The only difference between a small waggon and a coachee, is, that the latter is better finished, has varnished pannels, and doors at the side. The former has no doors; but the passengers scramble in, the best way they can, over the seat of the driver. These waggons are universally used for stage-carriages.

The accommodations at the *taverns*, in Philadelphia, are very indifferent; as, indeed, with very few exceptions, they are throughout the country. The mode of conducting them is nearly the same every where. The traveller, on his arrival, is shown into a room, which is common to every person in the house, and which is generally the one set apart for breakfast, dinner, and supper. All the strangers that are in the house sit down, to these meals, promiscuously; and, excepting in the large towns, the family of the house also forms a part of the company. It is seldom that a private parlour or drawing-room can be procured at taverns, even in the towns; and it is always with reluctance that breakfast or dinner is served up separately to any individual. If a separate bed-room can be procured, more ought not to be expected; and it is not always that even this is to be had; and persons who travel through the country must often submit to be crammed into rooms where there is scarcely sufficient space to walk between the beds.

The *Delaware*, on the banks of which this city is built, rises in the state of New York. At Philadelphia it is thirteen hundred and sixty yards wide, and is navigable for vessels of any burden. It is frozen in the winter months; a circumstance which materially affects the commercial interests of Philadelphia, and gives a great advantage to New York. The tide reaches as high as the falls of Trenton, thirty-five miles above Philadelphia, and one hundred and fifty-five miles from the sea. Six or seven steam-boats, of large size, ply on the Delaware, and form a communication with New York, by Trenton and Bordentown; and with Baltimore, by Wilmington and Newcastle. These vessels are all fitted up in an elegant manner.

Over the river *Schuylkil*, near Philadelphia, there is a singular bridge of iron wire. It is four hundred feet in length, and extends, from the window of a wire factory, to a tree on the opposite shore. The wires which form the curve are six in number; three on each side, and each three-eighths of an inch in diameter. The floor of the bridge is elevated sixteen feet above the water; and the whole weight of the wires is about four thousand seven hundred pounds. It is possible to construct a bridge of this kind in the space of a fortnight; and the whole expense would not exceed three hundred dollars.

About thirty miles north-east of Philadelphia, and betwixt that city and New York, is *Trenton*, the capital of New Jersey. Mr. Weld visited this place in the year 1796; and he says that it then contained only about eighty dwellings, in one long street. It had a college, which was in considerable repute. The number of students was about seventy; but, from their appearance, and the course of their studies, it more correctly deserved the appellation of a grammar-school, than a college. The library was a miserable one; and, for the most part, contained only old theological books. There were an orrery out of repair, and a few detached parts of philosophical apparatus. At the opposite end of the room were two small cupboards, which were shown as the museum. These contained two small alligators, stuffed, and a few fishes, in a wretched state of preservation.

Not far from Trenton, and on the bank of the Delaware, is the residence of Joseph Buonaparte, who, since the re-establishment of the ancient families on the thrones of Europe, has retired to America. The estate on which he lives he purchased for ten thousand dollars; and he is said to have expended, twenty thousand more in finishing the buildings, and laying out the grounds in a splendid style. At present it has much the appearance of the villa of a country gentleman in England.

Fifth Day's Instruction

UNITED STATES CONTINUED.

Narrative of Mr. Fearon's *Journey from Philadelphia to Pittsburgh.*

In the month of October, 1817, Mr. Fearon left Philadelphia for Pittsburgh. He passed through an extensive, fertile, well-cultivated, and beautiful tract of land called the *Great Valley*. Farms in this district are chiefly owned by Dutch and Germans, and their descendants. They consist of from fifty to two hundred acres each; and are purchasable at the rate of about £.46 sterling per acre, the buildings included; and, in well-improved land, the average produce of wheat may be estimated at twenty-five bushels.

At the distance of about twenty miles from Philadelphia there is a copper and zinc mine. Iron ore abounds throughout the state of Pennsylvania; and many of the rocks are of limestone. A coarse kind of grey marble is found in great quantity, and is used for steps and chimney-pieces.

The towns of *Lancaster, Harrisburgh,* and *Carlisle,* through which Mr. Fearon passed, are all considerable, both in extent and population. [*Lancaster* is nearly the largest inland town of North America. It contains upwards of nine hundred houses, built chiefly of brick and stone, and, in general, two stories high. It has also six churches, a market-house, and a gaol. The streets are laid out regularly, and cross each other at right angles. Several different kinds of wares are manufactured here, and chiefly by German mechanics. The rifled barrel guns made at this place are considered to have great excellence. In 1787, a college was founded at Lancaster, and named Franklin College, in honour of Dr. Franklin. The founders were an association of Germans, who were desirous of establishing a seminary for the education of their sons, in their own language and habits. But it has not flourished; and, in 1815, the number of students did not exceed fifty.]

Lancaster, Harrisburgh, and Carlisle, each contain many excellent brick buildings, and the usual erections of market-houses, gaols, and churches, all evincing an extent of national property, and an advancement to European establishments, truly extraordinary, when we recollect that this is a country which may be said to be but of yesterday. The German character is very prevalent throughout this state; and even the original language is preserved.

[At *Carlisle* there are many excellent shops and warehouses. This place has a college, which was founded in 1783, by Mr. John Dickenson of Pennsylvania. The number of students is about one hundred and forty; and there are professors of logic, metaphysics, languages, natural philosophy, and chemistry.]

Mr. Fearon next arrived at *Chambersburgh*, a town which contains about two hundred and forty houses, and two or three churches. He here secured a place, in the stage, to Pittsburgh, and set off the next morning at three o'clock. About eight he arrived at *Loudon*, a small town at the foot of the north mountain, one of the Alleghany ridges, and at this time containing seventeen log and twenty frame or brick houses. The tavern was cheerless and dirty.

On the road Mr. Fearon counted thirty regular stage-waggons, which were employed in conveying goods to and from Pittsburgh. Each of these was drawn by four horses; and the articles carried in them, were chiefly hardware, and silk, linen, cotton, and woollen goods. The waggons, in return, conveyed from Pittsburgh farming produce, and chiefly flour. It is, however, necessary to observe that this is the only trading waggon route to the whole western country; and that there is no water-carriage through this part of America.

The road, for a considerable distance, was excellent, and was part of a new national turnpike, which had been projected to extend from the head of the river Potomac to Wheeling. This road, when completed, will be of great advantage to the whole western country. The stage passed over the *North Mountain*, whence there was a most extensive view, of a wide and beautiful valley, containing several thousand acres, which have not yet been cultivated. The prospect combined some grand mountain-scenery, and was the most magnificent that Mr. Fearon had ever beheld. The travellers passed through a little town situated in the midst of this apparently trackless wild.

They afterwards overtook twenty small family waggons, those chiefly of emigrants from one part of the state to another. These persons were travelling in company, and thus formed an unity of interest, for the purpose of securing, when necessary, an interchange of assistance. The difficulties they experienced, in passing through this mountainous district, were very great.

Mr. Fearon and the other stage-passengers supped and slept at a place called *Bloody Run*, having, for several miles, proceeded over roads that were almost impassable. Early the next morning they again set out; and they arrived at *Bedford* about nine o'clock. [This little town, like most others on the great western road, trades in all kinds of corn, flour, and provisions.] They were not, however, permitted to stop here, as the stage-proprietor had a house further on, where they breakfasted. In passing over a range of mountains called the *Dry Ridge*, the view was peculiarly magnificent. The eye, at one glance, took in a varied and most interesting view of mountain scenery, intermingled with wooded vales, and much fertile land. The travellers continued to overtake many waggons of emigrants from different states.

About five o'clock in the afternoon they reached the top of the *Alleghany Mountains*. The road had of late been so bad, that they had walked more than sixteen miles, leaving the stage far behind. The character of the mountain *inhabitants* appeared to be cold, friendless, unfeeling, callous, and selfish. All the emigrants with whom Mr. Fearon conversed, complained of the enormous charges at taverns. Log-houses are the only habitations for many miles. These are formed of the trunks of trees, about twenty feet in length, and six inches in diameter, cut at the ends, and placed on each other. The roof is framed in a similar manner. In some houses there are windows; in others the door performs the double office of window and entrance. The chimney is erected on the outside, and in a similar manner to the body of the house. The hinges of the doors are generally of wood; and locks are not used. In some of the houses there are two apartments; in others but one, for all the various operations of cooking, eating, and sleeping; and even the pigs come in for their due share of the log residence. About eleven o'clock at night, the travellers safely arrived at *Somerset*, a small town distant two hundred and thirty-seven miles from Philadelphia.

In the morning of their third day's journey, they crossed *Laurel Hill*. The vegetation on this ridge appears superior to that of the Allegheny. The mountain called *Little Chesnut Ridge* succeeds Laurel Hill. The difficulties of the road were here extremely great. These arose not only from the height of the mountains, but from the enormous stones and deep mud-holes with which the road abounded. The trees on Chesnut Ridge are chiefly oak and chesnut; and the soil appeared to be chalky. At half past ten at night they arrived at *Greensburg*, [a town built upon the summit of a hill. The land, in its vicinity is, in general, very fertile; and the inhabitants, who are of German origin, cultivate wheat, rye, and oats, with great success.]

The party started, on the fourth day, at four in the morning, and with the high treat of a turnpike-road; but the advantages, arising from this, were but of short continuance. They had to descend *Turtle Creek Hill*, the road over which, in consequence of late rains, had become, if possible, even worse than those across Laurel Hill. The passengers all got out; and, up to their knees in mud, they took their turns, in holding up the stage. This tract bore decided evidence of being embedded with coal. About two o'clock they reached *Pittsburg*.

From Chambersburgh to Greensburgh the condition of the people is that of an absence of wealth and of the conveniences of life, with, however, the means of obtaining a sufficient quantity of food. The blacksmith and the tavern-keeper are almost the only occupations. The former earns from twenty shillings and sixpence to twenty-seven shillings per week; and the profits of the latter must be very great, if we may judge from the high charges and bad quality of the accommodations. From Greensburgh to Pittsburgh the improvement, in size and quality, of the houses, is evident, and the cultivation and condition of the land is much superior to those of the country through which the travellers had before past.

Pittsburg is, in several points of view, a most interesting town. Its situation, which is truly picturesque, is at the termination of two rivers, and at the commencement of a third river, that has a direct communication with the ocean, though at the immense distance of two thousand five hundred miles. This place possesses an exhaustless store of coal.

During the great American war, Pittsburg was an important military post called *Du Quesne*, and was remarkable for two signal defeats of the British troops. It is, at present, a place of great importance: the connecting link between *new* and *old* America; and though it is not a "Birmingham," as the natives bombastically style it, yet it certainly contains the seeds of numerous important and valuable manufactories.

Agricultural produce finds here a ready and advantageous market. Farming in this neighbourhood is not, indeed, the most profitable mode of employing capital; but here, as in other parts of the union, it is an independent mode of life. The farmer, however, must labour hard with his own hands. The labourers, or "helps," as they style themselves, are paid high wages, and are not to be relied on. In many instances they expect to sit down at table with their master, to live as well as he, and to be on terms of equality with every branch of the family.

Mr. Fearon remained at Pittsburgh several days, during which time the rain never ceased. The smoke, also, from the different manufactories, is extreme, giving, to the town and its inhabitants, a very sombre aspect. The articles manufactured here are various, and chiefly of copper, iron, and glass. In one of the glass-warehouses, Mr. Fearon saw chandeliers and numerous other articles, of a very splendid description, in cut glass. Among the latter was a pair of decanters, cut from a London pattern, the price of which was to be eight guineas. And it is remarkable that the demand for these articles of elegant luxury lies in the western states; the inhabitants of eastern America being still importers from the "old country." Not thirty years ago, the whole right bank of the Ohio was termed the "Indian side." Spots in Tenessee, in Ohio and Kentucky, which, within the lifetime of even young men, witnessed only the arrow and the scalping knife, now present, to the traveller, articles of elegance, and modes of luxury, which might rival the displays of London and of Paris: within the last half century, the beasts of the forest, and men more savage than the beasts, were the only inhabitants of the whole of that immense tract, which is peculiarly denominated the western country. This tract is now partially inhabited; and promises soon to be generally so, by civilized man, possessed of the arts and pursuits of civilized life.

On the whole, Pittsburgh is a very important town. When Mr. Fearon was here, it was supposed to contain about ten thousand inhabitants.

The face of the country, beyond this town, is an uninterrupted level, and many parts of it are occupied by agriculturists. Mr. Fearon, however, was informed that there were still for sale one million of acres of United States' land, at the rate of two dollars per acre, or one dollar and sixty-four cents for prompt payment. The principal towns are situated on the banks of the river. There are no canals, nor, indeed is there much occasion for them, as the whole state abounds with rivers and creeks, which fall into the Ohio.

The trees produced by the best kind of land are honey-locust, black walnut, and beech; by land of second quality, the sugar maple tree, sycamore, or butter-wood, and what is called white wood, which is used for building and joiner's work; and land of the third quality produces oak. There is but little underwood; for the great height and the spreading tops of the trees, prevent the sun from penetrating to the ground, and nourishing inferior articles of vegetation. The winters are severe, and of from three to four months continuance, with a keen and dry air, and cloudless sky. During summer excessive heat prevails, with heavy dews at night. In the spring there are cold and heavy rains. The autumns are fine, and are followed by what is called "Indian summer," which is truly delightful. Along the route that Mr. Fearon had travelled in this state, there was scarcely an elevation which could be called a hill, with exception of rising grounds on the margins of rivers. The dreary monotony of limited views, of such endless uniformity, produces sensations of the most depressing melancholy. The atmosphere, after a hot day, causes headaches, which frequently terminate in intermittent fevers.

Judging from the beds of the rivers, and the quality of the water, Mr. Fearon presumes that coal must be abundant. Salt is found in several situations, particularly on the Kenaway. There is much limestone. The wild animals, in this part of America, are neither numerous, nor troublesome.

The interior population of the United States, Mr. Fearon considers, may be divided into three classes: first, the "squatter," or man, who "sets himself down," upon land which is not his own, and for which he pays nothing; cultivates a sufficient extent of ground to supply himself and his family with the necessaries of life, remains until he is dissatisfied with his choice, has realized a sufficiency to become a land-owner, or is expelled by the real proprietor. Second, the small farmer, who has recently emigrated, and has had barely sufficient to pay the first instalment for his eighty or one hundred and sixty acres, of two-dollar land; cultivates, or, what he calls, improves, from ten to thirty acres; raises a sufficient "feed" for his family; is in a condition, which, if compelled by legislative acts, or by external force to endure, would be considered truly wretched; but, from being his own master, and having made his own choice, joined with the consciousness, that, though slowly, he is regularly advancing towards wealth, the breath of complaint is seldom heard to escape from his lips. Third, the wealthy, or "strong-handed" farmer, who owns from five to twelve hundred acres, has from one-fourth to one-third under cultivation, of a kind much superior to the former; raises live stock for the home, and Atlantic city markets; sends beef, pork, cheese, lard, and butter, to New Orleans: is a man of plain, business-like sense, though not in possession, nor desirous, of a very cultivated intellect; understands his own interest, and that of his country; and lives in sufficient affluence, and is possessed of comfort, according to the American acceptation of the term, but to which, an Englishman must feel inclined to take an exception.

The management of farms is here full a century behind that in England: there being a want of improved machinery for the promotion of economy in time and labour; and no regular attention being paid to the condition of live stock; while the mode of culture, in general, appears slovenly and unsystematic.

On the subject of emigration to America, Mr. Fearon remarks, that the capitalist will here receive legal interest of six or seven per cent. for his money; and perhaps eight per cent. might be made upon good security, as capital is wanted throughout the country. A London shopkeeper, with a capital of three thousand pounds or upwards, and who is well acquainted with the principles of business, might succeed. Lawyers, doctors, clerks, shopmen, literary men, artists, and schoolmasters, to use an American phrase, would "come to a bad market." Mechanics are able to obtain employment, but many who have emigrated have been lamentably deceived in their expectations. The person of small property, who is desirous to live on the interest of his money, and wants to remove to a cheaper country than England, should pause before the object of his choice is America. From what Mr. Fearon had hitherto seen of large towns, living is not, on the whole, cheaper than in the English cities. In the interior it may be less expensive than in the country parts of England; but such a man must, of necessity, have his ideas of happiness associated with many sources of comfort and gratification, which he would seek for in vain within the United States. With regard to certain Yorkshire and Leicestershire manufacturers, in whose welfare he was particularly interested, Mr. Fearon says, he was convinced that they could not profitably succeed here.

Sixth Day's Instruction

UNITED STATES CONTINUED.

Narrative of an Expedition from Pittsburg into the Illinois territory. From Notes on a Journey in America, by Morris Birkbeck.

Leaving Mr. Fearon at Pittsburgh, we will thence accompany Mr. Birkbeck on his tour into the western settlements of the United States. About the end of May, 1817, this gentleman and his family, consisting of nine persons, five male and four female, arrived at *Pittsburgh*; and, on the 5th of June, well mounted, and well furnished with saddle-bags and blankets, they set out on their journey westward, in search of a place where they might form an advantageous settlement. Each person had a blanket under his saddle, another upon it, and a pair of saddle-bags, with a great coat and an umbrella strapped behind.

In this manner, says Mr. Birkbeck, even women, and those of advanced age, often take long journeys without inconvenience. The day before he left Pittsburgh, he was told of a lady who was coming from Tenessee to Pittsburgh, twelve hundred miles; and, although she had with her an infant, she preferred travelling on horseback to boating up the river.

Seventeen miles of the ride from Pittsburgh on to *Cannonsburg,* was chiefly over clayey hills, well adapted for grass; but, in the present circumstances of the country, too stiff for profitable cultivation under the plough. From Cannonsburg to *Washington,* in Pennsylvania, eight miles, is a very desirable tract, containing much excellent land, with fine meadows.

Washington is a pretty, thriving town, which contains about two thousand five hundred inhabitants. It has a college, with about a hundred students; but, from the dirty condition of the schools, and the loitering habits of the young men, Mr. Birkbeck suspected it to be an ill-regulated institution.

From Washington, Mr. Birkbeck and his family proceeded still westward, and, on entering the *State of Ohio,* they found themselves in a country beautiful and fertile, and affording, to a plain, industrious, and thriving population, all that nature has decreed for the comfort of man. It contains rich land, good water, wholesome air; limestone, coal, mills, and navigation. It is also fully appropriated, and thickly settled; and land is worth from twenty to thirty dollars per acre: an advance of a thousand per cent. in about ten years!

A heavy fall of wet had rendered the roads muddy and unpleasant. On the 10th of June, the party arrived at *Wheeling*, a considerable but mean-looking town, of inns and stores, on the banks of the Ohio. Here they baited their horses, and took a repast of bread and milk. At this place the Ohio is divided into two channels, of five hundred yards each, by an island of three hundred acres.

Between Wheeling and St. Clairsville, they had sundry foaming creeks to ford; and sundry log-bridges to pass, which are a sort of commutation of danger. They had also a very muddy road, over hills of clay; and thunder and rain during nearly the whole of this their first stage: such thunder, and such rain, as they had heard of, but had seldom witnessed in England.

They were detained some days at *St. Clairsville*. This place consists of about one hundred and fifty houses; stores, taverns, doctors'-shops, and lawyers' offices, with the dwellings of sundry artisans; such as tailors, shoemakers, hatters, and smiths. Its chief street runs over one of the beautiful, round, and fertile hills which form this country. The court-house, a handsome brick edifice, on the summit, has a cheerful and a rather striking appearance. If the streets were paved, St. Clairsville would be a pleasant town, but, from the continued rains, they were, at this time, deep in mud.

The rich clay of this country is very favourable to grass, and the pastures are extremely fine. When the timber is destroyed, a beautiful turf takes immediate possession of the surface.

As they proceeded westward, towards Zanesville, the soil did not improve. It is here a yellow clay, well adapted for grass; but, when exhausted by repeated cropping, it will be unprofitable for tillage. In some places, the clay is over limestone, and exhibits marks of great and durable fertility.

During their journey, on the 13th of June, they met a group of nymphs, with their attendant swains, ten in number, on horseback: for no American walks who can obtain a horse; and there are few indeed who cannot. The young men were carrying umbrellas over the heads of their partners; and the appearance of the whole was very decent and respectable.

At the distance of eighteen miles east of Zanesville, whilst taking shelter from a thunder-storm, they were joined by four industrious pedestrians, who were returning eastward from a tour of observation through this state.

These all agreed in one sentiment, that there is no part of the Union, either in the new settlements or in the old, where an industrious man need be at a loss for the comforts of a good livelihood.

The land continued of the same character as before, a weak yellow clay, under a thin covering of vegetable mould, profitable for cultivation merely because it is new. The timber is chiefly oak. Little farms, of from eight to one hundred and sixty acres, with simple erections, a cabin and a stable, may be purchased, at the rate of from five to twenty dollars per acre. This is a hilly and romantic country; and affords many pleasant situations. Sand-stone is common; limestone more rare; but clay-slate appears to be the common basis.

The inhabitants are friendly and homely, not to say coarse; but they are well informed. This day the travellers passed various groups of emigrants, proceeding westward: one waggon, in particular, was the moving habitation of twenty souls.

Zanesville is a thriving town, on the beautiful *river Muskingum*, which is, at all times, navigable downward. The country around it is hilly and pleasant; not rich, but dry, and tolerably fertile. It abounds in coal and lime, and may, at some future period, become a grand station for manufactures.

At *Rushville* Mr. Birkbeck, another gentleman, and three children, sat down to a breakfast, consisting of the following articles: coffee, rolls, biscuits, dry toast, waffles, (a kind of soft hot cake, of German extraction, covered with butter,) salted pickerell, (a fish from Lake Huron,) veal-cutlets, broiled ham, gooseberry-pie, stewed currants, preserved cranberries, butter, and cheese: and Mr. Birkbeck, for himself and three children, and four gallons of oats, and a sufficient quantity of hay for four horses, was charged only six shillings and ninepence sterling.

South-west of Zanesville, instead of steep hills of yellow clay, the country assumes a more gently undulating surface; but it is sufficiently varied both for health and ornament, and has an absorbent, gravelly, or sandy soil, of moderate fertility.

Lancaster is on the edge of a marsh, or fen, which, at present, should seem to be a source of disease; though its bad effects, on the inhabitants of that town, are not by any means obvious.

The three towns, Zanesville, Lancaster, and *Chillicothe*, were founded by a sagacious man of the name of Zane, one of the earliest of the settlers. They are admirably placed, geographically, but with little regard to the health of their future inhabitants. The local advantages of Zanesville might have been equally secured, had the site of the town been on the higher, rather than the lower bank of the Muskingum: and the Sciota might have afforded equal facilities to the commerce of the inhabitants of Chillicothe, had they viewed it flowing beneath them, from those lovely eminences which adorn its opposite banks. Chillicothe is surrounded by the most charming elevations, but is itself in a bottom; and Lancaster is on the brink of an extensive marsh.

Seven miles north-west of Chillicothe the traveller enters on a tract of river bottom, the first rich land, for which this state, and indeed the whole western country, is so justly famous. It is agreeably varied in surface, occasionally rises into hills, and is never flat.

At Chillicothe there is an office for the several transactions regarding the disposal of the public lands of this district; and, on Mr. Birkbeck's arrival, he repaired to this office, for the purpose of inspecting a map of the district; and he found a great quantity of unentered lands, comprehending many entire townships, of eight miles square, lying about twenty miles south of Chillicothe; and, in several parts, abutting on the Sciota. Though it appeared certain that substantial objections had deterred purchasers from this extensive tract, in a country so much settled, yet Mr. Birkbeck, accompanied by his son, determined to visit it. They rode over twenty miles of fertile country, on the bank of the Sciota, and crossed that river to *Pike Town*; not far from which place was the land they were seeking.

Near Pike Town was a small cultivated prairie, the first Mr. Birkbeck had seen. It contained about two hundred acres of rich land, and was divided by a road, which ran through the middle; and nearly the whole of it was covered by fine Indian corn, neatly cultivated. The surrounding hills were crowned with woods. Nothing that Mr. Birkbeck had before seen in America at all resembled this delightful spot; but, from its low situation near the Sciota, it was unhealthy.

Pike Town was laid out, and received its name, about the year 1815. When Mr. Birkbeck was here, it contained a tavern, a store, and about twenty other dwellings.

The land of which Mr. Birkbeck came in quest was, as he supposed, of inferior quality. But though he found it unfit for his purpose, he had been repaid his trouble by the pleasure of his ride, through a fine portion of country. In leaving Chillicothe, to proceed towards Cincinnati, he and his party travelled through about seven miles of rich alluvial land, and over fertile uplands. But, as they proceeded, the country became level, with a cold heavy soil, better adapted to grass than tillage. Much of this tract remained in an unimproved state. They had passed some hills which were covered with the grandest white oak-timber imaginable. Within view from the road there were thousands of these magnificent trees, each of which measured fourteen or fifteen feet in circumference: their straight stems rising, without a branch, to the height of seventy or eighty feet, not tapering and slender, but surmounted by full, luxuriant heads.

For the space of a mile in breadth, a hurricane, which had traversed the entire western country in a north-east direction, about seven years before Mr. Birkbeck was here, had opened itself a passage through the forests, and had left a scene of extraordinary desolation. The trees lay tumbled over each other, like scattered stubble; some torn up by the roots, others broken off at different heights, or splintered only, and their tops bent over, and touching the ground. These hurricane tracts afford strong holes for game, and for all animals of savage kind.

As Mr. Birkbeck approached the *Little Miami River*, the country became more broken, much more fertile, and better settled than before. After crossing this rapid and clear stream, he had a pleasant ride to Lebanon, which is not a mountain of cedars, but a valley, so beautiful and fertile that, at its first opening on the view, it seemed rather a region of fancy than a real back-settlement scene.

Lebanon is itself one of those wonders which are the natural growth of these back woods. In fourteen years, from two or three cabins of half-savage hunters, it has grown to be the residence of a thousand persons, with habits and looks in no respect differing from their brethren of the east. Before Mr. Birkbeck and his party entered the town, they heard the supper-bells of the taverns; and they arrived just in time to take their seats at one of the tables, together with travellers like themselves, and several store-keepers, lawyers, and doctors; men who regularly board at taverns, and make up a standing company for the daily public table.

Mr. Birkbeck and his family next passed through *Cincinnati*, [a town which presents a scene of great life and activity. The market-house is an excellent building; and the market is under judicious regulations. Provisions are here plentiful and cheap; but articles of clothing, house-rent, and journeymen's wages are all very high.

This interesting town is situated on the banks of the *Ohio*, and contains from eight to ten thousand inhabitants, including blacks, who are numerous. It is built on the same plan as Philadelphia. There is a school, in which children are educated on the Lancasterian plan; and which, in 1817, contained one hundred and fifty children. Owing, however, to the "untamable insubordination of the scholars, it was found impossible to put in practice most of the punishments that are directed by the founder of the system. Two weekly newspapers are published at Cincinnati; one called "The Western Spy," and the other, "Liberty Hall."

There are, at this place, a woollen manufactory, a steam corn-mill, and a glass-house, on a tolerably large scale; and, in the main street, English goods abound in as great profusion as in Cheapside. The tradesmen import some of their goods direct from England, but they usually purchase them at Philadelphia; the journey to and from which place occupies three months; and goods are generally about fifty days in arriving.

There are, in Cincinnati, three banks; and paper-money is here so abundant, that specie, even of the smallest amount, is rarely to be seen. The little that does exist, consists chiefly of *cut* Spanish dollars. Notes of two shillings and two-pence, thirteen pence, sixpence halfpenny, and even of three-pence farthing, are very common: indeed, they constitute the chief part of the circulating medium.

Cincinnati is a very handsome town; a town, in fact, which must astonish every traveller, when he considers how recently it has been formed. Some of the houses are on a large scale; and the number of moderate-sized and well-built brick buildings is considerable. The churches are neat; and the post-office, in arrangement and management, would bear comparison with that of London.]

After having passed through Cincinnati, Mr. Birkbeck and his family entered the *state of Indiana*, and proceeded towards Vincennes. Indiana was, evidently, newer than the state of Ohio; and the character of the settlers appeared superior to that of the settlers in Ohio, who, in general, were a very indigent people. Those who fix themselves in Indiana, bring with them habits of comfort and the means of procuring the conveniences of life. These are observable in the construction of their cabins, and the neatness surrounding them; and, especially, in their well-stocked gardens, so frequent here, and so rare in the state of Ohio.

The country, from the town of Madison to the *Camp Tavern*, is not interesting, and a great part of the land is but of medium quality. At the latter place commences a broken country, approaching to mountainous, which, if well watered, would form a fine grazing district. In their progress, Mr. Birkbeck, one of the ladies, and a servant boy, were benighted at the foot of one of these rugged hills; and, without being well provided, they were compelled to make their first experiment of "camping out," as it is called.

A traveller, in the woods, says this gentleman, should always carry with him a flint, steel, tinder, and matches; a few biscuits, a half-pint vial of spirits, a tin cup, and a large knife or tomahawk; then, with his two blankets, and his great coat and umbrella, he need not be uneasy, should any unforeseen delay require his sleeping under a tree.

In the present instance, the important articles of tinder and matches were in the baggage of the division that had proceeded; and, as the night was rainy and excessively dark, the benighted party were, for some time, under considerable apprehension, lest they should be deprived of the comfort and security of a fire. Fortunately, Mr. Birkbeck's powder-flask was in his saddle-bags, and he succeeded in supplying the place of tinder, by moistening a piece of paper, and rubbing it with gunpowder. He then placed the touchpaper on an old cambric handkerchief. On this he scattered gunpowder pretty copiously, and with a flint and steel he soon succeeded in raising a flame: then, collecting together a quantity of dry wood, he made a noble fire. There was a mattress for the lady, a bear-skin for Mr. Birkbeck, and the load of the pack-horse served as a pallet for the boy. Thus, by means of great coats and blankets, and their umbrellas spread over their heads, they made their quarters tolerably comfortable; and, placing themselves to the leeward of the fire, with their feet towards it, they lay more at ease than they could have done in the generality of taverns. They had a few biscuits, a small bottle of spirits, and a phial of oil. By twisting some cord very hard, and dipping it in the oil, they contrived to make torches; and, after several fruitless attempts, they succeeded in finding water. "Camping out," when the tents are pitched by day-light, and the party are furnished with the articles, which Mr. Birkbeck was obliged to supply by expedients, is pleasant in fine weather. The lady was exceedingly ill, which had in fact occasioned their being benighted; and never was the night's charge of a sick friend undertaken with more dismal forebodings. The rain, however, having ceased, the invalid passed the night in safety; so that the morning found them more comfortable than they could have anticipated.

The town of *Vincennes* is scattered over a plain, lying some feet lower than the banks of the *Wabash*: a situation seemingly unfavourable to health; and, in fact, agues and bilious fevers are frequent here during the autumn.

The road from Sholt's Tavern to this place, thirty-six miles distant, lies partly across "barrens," that is, land of middling quality, thinly set with timber, or covered with long grass and shrubby underwood; generally level and dry, and gaudy with marigolds, sunflowers, martagon lilies, and many other beautiful flowers. On the whole, the country is tame, poorly watered, and not desirable as a place of settlement; but, from its varied character, it is pleasant to travel over. Vincennes exhibits a motley assemblage of inhabitants as well as visitors. The inhabitants are Americans, French Canadians, and Negroes. The visitors are chiefly Americans from various states; and Indians from various nations: Shawnees, Delawares, and Miamies, who live about a hundred miles northward, and who come here to trade for skins. The Indians were encamped, in considerable numbers, round the town, and were continually riding into the place, to the stores and the whiskey-shops. Their horses and accoutrements were generally mean, and their persons disagreeable. Their faces were painted in various ways, which gave an appearance of ferocity to their countenances.

One of them, a Shawnee, had his eyes, or rather his eyelids and the surrounding parts, daubed with vermilion. He thus looked hideous enough at a distance; but, on a nearer view, he had good features, and was a fine, stout, and fierce-looking man. Some of the Indians were well dressed. One young man, in particular, of the Miami nation, wore a clear, light blue cotton vest, with sleeves; and had his head ornamented with black feathers.

They all wear pantaloons, or rather long moccasins of buck-skin, covering the foot and leg, and reaching half way up the thigh, which is bare: a covering of cloth, a foot square, passes between the thighs, and hangs behind like an apron. Their complexion was various: some were dark, and others were not so swarthy as even Mr. Birkbeck; but he saw none of the copper-colour, which he had imagined to be their distinguishing characteristic. These Indians are addicted to drinking spirits, and are often intoxicated. They use much action in their discourse, and laugh immoderately. Their hair is straight and black, and their eyes are dark. Many of the women are decently dressed and good-looking.

Mr. Birkbeck remarks that, in Great Britain, the people are so circumscribed in their movements, that, with them, miles seem equal to tens of miles in America. He says that, in America, travellers will start on an expedition of three thousand miles, by boats, on horseback, or on foot, with as little deliberation or anxiety, as an Englishman would set out on a journey of three hundred.

At Vincennes, the foundation had just been laid of a large establishment of mills to be worked by steam. Water-mills of great power were building on the Wabash, near Harmony; and undertakings of similar kind will, no doubt, be called for and executed, along the banks of this river, and of its various tributary streams.

On entering Vincennes there is nothing which tends to make a favourable impression on a stranger; but it improves on acquaintance, for it contains agreeable people: and there is a spirit of cleanliness, and even of neatness, in the houses and manner of living. There is also a strain of politeness in the inhabitants, which marks the origin of this settlement to be French.

At *Princeton*, a place scarcely three years old, Mr. Birkbeck and his family went to a log-tavern, where neatness was as well observed as at many taverns in the cities of England. The people of this town belong to

America in dress and manners; but they would not disgrace old England in the general decorum of their deportment.

Mr. Birkbeck lamented here, as in other parts of America, the small account that is had of time. Subsistence is easily secured, and liberal pursuits are yet too rare to operate as a general stimulus to exertion: the consequence is, that life is whiled away in a painful state of yawning lassitude.

Twenty or thirty miles west of this place, in the Illinois territory, is a large country where settlements were beginning; and where, Mr. Birkbeck says, there was an abundant choice of unentered lands, of a description, which, if the statements of travellers and surveyors, even after great abatements, can be relied on, he imagined would satisfy his wishes.

Princeton affords a very encouraging situation for a temporary abode. It stands on an elevated spot, in an uneven country, ten miles from the river Wabash, and two from the navigable stream of the Patok; but the country is rich, and the timber is vast in bulk and height.

The small-pox is likely soon to be excluded from this state; for vaccination is very generally adopted, and inoculation for the small-pox is prohibited altogether; not by law, but by common consent. If it should be known that an individual had undergone this operation, the inhabitants would compel him to withdraw from society. If he lived in a town, he must absent himself, or he would be driven away.

On the 25th of July, Mr. Birkbeck explored the country as far as *Harmony* and the banks of the Ohio. He lodged in a cabin, at a very new town, on the banks of the Ohio, called *Mount Vernon*. Here he found the people of a character which confirmed the aversion he had previously entertained to a settlement in the immediate vicinity of a large navigable river. Every hamlet was demoralized, and every plantation was liable to outrage, within a short distance of such a thoroughfare.

Yet, to persons who had been long buried in deep forests, the view of that noble expanse was like the opening of a bright day upon the gloom of night. To travel, day after day, among trees a hundred feet high, without a glimpse of the surrounding country, is oppressive to a degree which those cannot conceive who have not experienced it.

Mr. Birkbeck left Harmony after breakfast, on the ensuing day, and, crossing the Wabash, at a ferry, he proceeded to the *Big Prairie*, where, to his astonishment, he beheld a fertile plain of grass and arable; and some thousand acres of land covered with corn, more luxuriant than any he had before seen. The scene reminded him of some open well-cultivated vale in Europe, surrounded by wooded uplands. But the illusion vanished on his arrival at the habitation of Mr. Williams, the owner of an estate, on which, at this time, there were nearly three hundred acres of beautiful corn in one field; for this man lived in a way apparently as remote from comfort, as the settler of one year, who thinks only of the means of supporting existence.

The inhabitants of the Prairie are healthy, and the females and children are better complexioned than their neighbours of the timber country. It is evident that they breathe better air: but they are in a low state of civilization, being about half Indian in their mode of life. They are hunters by profession, and would have the whole range of the forests for themselves and their cattle. Strangers appear, to them, invaders of their privileges; as they have intruded on the better founded and exclusive privileges of their Indian predecessors.

After viewing several Prairies, which, with their surrounding woods, were so beautiful as to seem like the creation of fancy; (gardens of delight in a dreary wilderness;) and after losing their horses, and spending two days in recovering them, Mr. Birkbeck and his party took a hunter, as their guide, and proceeded across the little Wabash, to explore the country between that river and the Skillet Fork.

The lonely settlers, in the districts north of Big Prairie, are in a miserable state: their bread-corn must be ground thirty miles off; and it occupied three days to carry to the mill, and bring back, the small horse-load of three bushels. To struggle with privations has now become the habit of their lives, most of them having made several successive plunges into the wilderness.

Mr. Birkbeck's journey across the little Wabash was a complete departure from all mark of civilization. Wandering without track, where even the sagacity of the hunter-guide had nearly failed, they at length arrived at the cabin of another hunter, in which they lodged. This man, his wife, his eldest son, a tall, half-naked youth, just initiated in the hunter's arts; his three daughters, growing up into great rude girls, and a squalling tribe of dirty brats, of both sexes, were of one pale yellow colour, without the slightest tint of healthful bloom. They were remarkable instances of the effect, on the complexion, produced by living perpetually in the midst of woods.

Their cabin, which may serve as a specimen of these rudiments of houses, was formed of round logs, with apertures of three or four inches: there was no chimney, but large intervals were left between the "clapboards," for the escape of the smoke. The roof, however, was a more effectual covering, than Mr. Birkbeck had generally experienced, as it protected him and his party very tolerably from a drenching night. Two bedsteads, formed of unhewn logs, and cleft boards laid across; two chairs, (one of them without a bottom,) and a low stool, were all the furniture possessed by this numerous family. A string of buffalo-hide, stretched across the hovel, was a wardrobe for their rags; and their utensils, consisting of a large iron-pot, some baskets, one good rifle, and two that were useless, stood about in corners; and a fiddle, which was seldom silent, except when the inhabitants were asleep, hung by them.

These hunters, in the back-settlements of America, are as persevering as savages, and as indolent. They cultivate indolence as a privilege: "You English (they say) are industrious, but we have freedom." And thus they exist, in yawning indifference, surrounded by nuisances and petty wants; the former of which might be removed, and the latter supplied, by the application of one tenth part of the time that is loitered away in their innumerable idle days.

The *Little Wabash*, which Mr. Birkbeck crossed in search of some Prairies, that had been described to him in glowing colours, was, at this season, a sluggish and scanty stream; but, for three months of the latter part of winter and the beginning of spring, it covers a great space of ground, by the overflow of waters collected in its long course. The *Skillet Fork* is a river of similar character; and the country that lies between them must labour under the inconvenience of absolute seclusion, for many months every year, until bridges and ferries are established. Having made his way through this wildest of wildernesses to the Skillet Fork, Mr. Birkbeck crossed that river at a shoal. The country, on each side of it, is flat and swampy; so that the water, in many places, even at this season, rendered travelling disagreeable; yet here and there, at ten miles' distance, perhaps, the very solitude tempts persons to pitch their tents for a season.

At one of these lone dwellings Mr. Birkbeck found a neat, respectable looking female, spinning under the little piazza at one side of the cabin, which shaded her from the sun. Her husband was absent on business, which would detain him some weeks: she had no family, and no companion except her husband's dog, which usually attended him during his bear-hunting, in the winter. She said she was quite overcome with "lone," and hoped the party would tie their horses in the wood, and sit awhile with her, during the heat of the day. They did so, and she rewarded them with a basin of coffee. She said her husband was kind and good, and never left her without necessity. He was a true lover of bear-hunting; and, in the preceding winter, had killed a great number of bears.

On the second of August the party lodged at another cabin, where similar neatness prevailed, both within and without. The woman was neat, and the children were clean in skin, and whole in their clothes. The man possessed good sense and sound notions, and was ingenious and industrious. He lived on the edge of the Seven Miles' Prairie, a spot charming to the eye, but deficient in water.

Mr. Birkbeck considers *Shawnee Town* as a phænomenon, evincing the pertinacious adherence of man to the spot where he has once established himself. Once a year, for many successive springs, the Ohio, in its annual overflowings, has carried away the fences from the cleared lands of the inhabitants, till at length they have given them up, and ceased to cultivate them. Once a year the inhabitants of Shawnee Town either make their escape to higher lands, or take refuge in the upper stories of their houses, until the waters subside, when they recover their position on this desolate sand-bank.

At Shawnee Town there is an office for the south-east district of Illinois. Here Mr. Birkbeck constituted himself a land-owner, by paying seven hundred and twenty dollars, as one-fourth part of the purchase-money of fourteen hundred and forty acres. This land, with a similar purchase made by a Mr. Flower, constituted part of a beautiful and rich Prairie, about six miles distant from the Big Wabash, and the same distance from the Little Wabash.

The land was rich, natural meadow, bounded by timbered ground: it was within reach of two navigable rivers; and, at a small expence, was capable of being rendered immediately productive.

The geographical position of this portion of territory appeared to be extremely favourable. The Big Wabash, a noble stream, which forms its eastern boundary, runs four hundred miles, through one of the most fertile portions of this most fertile region. By means of a portage of eight miles to the Miami of the lakes, it has a communication, well known to the Indian traders, with Lake Huron, and with all the navigation of the north.

Mr. Birkbeck left Shawnee town on the third of August. He had found here something of river-barbarism, the genuine Ohio character; but he had met with a greater number, than he had expected, of agreeable individuals: and the kind and hospitable treatment he experienced at the tavern, formed a good contrast to the rude society and wretched fare he had left at the Skillet Fork.

On his return to *Harmony*, the day being Sunday, he had an opportunity of seeing, grouped and in their best attire, a large part of the members of this wonderful community. It was evening when he arrived, and he observed no human creature about the streets: soon the entire body of the people, about seven hundred in number, poured out of the church, and exhibited the appearance of health, neatness, and peace.

This colony is useful to the neighbourhood. It furnishes, from its store, many articles of great value, not so well supplied elsewhere; and it is a market for all spare produce. Many kinds of culinary plants, and many fruit-trees are cultivated here; and the Harmonites set a good example of neatness and industry. When we contrast their neatness and order, with the slovenly habits of their neighbours, we see (says Mr. Birkbeck) the good that arises from association, which advances these poor people a century, at least, on the social scale, beyond the solitary beings who build their huts in the wilderness.

At Harmony Mr. Birkbeck and his family lived at the tavern, and their board there cost two dollars per week, each person: for these they received twenty-one meals. Excellent coffee and tea, with broiled chickens, bacon, &c. for breakfast and supper, and a variety of good, but simple fare at dinner. Except coffee, tea, or milk, no liquor but water is thought of at meals in this country.

Mr. Birkbeck observes that, when the back country of America is mentioned in England, musquitoes by night, and rattlesnakes by day, never fail to alarm the imagination: to say nothing of wolves and bears, and panthers, and Indians still more ferocious than these. His course of travelling, from the mouth of James River, and over the mountains, up to Pittsburg, about five hundred miles; then three hundred miles through the woods of the state of Ohio, down to Cincinnati; next, across the entire wilderness of Indiana, and to the extreme south of the Illinois: — this long and deliberate journey, (he says,) one would suppose, might have introduced his party to an intimate acquaintance with some of these pests of America. It is true that they killed several of the serpent tribe; black snakes, garter-snakes, &c. and that they saw one rattlesnake of extraordinary size. They experienced inconvenience from musquitoes in a few damp spots, just as they would have done from gnats in England. In their late expeditions in the Illinois, where they led the lives of thorough backwoods-men, if they were so unfortunate as to pitch their tent on the edge of a creek, or near a swamp, and mismanaged their fire, they were teased with musquitoes, as they would have been in the fens of Cambridgeshire: but this was the sum total of their experience of these reported plagues.

Wolves and bears are extremely numerous, and commit much injury in the newly-settled districts. Hogs, which are a main dependance for food as well as profit, are the constant prey of the bears; and the holds of these animals are so strong, that the hunters are unable to keep down their numbers.

[In the autumn of the year 1817, Mr. Birkbeck removed, with his family, to the property he had purchased, between the Great and Little Wabash, and to which he has given the name of *English Prairie*." In his "Notes on America," and in his "Letters from the Illinois," he has described, in an interesting manner, the face of the country, its soil, productions, mode of culture, and capacities of improvement; and has pointed out the great advantages which it offers to settlers, especially to labourers and to farmers with small capital. The confidence that is reposed in his judgment and agricultural skill, has already induced several persons to emigrate into the same neighbourhood, both from England and the United States; but the singularity of his religious opinions, and his objection to the admission of religious instructors of any description into his settlement, had prevented many conscientious persons from joining him, who might have proved useful members of his little community.]

From this place we must return to *Philadelphia*, for the purpose of accompanying Mr. Weld on a journey to Washington, the federal city or metropolis of the United States.

Seventh Day's Instruction

UNITED STATES CONTINUED.

Narrative of Mr. Weld's *Excursion from Philadelphia to Washington.*

On the 16th of November, 1795, Mr. Weld left *Philadelphia* in one of the public stage-waggons. The country around this city was well cultivated, and abounded with neat villas and farm-houses; but it had a naked appearance, for all the trees had been cut down, either for fuel or to make way for the plough.

The road to Baltimore passed over the lowest of three floating bridges, which had been thrown across the *river Schuylkill.* The view, on crossing this river, which is about two hundred and fifty yards wide, is peculiarly beautiful. The banks on each side are high, and, for many miles, afford extremely delightful situations for villas.

The country, after passing the Schuylkill, is pleasingly diversified with rising grounds and woods; and appears to be in a good state of cultivation. The first town of any note at which Mr. Weld arrived, was *Chester;* which at this time contained about sixty dwellings, and was remarkable for being the place where the first colonial assembly sat. From the vicinity of Chester, there is a grand view of the river Delaware.

About half a mile from Wilmington is *Brandywine River,* remarkable for its mills: no fewer than thirteen having been built, almost close to each other, upon it.

Wilmington is the capital of the state of Delaware, and contained, at this time, about six hundred houses, which were chiefly of brick. The streets are laid out in a manner somewhat similar to those of Philadelphia. There is, however, nothing very interesting in this town, and the country around it is flat and unpleasant. *Elkton,* twenty-one miles from Wilmington, and the first town in Maryland, is a dirty and disagreeable place; which contains about ninety indifferent houses, that are built without any regularity.

Every ten or twelve miles upon this road there are taverns. These are all built of wood, and much in the same style; with a porch in front, which extends the entire length of the house. Few of them have any signs, and they are only to be distinguished from other houses, by a number of handbills pasted upon the walls near the door. Each of them is named, not from the sign, but from the person who keeps it; as Jones's, Brown's, &c. and all are kept nearly in the same manner. At each house there are regular hours for breakfast, dinner, and supper: and, if a traveller arrive somewhat before the time appointed for any one of these meals, it is in vain to desire a separate repast for himself: he must patiently wait till the regulated hour; and must then sit down with such other guests as happen to be in the house.

The *Susquehannah* river is crossed, on the way to Baltimore, at a ferry five miles above its entrance into the Chesapeak. The river is here about a mile and a quarter wide, and deep enough for vessels of any burden. The banks are high and thickly wooded, and the scenery is grand and picturesque. A small town, called *Havre de Grace*, which contains about forty houses, stands on this river at the ferry. From Havre to Baltimore the country is extremely poor; the soil is of a yellow gravel mixed with clay, and the road is execrable.

Baltimore is supposed to have, at this time, contained about sixteen thousand *inhabitants*. Though not the capital of the state, it is the largest town in Maryland; and, after Philadelphia and New York, is the most considerable place of trade in North America. [It is built round the head of a bay or inlet of the *river Patuxent,* and about eight miles above its junction with the Chesapeak.] The *plan* of the town is somewhat similar to that of Philadelphia. Most of the *streets* cross each other at right angles. The main street, which runs nearly east and west, is about eighty feet wide, and the others measure from forty to sixty feet. The streets are not all paved, so that, in wet weather, they are almost impassable; the soil being a stiff yellow clay, which retains the water a long time. On the south of the town is the harbour, which affords about nine feet water, and is large enough to contain two thousand sail of merchant-vessels.

The greatest number of private *houses* in Baltimore, are of brick; but many, particularly in the skirts of the town, are of wood. In some of the new streets, a few appeared to be well built; but, in general, they are small, heavy, and inconvenient. [The public buildings have very little architectural beauty.

In the year 1817, Baltimore contained fifty thousand inhabitants; and was still rapidly increasing.] Among the inhabitants are to be found English, Irish, Scotch, and French; but the Irish appear to be most numerous. With a few exceptions, they are all engaged in trade; and they are, for the most part, a plain people, sociable among themselves, and friendly and hospitable towards strangers. Cards and dancing are here favourite amusements. During the autumn, Baltimore is unhealthy, and such persons as can afford it, retire to country-seats in the neighbourhood, some of which are delightfully situated.

From Baltimore to Washington, a distance of forty miles, the country has but a poor appearance. The soil, in some parts, consists of yellow clay mixed with gravel: in other parts it is sandy. In the neighbourhood of the creeks, and between the hills, there are patches of rich black earth, called bottoms, the trees upon which grow to a large size.

A description of the City of Washington.

This city was laid out in the year 1792; and was expressly designed for the seat of government, and the metropolis of the United States. Accordingly, in the month of November, 1800, the congress assembled here for the first time. It stands on a neck of land, between the forks formed by the eastern and western branches of the river *Potomac*. This neck of land, together with an adjacent territory, ten miles square, was ceded to the American congress by the states of Maryland and Virginia. The ground on which the city has been built, was the property of private individuals, who readily relinquished their claim to one half of it in favour of congress, conscious that the value of what was left to them would increase, and amply compensate them for their loss.

The *plan* of the buildings was drawn by a Frenchman, whose name was L'Enfant; and the ground, marked out for them, was fourteen miles in circumference. The *streets* run north and south, east and west; but, to prevent that sameness which would result from their all crossing each other at right angles, several avenues have been laid out, in different parts of the city, which run transversely. The streets are, in general, from ninety to a hundred feet, and the avenues one hundred and sixty feet wide. There is also an arrangement for several squares.

Including the suburb of George Town, this city contains about twenty thousand *inhabitants*, who are scattered over a vast space, in detached masses of buildings, which appear like petty hamlets in a populous country. The intended *streets* are, for the most part, only distinguishable from the rugged waste, by a slight trace, like that of a newly-formed road; or, in some instances, by rows of poplar trees, which afford neither ornament nor shade.

The *Capitol*, and the house appropriated to the president of the United States, are situated on opposite hills, and are the chief public buildings in Washington. During the late war, they were both nearly destroyed by the British forces; but they are now rising into increased splendour. The capitol, in which are the houses of the legislature, and several public offices, stands on a bank of the Potomac, seventy feet above the level of that river. It as yet consists of only two wings; but these are intended to be connected by a centre, surmounted by a dome.

The *president's house* is at the opposite end of "Pennsylvania Avenue," and commands a most beautiful prospect. On each side of it stands a large brick building: one of which is the treasury, and the other is appropriated to the war and navy offices. These are hereafter to be connected with the palace.

The *post office* is a large brick edifice, situated at about an equal distance from the president's house and the capitol. Under the same roof is the patent-office, and the national library, for the use of members of the congress. In 1817 there were, in Washington, many brick buildings, two and three stories high. There were also some small wooden houses; though, according to the original plan, no houses were to be built less than three stories high, and all were to have marble steps.

The *river Potomac*, at Washington, is navigable only for small craft; but, besides this, there is a river, about the width of the Paddington canal, which is dignified by the name of *Tiber*. The ridiculous, though characteristic vanity displayed in changing its original appellation from "Goose-creek" to that of "Tiber," has been happily exposed by the English poet Moore. Speaking of this city, he says,

> In fancy now, beneath the twilight gloom,
> Come, let me lead thee o'er this modern Rome,
> Where tribunes rule, where dusky Davi bow,
> And what was Goose-creek once is Tiber now.
> This fam'd metropolis, where fancy sees
> Squares in morasses, obelisks in trees.

There are, at Washington, four market-days in the week, and negroes are the chief sellers of provisions; but the supplies are neither good nor various. In this city rents are very high; and mechanics are fully employed and well paid. Shopkeepers too are numerous; but its increase cannot be rapid, for it has no decidedly great natural advantages. It has little external commerce, a barren soil, and a scanty population; is enfeebled by the deadly weight of absolute slavery, and has no direct communication with the western country.

With regard to the manners of the *inhabitants*, it is remarked that both sexes, whether on horseback or on foot, carry umbrellas at all seasons: in summer, to keep off the sunbeams; in winter, as a shelter from the rain and snow; and in spring and autumn, to intercept the dews of the evening. At dinner and at tea parties, the ladies sit together, and seldom mix with the gentlemen, whose conversation usually turns upon political subjects. In almost all houses toddy, or spirits and water, is offered to guests a few minutes before dinner. Boarders in boarding-houses, or in taverns, sometimes throw off their coats during the heat of summer; and, in winter, their shoes, for the purpose of warming their feet at the fire; customs which the climate only can excuse. The barber always arrives on horseback, to perform the operation of shaving; and here, as in some towns of Europe, he is the organ of all the news and scandal of the place.

In the year 1817, when Mr. Fearon was in Washington, the congress was sitting, and that gentleman several times attended the debates. The place of meeting was a temporary one: it had been designed for an hotel, and was in the immediate vicinity of the capitol. The congress assembled at eleven o'clock in the morning, and adjourned at four in the afternoon. Mr. Fearon's first visit was to the *senate*. This body is composed of forty members, the states having increased their original number of thirteen to that of twenty; and each state, regardless of its population, sends two. The gallery of the senate-house is open to all; and the only form observed, is that of taking off the hat. When Mr. Fearon was at Washington, the chairman's seat was central, under a handsome canopy; and the members were seated, on rich scarlet cushions, some at double, and some at single desks. There were two large fires; and the room was carpeted, as was also the gallery. In the congress, the forms of business, with a few minor exceptions, are taken from those of the British parliament. There is, however, one point of variation: every speech is apparently listened to; and all the speeches, whether good or bad, seem regarded with equal apathy, and with a complete lifeless endurance, neither applause nor censure being allowed.

The *Representative Chamber* was in the same building, and about twice the extent. A gallery was here also open to the public of both sexes. This assembly consists of nearly two hundred members. These want, in appearance, the age, experience, dignity, and respectability, which an Englishman associates with the idea of legislators, and which are possessed by the superior branch of the congress. The members sat on very common chairs, and at unpainted desks, which were placed in rows. A few of the speakers commanded attention; but others talked on as long they pleased, while the rest were occupied in writing letters or reading newspapers. A spitting-box was placed at the feet of each member, and, contrary to the practice of the upper house, both the members and visitors wore their hats.

During the sitting of congress, the president, or rather his lady, holds a drawing-room weekly. He takes by the hand all those persons who are presented to him; shaking of hands being here considered more rational and more manly than kissing them.

George Town may be described as a suburb of Washington. It is finely situated, on the north-east side of the Potomac river, and is divided, from Washington, by the Rock Creek, over which are two bridges. The houses are chiefly of brick, and have a neat appearance. Several of them were built before the streets were formed, which gave rise to an observation by a French lady, that "George Town had houses without streets; Washington, streets without houses."

Alexandria, formerly called Belhaven, is a small, but peculiarly neat town, on the western side of the Potomac, and about six miles south of Washington. Its streets, like those of Philadelphia, run in straight lines, and intersect each other at right angles. The houses are of neat construction. The public buildings are an episcopal church, an academy, a court-house, a bank, and gaol. This place carries on a considerable trade; and the warehouses and wharfs are very commodious. The distance from Alexandria to George Town is about ten miles; and there is a daily communication between the two places, by means of a packet-boat.

Nine miles below Alexandria, and also on the bank of the Potomac, stands *Mount Vernon*, formerly the country-seat of general Washington. The house is of wood, but cut and painted so as to resemble stone. It has a lawn in front; and, when Mr. Weld was here, the garden had the appearance of a nursery-ground.

Narrative of Mr. Weld's Journey from Washington to Richmond in Virginia.

In proceeding from Washington southward, Mr. Weld passed through a part of the country which was flat, sandy, and had a most dreary aspect. For many successive miles nothing was to be seen but extensive plains, that had been worn out by the culture of tobacco, and were overgrown with yellow sedge, and interspersed with groves of pine and cedar-trees, the dark green colour of which formed a singular contrast with the yellow of the sedge. In the midst of these plains there were, however, the remains of several good houses, which showed that the country had once been in a flourishing state.

Mr. Weld crossed the Potomac at a place called *Hoe's Ferry*, The ferry-man told him that, in the river, was a bank of oysters, and that, if he wished it, the men should take up some. The singularity of obtaining oysters from fresh water induced Mr. Weld to stop at the bank; and the men, in a few minutes, collected as many as would have filled a bushel. The oysters were extremely good when cooked, but were disagreeable when eaten raw. The Potomac, as well as the other rivers in Virginia, abounds with excellent fish of various kinds. At the ferry it is about three miles wide.

Mr. Weld prevailed with the ferry-man to take him about ten miles down the river, and land him on the Virginian shore, in a part of the country which appeared to be a perfect wilderness. No traces of a road or pathway were visible on the loose white sand; and the cedar and pine-trees grew so closely together, on all sides, that it was scarcely possible to see further forward, in any direction, than a hundred yards. Taking a course, as nearly as he could guess, in a direct line from the river, at the end of about an hour, he found a narrow road, which led to a large and ancient brick house. The master of it was from home, and Mr. Weld was obliged to proceed onward, several miles further, to a wretched hovel which had the name of a tavern. On the ensuing morning he proceeded to the residence of a gentleman, which was between the rivers Potomac and *Rappahannoc*, and where he had been invited to pass a few weeks.

The principal planters in Virginia possess large estates, and have, on them, nearly every thing they can want. Among their slaves are found tailors, shoemakers, carpenters, smiths, turners, wheelwrights, weavers, and tanners. Woollen cloths and cotton goods, of several kinds, are manufactured at this province. Cotton grows here in great luxuriance: the plants, indeed, are often killed by the frost in winter, but they always produce abundantly, the first year in which they are sown.

The large estates in Virginia are managed by stewards and overseers; and the work is done wholly by slaves. The cottages of the slaves are usually at the distance of a few hundred yards from the dwelling-house, and give the appearance of a village, to the residence of every planter. Adjoining to these cottages the slaves usually have small gardens, and yards for poultry. They have ample time to attend to their own concerns: their gardens are generally well stocked, and their flocks of poultry numerous. Many of their little huts are comfortably furnished, and they are themselves, in general, well clad. But Mr. Weld remarked, that this class of persons is much more kindly treated in Virginia, than in the other states of America.

The part of Virginia in which Mr. Weld was now passing his time, was, in general, flat and sandy, and abounded in pine and cedar-trees: some districts, however, were well cultivated, and afforded good crops of corn; but these were intermixed with extensive tracts of waste land, worn out by the culture of tobacco, and almost destitute of verdure.

The common people, in the lower parts of Virginia, have very sallow complexions, owing to the burning rays of the sun in summer, and the bilious complaints to which they are subject during the fall of the year; but those in the upper parts of the country, towards the mountains, have a healthy and comely appearance.

After Mr. Weld had left the house of his friend, he crossed the *Rappahannoc River*, to a small town called *Tappahannoc*, or *Hob's Hole*, containing about one hundred houses. The river is here about three quarters of a mile wide, and, though the distance from its mouth is seventy miles, sharks are very often seen.

From Tappahannoc to *Urbanna*, another small town on the Rappahannoc, and about twenty-five miles lower down, the country wears but a poor aspect. The road, which is level and sandy, runs, for many successive miles, through woods. The habitations that are seen from it are but few, and these of the poorest description. The woods chiefly consist of black oak, pine, and cedar-trees, which only grow on land of the worst quality.

Mr. Weld observed many traces of fires in the woods. Such fires, he was informed, were frequent in the spring of the year; and they were usually occasioned by the negligence of people who burnt the underwood, for the purpose of clearing the lands. He was himself witness to one of them. The day had been remarkably serene, and the underwood had been fired in several places. During the afternoon, the weather was sultry, and, about five o'clock, the horizon, towards the north, became dark, and a terrible whirlwind arose. Mr. Weld was standing, with some gentlemen, on an eminence, and perceived it gradually advancing. It carried along with it a cloud of dust, dried leaves, and pieces of rotten wood; and, in many places, as it passed along, it levelled the fence-rails, and unroofed the cattle-sheds. Mr. Weld and his friends endeavoured, but in vain, to reach a place of shelter. In the course of two minutes the whirlwind overtook them: the shock was violent; it was hardly possible to stand, and was difficult to breathe. It passed over in about three minutes; but a storm, accompanied by heavy thunder and lightning, succeeded: this lasted more than half an hour. On looking round, immediately after the whirlwind had passed, a prodigious column of fire appeared in a part of the wood where some underwood had been burning. In many places the flames rose considerably above the summit of the trees, which were of large growth. It was a tremendous, and, at the same time, a sublime sight. The Negroes, on the surrounding plantations, were all assembled with their hoes; and guards were stationed, at every corner, to give alarm, if the fire appeared elsewhere, lest the conflagration should become general. To one plantation a spark was carried by the wind more than half a mile; happily, however, a torrent of rain, shortly afterwards, came pouring down, and enabled the people to extinguish the flames in every quarter.

The country between Urbanna and Gloucester is neither so sandy nor so flat as that bordering upon the Rappahannoc. The trees, chiefly pines, are of large size, and afford abundance of turpentine, which is extracted from them, in great quantities, by the inhabitants.

Gloucester contained, at this time, only ten or twelve houses. It is situated on a neck of land nearly opposite to the town of York, and on the bank of the *York River*, here about a mile and half wide. *York* consisted of about seventy houses, an episcopalian church, and a gaol. It is remarkable for having been the place where lord Cornwallis surrendered his army to the combined forces of the Americans and French. The banks of the river are, for the most part, high and inaccessible; and the principal part of the town is built upon them; only a few fishing-huts and store-houses standing at the bottom.

Twelve miles from York is *Williamsburgh*, formerly the seat of government in Virginia. At this time it consisted of one principal street, and two others, which ran parallel to it. At one end of the main street stands the college, and, at the other end, the old capitol or State-house, a capacious building of brick, which was crumbling to pieces, from neglect. The houses around it were mostly uninhabited, and presented a melancholy appearance.

The college of William and Mary, as it is still called, is at the opposite end of the main street: it is a heavy pile of building, somewhat resembling a large brick-kiln. The students were, at this time, about thirty in number; but, from their boyish appearance, the seminary ought rather to be termed a grammar-school than a college.

Mr. Weld dined with the president of the college. Half a dozen, or more, of the students, the eldest about twelve years old, were at table; some without shoes and stockings, and others without coats. A couple of dishes of salted meat, and some oyster-soup, formed the whole of the repast.

The town of Williamsburgh contained, at this time, about twelve hundred inhabitants; and the society in it was thought to be more extensive, and at the same time more genteel, than in any other place of its size in America. No manufactures were carried on here, and there was scarcely any trade.

From Williamsburgh to Hampton the country is flat and uninteresting. *Hampton* is a small town, situated at the head of a bay, near the mouth of James River. It contained about thirty houses and an episcopal church; and was a dirty, disagreeable place.

From this town there is a regular ferry to Norfolk, across Hampton Roads, eighteen miles over. *Norfolk* stands nearly at the mouth of the eastern branch of Elizabeth River, the most southern of the rivers which fall into *Chesapeak Bay*. This is the largest commercial town in Virginia, and carries on a flourishing trade to the West Indies. Its exports consist principally of tobacco, flour, and corn, and various kinds of timber. Of the latter it derives an inexhaustible supply, from the great "Dismal Swamp," which is immediately in its neighbourhood.

The houses in Norfolk were about five hundred in number; but most of them were of wood, and meanly built. These had all been erected since the year 1776; when the place had been totally burnt, by order of lord Dunmore, then the British governor of Virginia. The losses sustained, on this occasion, were estimated at three hundred thousand pounds sterling. Near the harbour the streets are narrow and irregular: in the other parts of the town they are tolerably wide. None of them, however, are paved, and all are filthy. During the hot months of summer, the stench that proceeds from some of them is horrid.

There were, at this time, two churches, one for episcopalians, and the other for methodists; but, in the former, service was not performed more than once in two or three weeks. Indeed, throughout all the lower parts of Virginia, that is, between the mountains, and the sea, the people seemed to have scarcely any sense of religion; and, in the country districts, all the churches were falling into decay.

From Norfolk Mr. Weld went to the *Dismal Swamp*. This commences at the distance of nine miles from the town, extends into North Carolina, and occupies, in the whole, about one hundred and fifty thousand acres. The entire tract is covered with trees, some of which are of enormous size; and between them, the underwood springs up so thick, that the swamp is, in many parts, absolutely impervious. It abounds also with cane-reeds, and with long rich grass, on which cattle feed with great avidity, and become fat in a short time. In the interior of the swamp, large herds of wild cattle are found; the offspring, probably, of animals which have at different times been lost, or turned out to feed. Bears, wolves, deer, and other wild indigenous animals, are also found here.

As the Dismal Swamp lies so very near to Norfolk, where there is a constant demand for timber, staves, and other similar articles, for exportation; and, as the best of these are made from trees grown upon the swamp, it of course becomes a valuable species of property. A canal, which the inhabitants of Norfolk were, at this time, cutting through it, would also tend to enhance its value.

From the Dismal Swamp to Richmond, a distance of about one hundred and forty miles, along the south side of *James River*, the country is flat and sandy, and, for many successive miles, is covered with pine-trees. In some parts there are peach-orchards, which are very profitable. From the peaches, the inhabitants make brandy, which, when properly matured, is an excellent liquor, and much esteemed: they give it a delicious flavour by infusing dried pears in it.

The accommodation at the taverns along this road, was most wretched; nothing was to be had but rancid fish, fat salt pork, and bread made of Indian corn. Mr. Weld's horses were almost starved. Hay is scarcely ever used in this part of the country, but, in place of it, the inhabitants feed their cattle with what they call fodder, the leaves of the Indian corn-plant. Not a bit of fodder, however, was to be had on the whole road from Norfolk to Richmond, except at two places.

Petersburgh stands at the head of the navigable part of *Appommattox River*, and is the only place of importance between Norfolk and Richmond. The houses in Petersburgh were about three hundred in number, and built without regularity. A flourishing trade was carried on in this place. About two thousand four hundred hogsheads of tobacco were inspected annually at the warehouses; and, at the falls of the Appamatox, near the upper end of the town, were some of the best flour-mills in Virginia.

Richmond, the capital of Virginia, is situated immediately below the Falls of *James River*, which is here about four hundred yards wide, and was at this time crossed by two bridges, separated from each other by an island. The houses in Richmond were not more than seven hundred in number, yet they extended nearly a mile and a half along the banks of the river. The lower part of the town is built close to the water; and opposite to it, lies the shipping. It is connected with the upper town by a long street, which runs parallel to the course of the river, and about fifty yards from the banks. The situation of the upper town is very pleasing: it is on an elevated spot, and commands a fine prospect of the falls of the river, and of the adjacent country. The best houses stand here, and also the capitol or state-house, which is a clumsy, ill-shaped edifice. Richmond, at this time, contained about four thousand inhabitants, one half of whom were slaves.

The *Falls* in the river, or the *Rapids*, as they ought to be called, extend six miles above the city. Here the river is full of large rocks; and the water rushes along in some places with great impetuosity. At the north side of the falls is a canal, which renders the navigation complete from Richmond to the Blue Mountains.

There is, perhaps, no place in the world of equal size, in which more gambling is carried on, than in Richmond. Mr. Weld had scarcely alighted from his horse, when the landlord of the tavern at which he stopped, inquired what game he was most partial to, as in such a room there was a faro-table, in another a hazard-table, in a third a billiard-table; to any of which he was ready to conduct him. Not the slightest secrecy is employed in keeping these tables. They are always crowded with people, and the doors of the apartments are only closed to prevent the rabble from entering. Cock-fighting is another favourite diversion. The lower classes of people, however, are those chiefly who partake of such amusements; but the circumstance of having the taverns thus infested, renders travelling extremely unpleasant.

The common people of Virginia are usually represented to be more quarrelsome than those of any other American state; and, when they come to blows, they fight like wild beasts. They bite and kick each other with indescribable fury; and endeavour to tear each other's eyes out with their nails.

Eighth Day's Instruction

UNITED STATES CONTINUED.

Narrative of Mr. Weld's *return from Richmond to Philadelphia, through the central parts of Virginia.*

Having continued at *Richmond* somewhat more than a week, Mr. Weld mounted his horse, and, accompanied by his servant, proceeded towards the *South-west* or *Green Mountains.*

The country around Richmond is sandy; but it is not so much so, nor so flat, as on the south side of James River, towards the sea. When Mr. Weld was here it wore a most pleasing aspect. The first week in May had arrived; the trees had acquired a considerable part of their foliage; and the air, in the woods, was perfumed with the fragrant smell of numberless flowers and flowering shrubs. The music of the birds also was delightful: the notes of the mocking-bird or Virginia nightingale, in particular, were extremely melodious.

In this part of America there is a singular bird, called whipper-will, or whip-poor-will, which has obtained its name from the plaintive noise that it makes. This it commences every evening about dusk, and continues through the greatest part of the night. The frogs in America make a most singular noise. Some of them absolutely whistle; and others croak so loudly, that it is difficult, at times, to tell whether the sound proceeds from a calf or a frog. Mr. Weld, whilst walking in the meadows, was more than once deceived by it. The largest kinds are called bull-frogs: they chiefly live in pairs, and are never found but where there is good water; their bodies measure from four to seven inches, and their legs are of proportionate length. These animals are extremely active, and take prodigious leaps.

In one part of his journey, the road extended almost wholly through pine-forests, and was very lonely. Night came on before he reached the end of it; and, as commonly happens with travellers in this part of the world, he soon lost his way. A light, however, seen through the trees, seemed to indicate that a house was not far distant. His servant eagerly rode up to it, but the poor fellow's consternation was great indeed when he observed it moving from him, presently coming back, and then, with swiftness, departing into the woods. Mr. Weld was himself at a loss to account for this singular appearance, till, after having proceeded a little further, he observed the same sort of light in many other places; and, dismounting from his horse to examine a bush, where one of these sparks appeared to have fallen, he found that it proceeded from a fire-fly. In the present instance Mr. Weld was much surprised; but, as the summer advanced, these flies appeared every night. After a light shower in the afternoon, this gentleman says he has seen the woods sparkling with them in every direction. The light is emitted from the tail, and the animal has the power of emitting it or not at pleasure.

After wandering about till near eleven o'clock, he came at last to a house, where he obtained information respecting the road: and, about midnight, he arrived at a miserable tavern. During the next day's ride he observed a great number of snakes, which were now beginning to come forth from their holes.

The *South-west Mountains* run nearly parallel to the *Blue Ridge*, and are the first that are seen in Virginia, on going up the country, from the sea-coast. They are not lofty, and ought indeed rather to be called hills than mountains. These mountains are not seen till the traveller comes within a few miles of them; and the ascent is so gradual, that he reaches their top almost without perceiving it.

The soil is here a deep clay, particularly well suited to the culture of grain and clover, and it produces abundant crops.

The salubrity of the climate, in this part of Virginia, is equal also to that of any part of the United States; and the inhabitants have, in consequence, a healthy and ruddy appearance, totally different from that of the residents in the low country.

In these mountains live several gentlemen of large property, who farm their own land. Among the number was Mr. Jefferson, the vice-president of the United States. His house was about three miles from Charlottesville, and was most singularly situated, being built on the top of a small mountain, the apex of which had been cut off. At this time it was in an unfinished state; but, if carried on, according to a plan which had been laid down, it promised to be one of the most elegant private habitations in America. Several attempts have been made in this neighbourhood, to bring the manufacture of wine to perfection; none of them, however, have succeeded to the wish of the parties concerned in it.

The country between the South-west Mountains and the Blue Ridge is very fertile, and is much more closely inhabited than that in the lower parts of Virginia. The climate is good, and the people have a healthy and robust appearance. Several valuable mines of iron and copper have been discovered here.

Having crossed the South-west Mountains, Mr. Weld proceeded to *Lynchburgh*, a town on the south side of *Fluvanna River*, and one hundred and fifty miles beyond Richmond. This town contained about one hundred houses; and a warehouse for the inspection of tobacco, where about two thousand hogsheads were annually inspected. It had been built within the last fifteen years, and, in consequence of its advantageous situation for trade, was rapidly increasing.

Between Lynchburgh and the Blue Mountains, the country is rough and hilly, and but thinly inhabited. The few inhabitants, however, who are seen here, are uncommonly robust and tall: it is rare to observe a man amongst them who is not six feet high. The Blue Ridge is thickly covered with large trees, to the very summit. Some of the mountains are rugged and stony; others are not so; and on the latter the soil is rich and fertile. It is only in particular places that this ridge can be crossed; and at some of the gaps the ascent is steep and difficult.

The *Peaks of Otter*, near which Mr. Weld crossed it, are the highest mountains in the Blue Ridge, and, measured from their bases, they are supposed to be more lofty than any others in North America. The principal peak is said to be about four thousand feet in perpendicular height.

Beyond the Blue Ridge, Mr. Weld observed very few settlements, till he approached *Fincastle*. This town is about twenty miles from the mountains, and fifteen south of *Fluvanna River*. It was only begun about the year 1790; yet, when Mr. Weld was there, it contained sixty houses, and was rapidly increasing. The inhabitants consisted principally of Germans.

On the eastern side of the Blue Mountains, cotton grows extremely well; and, in winter, the snow scarcely ever remains more than a day or two upon the ground. On the opposite side, cotton never comes to perfection; the winters are severe, and the fields are covered with snow for many successive weeks. In every farm-yard are seen sleighs or sledges, a kind of carriages that are used for travelling upon the snow.

In this part of America, the soil consists chiefly of a rich brown mould, in which white clover grows spontaneously. To have a fertile meadow, it is only necessary to leave a piece of ground to the hand of nature for one year. A bed of limestone also runs entirely through the country.

It appeared to Mr. Weld that there was no part of America where the climate would be more congenial to the constitution of a native of Great Britain or Ireland than this. The frost in winter is more regular, but is not more severe than what commonly takes place in those islands. During summer the heat is somewhat greater; but there is not a night in the year in which a blanket is not found comfortable. Fever and ague are disorders here unknown; and the air is so salubrious, that persons who come from the low country, afflicted with those disorders; get rid of them in a short time.

In the western part of the country there are several medicinal springs, to which, about the end of summer, great numbers of people resort, as much for the sake of escaping the heat in the low country, as for drinking the waters. Those that are most frequented are called the *Sweet Springs*; but there are others in *Jackson's Mountains*, a ridge that runs between the Blue Mountains and the Alleghany. One of these is warm, and another quite hot. There is also a sulphur spring near them, into which, if the leaves of trees fall, they become thickly incrusted with sulphur, in a very short time; and silver, if put into them, will be turned black almost immediately.

Mr. Weld, now bending his course in a northerly direction, again crossed the *Fluvanna River*. About ten miles from this stream, there is, among the mountains, a deep cleft or chasm, about two miles long, and, in some places, three hundred feet deep. Over one part of this is a natural arch, called *Rockbridge*, which consists of a solid mass of stone, or of several stones so strongly cemented together that they appear but as one. The road extends over this natural bridge. On one side of it is a parapet or wall of fixed rocks, but on the other there is a gradual slope, to the very brink of the chasm. The slope is thickly covered with large trees, principally cedars and pines. The whole width of the bridge is about eighty feet: the road runs nearly along the middle of it, and is passed daily by waggons.

At the distance of a few yards from the bridge there is a narrow path, which winds, along the sides of the fissure, and amidst immense rocks and trees, down to the bottom of the chasm. Here the stupendous arch appears in all its glory, and seems even to touch the skies. The height, to the top of the parapet, is two hundred and thirteen feet. The rocks are of limestone, and nearly perpendicular; and the sides of the chasm are thickly clad with trees, wherever there is space sufficient to admit of their growth. A small stream runs at the bottom of the fissure, over beds of rock, and adds much to the beauty of the scene.

About fifty miles beyond Rockbridge, there is another remarkable natural curiosity: a large cavern, known by the name of *Maddison's Cave*. It is in the heart of a mountain, and about two hundred feet high. Persons who reside in a house, not far distant from this cave, act as guides, and use, as lights, splinters from the wood of the pitch pine-tree, a bundle of which they carry with them for this purpose. This cave is of great extent, and is divided into many large, and singularly-shaped apartments, covered with stalactites, or petrifactions, at the top and sides. Before these were blackened by the smoke of the torches, they are said to have been extremely beautiful. The floor is of a deep sandy earth, which has been repeatedly dug up, for the purpose of obtaining saltpetre, with which it is strongly impregnated.

The country immediately behind the Blue Mountains, is agreeably diversified with hill and dale, and abounds in extensive tracts of rich land. Clover grows here in great luxuriance. Wheat also is raised, and in crops as abundant as in any part of the United States. Tobacco is not grown, except for private use. The climate is not here so warm as in the lower parts of the country, on the eastern side of the mountains.

As Mr. Weld passed along, he met great numbers of people who were proceeding from Kentucky, and from the state of Tenessee, towards Philadelphia and Baltimore. He also saw many others, who were going in a contrary direction, to "explore," as they called it; that is, to search for, lands in the western country, conveniently situated for new settlements. These all travelled on horseback, armed with pistols and swords; and each had a large blanket, folded up under his saddle, for sleeping in, whenever they were obliged to pass the night in the woods.

Of all the uncouth human beings that Mr. Weld met with in America, the people from the western country were the most so. Their curiosity was boundless. Often has he been stopped abruptly by them, even in solitary parts of the road; and, without any further preface, has been asked where he came from? if he was acquainted with any news? where bound to? and what was his name?

The first town that Mr. Weld reached was *Lexington*, a neat little place, which had contained about one hundred dwelling-houses, a court-house, and a gaol; but most of these had been destroyed by fire, just before he was there. Great numbers of Irish are settled in this place. Thirty miles further on is *Staunton*. This town carries on a considerable trade with the back country, and contains nearly two hundred dwellings, mostly built of stone.

Winchester stands one hundred miles north of Staunton, and is the largest town in the United States, on the western side of the Blue Mountains. The houses were, at this time, estimated at three hundred and fifty, and the inhabitants at two thousand. There were four churches, which, as well as the houses, were plainly built. The streets were regular, but very narrow. There was nothing particularly deserving of attention, either in this place, or in any of the small towns that have been mentioned.

Mr. Weld reached the *Potomac*, at the place where that river passes through the Blue Ridge; and where a scene is exhibited which has been represented as one of the most "stupendous in nature, and even worth a voyage across the Atlantic." The approach towards it is wild and romantic. After crossing a number of small hills, which rise in succession, one above another, the traveller at last perceives a break in the Blue Ridge; at the same time, the road, suddenly turning, winds down a long and steep hill, shaded with lofty trees, whose branches unite above. On one side of the road are large heaps of rocks, overhead, which threaten destruction to any one who passes beneath them; on the other, a deep precipice presents itself, at the bottom of which is heard the roaring of the waters, that are concealed from the eye, by the thickness of the foliage. Towards the end of this hill, about sixty feet above the level of the water, stand a tavern and a few houses; and from some fields in the rear of them, the passage of the river, through the mountain, is seen to great advantage.

The Potomac, on the left, winds through a fertile country, towards the mountain. On the right flows the *Shenandoah*. Uniting together, they roll on, in conjunction, through the gap; then, suddenly expanding to the breadth of about four hundred yards, they pass on towards the sea, and are finally lost to the view, amidst surrounding hills.

After crossing the Potomac, Mr. Weld passed on to *Frederic*, in Maryland, which has already been mentioned, and thence to Baltimore. The country between Frederic and Baltimore is by no means so rich as that west of the Blue Ridge, but it is tolerably well cultivated. Iron and copper are found here in many places.

From Baltimore Mr. Weld returned to *Philadelphia*, where he arrived on the fourteenth of June, after an absence of about three months.

We must now return to Pittsburgh, for the purpose of proceeding, from that place, with M. Michaux a French naturalist of considerable eminence, in a journey through Kentucky, Tenessee, North and South Carolina.

Ninth Day's Instruction

UNITED STATES CONTINUED.

Narrative of a Journey from Pittsburgh to Lexington in Kentucky. From Travels in North America, by F. A. Michaux.

This gentleman, in company with a Mr. Craft, set out from Pittsburgh, on the 14th of July, 1802; and, two days afterwards, arrived at Wheeling, a small town on the bank of the Ohio, and about eighty miles distant from Pittsburgh. *Wheeling* had not been more than twelve years in existence, yet it contained, at this time, about seventy houses, built of wood. It is bounded by a long hill, nearly two hundred fathoms high, and the base of which is not more than four hundred yards from the river. In this space the houses are built: they form but one street, along which runs the main road. From fifteen to twenty large shops supply the inhabitants, twenty miles, round, with provisions. This little town shares largely in the export trade that is carried on with the western country at Pittsburgh.

At Wheeling the travellers purchased a canoe, twenty-four feet long, eighteen inches wide, and about as many in depth. Canoes of this description are made from the single trunk of a tree: they are too narrow for the use of oars, and, in shallow water, they are generally forced along either with a paddle or a staff. As a shelter from the sun, M. Michaux and his friend covered their canoe, a quarter of its length, with a piece of cloth thrown upon two hoops; and, having placed on board of it a sufficient stock of provisions, they embarked about five o'clock in the afternoon of the ensuing day. They floated twelve miles down the stream that evening, and slept on the right bank of the Ohio. Both M. Michaux and his friend were excessively fatigued with their first day's voyage; but not so much by paddling their canoe along, as by remaining constantly seated in one position. For, the canoe being very narrow at the bottom, they were obliged to keep their legs extended; as the least motion of the vessel would have exposed them to the danger of being overset. In the course, however, of a few days, they became accustomed to these inconveniences, and attained the art of travelling comfortably.

They were three days and a half in proceeding to *Marietta*, about a hundred miles from Wheeling. This town is situated on the right bank of the

Great Muskingum, and near the place of its junction with the Ohio. Although fifteen years before M. Michaux was here, it was not in existence, Marietta now contained more than two hundred houses, some of which were built of brick; but the greatest number were of wood. Several of them were from two to three stories high, and somewhat elegantly constructed. The mountains which, from Pittsburgh, extend along the side of the river, are, at Marietta, distant from its banks, and leave a considerable space of level ground, which will facilitate, in every respect, the enlarging of the town.

The inhabitants of Marietta were the first, in the interior of America, who entertained an idea of exporting, directly to the Caribbee Islands, the produce of their country. This they did in a vessel, built in their own town. The vessel was sent to Jamaica, and the success which crowned this first attempt, excited great emulation among the inhabitants of the western country. The ship-yard at Marietta is near the town, on the great Muskingum. When M. Michaux was there, the inhabitants were building three brigs, one of which was of two hundred and twenty tons burden.

On the 21st of July the voyagers set out from Marietta, for Gallipoli, distant about a hundred miles. On the 23rd, at ten in the morning, they discovered *Point Pleasant*, situated a little above the mouth of the *Great Kenaway*, and on a promontory which is formed by the right bank of that river. Its situation is peculiarly beautiful. The Ohio, into which the Kenaway falls, is here four hundred fathoms wide, and continues of the same width for four or five miles. Its borders, sloping and elevated from twenty-five to forty feet, are, in the whole of its windings, overgrown, at their base, with willow, from fifteen to eighteen feet in height, the drooping branches and foliage of which form a pleasing contrast to the sugar-maples, red-maples, and ash-trees, which are seen immediately above. The latter are overhung by palms, poplars, beeches, and magnolias, of the highest elevation; the enormous branches of which, attracted by a more splendid light and an easier expansion, extend towards the borders, overshadowing the river, at the same time that they completely cover the trees that are beneath them. This natural display, which reigns upon the two banks, forms, from each side, a regular arch, the shadow of which, reflected by the stream, embellishes, in an extraordinary degree, the magnificent *coup d'œil*.

Gallipoli is on the right bank of the Ohio, four miles below Point Pleasant. It was, at this time, composed of about sixty log-houses, most of which, being uninhabited, were falling into ruins; the rest were occupied by Frenchmen, two only of whom appeared to enjoy the smallest comfort.

On the 25th of July, M. Michaux and his friend set out, in their canoe, for *Alexandria*, about a hundred and four miles distant; and they arrived there in three days and a half. The ground designed for this town is at the mouth of the *Great Scioto,* and in the angle which the right bank of this river forms with the north-west border of the Ohio. Although the plan of Alexandria had long been laid out, few people had settled there: the number of its edifices was not, at this time, more than twenty, and the major part of these were constructed of wood. The inhabitants are subject, every autumn, to intermittent fevers, which seldom abate till the approach of winter.

On the 1st of April the voyagers arrived at *Limestone* in Kentucky, fifty miles lower than Alexandria; and, at this place, their voyage on the Ohio terminated. They had floated, in their canoe, three hundred and forty miles from Wheeling; and, during the ten days which their voyage had occupied, they had been obliged, almost incessantly, to paddle their vessel along. This labour, although in itself painful to persons who are unaccustomed to it, was, in the present instance, still more so, on account of the intense heat which prevailed. They also suffered much inconvenience from thirst, not being able to procure any thing to drink, but by stopping at the plantations on the banks of the river; for, during summer, the water of the Ohio acquires such a degree of heat, that it is not fit to be drunk till it has been kept twenty-four hours. At Limestone M. Michaux relinquished an intention which he had formed of proceeding further down the Ohio; and here he took leave of Mr. Craft, who prosecuted the remaining part of the voyage alone.

The banks of the Ohio, though elevated from twenty to sixty feet, scarcely afford any hard substances, betwixt Pittsburgh and Limestone; except large detached stones, of a greyish colour, which M. Michaux observed, in an extent of ten or twelve miles, below Wheeling: the remainder of the country seems wholly covered with vegetable earth. A few miles before this gentleman reached Limestone, he observed a chalky bank, the thickness of which, being very considerable, left no room to doubt that it must be of great extent. The Ohio abounds in fish, some of which are of great size and weight.

Till the years 1796 and 1797, the banks of the Ohio were so little populated, that there were scarcely thirty families in the space of four hundred miles; but, since that time, a great number of emigrants had settled here, from the mountainous parts of Pennsylvania and Virginia; consequently the plantations had, at this time, so much increased, that they were not further than two or three miles asunder; and, when M. Michaux was on the river, he always had some of them in view.

The inhabitants of the banks of the Ohio employ the greatest part of their time in stag and bear-hunting, for the sake of the skins, which are important articles of traffic. The dwellings of this people are, for the most part, in pleasant situations; but they are only log-houses, without windows, and so small that they hold no more than two beds each. A couple of men, in less than ten days, could erect and finish one of them. No attention is here paid to any other culture than that of Indian corn.

The favourable situation of the Ohio entitles this river to be considered as the centre of commercial activity, between the eastern and western states; and it is the only open communication with the ocean, for the exportation of provisions, from that part of the United States, which is comprised between the Alleghany Mountains, the lakes, and the left bank of the Mississippi.

All these advantages, blended with the salubrity of the climate and the general beauty of the country, induced M. Michaux to imagine that, in the course of twenty years, the banks of the Ohio, from Pittsburgh to Louisville, would become the most populous and the most commercial part of the United States. *Limestone* consisted only of thirty or forty houses, constructed with wood. This little town had been built upwards of fifteen years. It was for some time the place where such emigrants landed as came from the northern states, by way of Pittsburgh: it was also the mart for merchandise, sent from Philadelphia and Baltimore to Kentucky.

M. Michaux resolved to travel on foot, from this place to Lexington. The distance is sixty-five miles, and he performed the journey in two days and a half. In his journey he passed through *Mays Lick*, where there is a salt-work. The wells that supply the salt-water are about twenty feet in depth, and not more than fifty or sixty fathoms from the *River Salt Lick*; the waters of which, during the summer, are somewhat brackish. In this part of the country salt-springs are usually found in places which are described by the name of *Licks*; and where, before the arrival of Europeans, the bisons, elks, and stags, that existed in Kentucky, went, by hundreds, to lick the saline particles; with which the soil is impregnated.

In the country around Mays Lick the soil is dry and sandy; and the road is covered with large, flat, chalky stones, of a bluish colour within, and the edges of which are round. The only trees that M. Michaux observed here, were white oaks and hickory; and the stinted growth and wretched appearance of these, clearly indicated the sterility of the soil.

In the year 1796, *Lexington* consisted of only eighteen houses; but it now contained more than a hundred and fifty, half of which were of brick. This town is situated on a delightful plain, and is watered by a small river, near which were several corn-mills. Every thing seemed to announce the comfort of its inhabitants. It is built on a regular plan. The streets are broad, and cross each other at right angles. The want of pavement, however, renders it very muddy in winter. There were, at this time, in Lexington, two printing-offices, at each of which a newspaper was published twice a week. Two extensive rope-walks, constantly in employ, supplied, with rigging, the ships that were built upon the Ohio. Independently of other manufactories which had been established in this town, there were several common potteries, and one or two gunpowder-mills. The sulphur for the latter was obtained from Philadelphia, and the saltpetre was manufactured from substances dug out of grottos, or caverns, that are found on the declivity of lofty hills, in the mountainous parts of the state. The soil of these is extremely rich in nitrous particles.

[About fifty miles west of Lexington, on the bank of the Ohio, and near the falls of that river, is the town of *Louisville*. This place forms a connecting link between New Orleans and the whole western parts of the United States. Mechanics can here obtain full employment, and they are able to earn from forty to fifty-four shillings a week. Every article of clothing is excessively expensive; and the rents of houses are very high. This place was formerly very unhealthy, the inhabitants being subject to fevers, agues, and other complaints; but it is said to be improving in healthiness. Mr. Fearon, who visited this place in the year 1817, does not speak favourably of the character of the Kentuckians. He says they drink a great deal, swear a great deal, and gamble a great deal; and that even their amusements are sometimes conducted with excessive barbarity. The expence of sending goods, by water, from New Orleans to Louisville, is about twenty shillings per hundred weight; and down the stream, to New Orleans, about four shillings. The boats usually make the voyage upward in about ninety days; and downward in twenty-eight days. Steam-vessels accomplish the former voyage in thirty-six, and the latter in twenty-eight days.

There are in Louisville, two great hotels, one of which has, on an average, one hundred and forty, and the other eighty boarders. A person, on going to either of them, applies to the bar-keeper for admittance: and the accommodations are very different from those in an English hotel. The place for washing is not, as with us, in the bed-rooms; but in the court-yard, where there are a large cistern, several towels and a negro in attendance. The sleeping-room usually contains from four to eight bedsteads, having mattresses and not feather-beds; sheets of calico, two blankets, and a quilt: the bedsteads have no curtains. The public rooms are, a news-room, a boot-room, (in which the bar is situated,) and a dining-room. The fires are generally surrounded by parties of about six persons. The usual custom with Americans is to pace up and down the news-room, in a manner similar to walking the deck of a ship at sea. Smoking segars is practised by all, and at every hour of the day. Argument or discussion, in this part of the world, is of very rare occurrence; social intercourse seems still more unusual; conversation on general topics, or taking enlarged and enlightened views of things, rarely occurs: each man is in pursuit of his own individual interest. At half past seven, the first bell rings for the purpose of collecting all the boarders, and, at eight, the second bell rings; breakfast is then set, the dining-room is unlocked, a general rush commences, and some activity, as well as dexterity, is necessary to obtain a seat at the table. The breakfast consists of a profuse supply of fish, flesh, and fowl, which is consumed with a rapidity truly extraordinary. At half-past one, the first bell rings, announcing the approach of dinner; the avenues to the dining-room become thronged. At two o'clock the second bell rings, the doors are thrown open, and a repetition of the breakfast-scene succeeds. At six, tea, or what is here called supper, is announced, and partaken of in the same manner. This is the last meal, and it usually affords the same fare as breakfast. At table there is neither conversation nor drinking: the latter is effected by individuals taking their liquor at the bar, the keeper of which is in full employ from sunrise to bed-time. A large tub of water, with a ladle, is placed at the bar; and to this the customers go and help themselves. When spirits are called for, the decanter is handed; the person calling for them takes what quantity he pleases, and the charge is sixpence-halfpenny. The life of boarders at an American tavern, presents a senseless and comfortless mode of killing time. Most houses of this description are thronged to excess; and few of the persons who frequent them, appear to have any other object in view than spitting and smoking.

In the state of Kentucky there are several subterraneous *caverns*, which have attracted much attention, and which are described as among the most extraordinary natural curiosities in the world. They are also of considerable importance in a commercial view, from the quantity of nitre they afford. The great cave, near Crooked Creek, is supposed to contain a million pounds of nitre. This cave has two mouths or entrances, about six hundred and fifty yards from each other, and one hundred and fifty yards from the creek.]

Tenth Day's Instruction

UNITED STATES CONTINUED.

Narrative of the Journey of M. Michaux, from
Lexington to Charleston in South Carolina.

On the tenth of August, M. Michaux set out from Lexington to Nasheville, in the state of Tenessee; and, as an establishment for the purpose of naturalizing the vine in Kentucky, was not very far out of his road, he resolved to visit it. Consequently, about fourteen miles from Lexington, he quitted the road, turned to the left, strolled through some woods, and reached the vineyard in the evening. It was, at this time, under the superintendance of a M. Dufoux, the principal person of a small Swiss colony, which had settled in Kentucky some years before. The vines had been selected chiefly from the vicinity of New York and Philadelphia. Many of them had failed; but those of the kinds which produce the Madeira wines, appeared to give considerable hopes of success. The whole of the vines occupied a space of about six acres; and they were planted and fixed with props similar to those in the environs of Paris.

From this place M. Michaux was conducted, through the woods, to a ferry over the *Kentucky River*. The borders of the river at this ferry are formed by an enormous mass of chalky stones, remarkably peaked, and about a hundred and fifty feet high.

Near *Harrodsburgh* M. Michaux visited the plantation and residence of General Adair. A spacious and commodious house, a great number of black servants, equipages: every thing announced the opulence of the general. Magnificent peach-orchards, and immense fields of Indian wheat, surrounded the house. The soil was extremely fertile, as was evident from the largeness of the blades of corn, their extraordinary height, and the abundance of the crops.

About forty miles beyond the general's plantation, M. Michaux passed over *Mulder Hill*, a steep and lofty mountain, that forms a kind of amphitheatre. From its summit the neighbouring country presents the aspect of an immense valley, covered with forests of imperceptible extent.

As far as the eye can reach, nothing but a gloomy verdant space is seen, formed by the tops of the close-connected trees, and, through which, not even the vestige of a plantation can be discerned. The profound silence that reigns in these woods, uninhabited by savage beasts, and the security of the place, forms an *ensemble* rarely to be seen in other countries.

About ten miles beyond *Green River* commence what are called the *Barrens*, or *Kentucky Meadows*. On the first day of his journey over them, M. Michaux travelled fifteen miles; and, on the ensuing morning, having wandered to some distance out of the road, in search of a spring, at which to water his horse, he discovered a plantation in a low and narrow valley. The mistress of the house told him that she had resided there upwards of three years, and that, for eighteen months, she had not seen any individual except of her own family: that, weary of living thus isolated, her husband had been more than two months from home in quest of another spot, towards the mouth of the Ohio. A daughter, about fourteen years of age, and two children, considerably younger, were all the company she had: her house was abundantly stocked with vegetables and corn.

This part of the Barrens was precisely similar to that which M. Michaux had traversed the day before; and the same kind of country extends as far as the line which separates the state of Tenessee from that of Kentucky. Here, to the great satisfaction of M. Michaux, he once more entered the woods. Nothing, he says, can be more tiresome than the doleful uniformity of these immense meadows, where there is no human creature to be met with; and where, except a great number of partridges, no species of living beings are to be seen.

The Barrens comprise a portion of country from sixty to seventy miles in length, by sixty miles in breadth. According to the signification of the name, M. Michaux had imagined that he should have to cross a naked space, scattered here and there with a few plants; but he was agreeably surprised to find a beautiful meadow, where the grass was from two to three feet high. He here discovered a great variety of interesting plants. In some parts he observed several species of wild vines, and, in particular, one which is called by the inhabitants "summer grapes:" the bunches of fruit were as large, and the grapes as good in quality, as those in the vineyards round Paris. And it appeared to M. Michaux that the attempts which had been made in Kentucky, to establish the culture of the vine, would have been more successful in the Barrens, the soil of which appeared to him better adapted for this kind of culture, than that on the banks of the Kentucky. The Barrens are very thinly populated; for, on the road where the plantations are closest together, M. Michaux counted but eighteen in a space of sixty or seventy miles.

Nasheville, the principal and the oldest town in this part of Tenessee, is situated on the *river Cumberland*, the borders of which are here formed by a mass of chalky stone, upwards of sixty feet in height. Except seven or eight houses, built of brick, the rest, to the number of about a hundred and twenty, were constructed of wood, and were distributed over a surface of twenty-five or thirty acres, where the rock appeared almost naked in every part.

This little town, although it had been built more than fifteen years, contained no kind of manufactory or public establishment; but there was a printing-office, at which a newspaper was published once a week. A college had also been founded here; but it was yet in its infancy, having not more than seven or eight students, and only one professor.

The price of labour in the vicinity of Nasheville was higher than at Lexington. There appeared to be from fifteen to twenty shops, which were supplied from Philadelphia and Baltimore; but they did not seem so well stocked as those of Lexington, and the articles, though dearer, were of inferior quality.

All the inhabitants of the western country, who go by the river to New Orleans, return by land and pass through Nasheville, which is the first town beyond Natchez. The interval which separates these towns is about six hundred miles, and was, at this time, entirely uninhabited. Several persons who had travelled this road, assured M. Michaux that, for a space of four or five hundred miles beyond Natchez, the country was very irregular; that the soil was sandy, in some parts covered with pines, and not much adapted for culture; but that, on the contrary, the borders of the river Tenessee were fertile, and superior even to the richest parts of Kentucky.

On the fifth of September, M. Michaux set out from Nasheville for Knoxville. He was accompanied by a Mr. Fisk, one of the commissioners who had been appointed to determine the boundaries between the states of Tenessee and Kentucky. They stopped on the road, with different friends of Mr. Fisk; among others, with General Smith, one of the oldest inhabitants of the country. M. Michaux saw, *en passant*, General Winchester. He was at a stone house which was building for him on the road. This mansion, the state of the country considered, bore the external marks of grandeur: it consisted of four large rooms on the ground-floor, one story, and a garret. The workmen employed to finish the inside had come from Baltimore, a distance of near seven hundred miles.

A few miles from the residence of General Winchester, and at a short distance from the road, is a small town which had been founded but a few years, and to which the inhabitants had given the name of *Cairo*, in memory of the taking of Cairo by the French.

Between Nasheville and Fort Blount the plantations, though always isolated in the woods, were, nevertheless, by the side of the road, and within two or three miles of each other: the inhabitants resided in log-houses, and most of them kept negroes, and appeared to live happily and in abundance. Through the whole of this space the soil was but slightly undulated: in some places it was level, and in general it was excellent.

Fort Blount had been constructed about eighteen years before M. Michaux was in America. It had been built for the purpose of protecting, against the attacks of the Indians, such emigrants as came, at that time, to settle in its vicinity. But peace having been concluded with the Indians, and the population having much increased, the fortifications now no longer existed.

On the eleventh of September M. Michaux and Mr. Fisk left Fort Blount; and, at the house of Major Russel, some miles distant, they were obligingly furnished with provisions for two days' journey through the territory of the Cherokees.

The country became now so mountainous, that they could not proceed more than forty-five miles the first day, though they travelled till midnight. They encamped near a small river, where there was an abundance of grass; and, after having lighted a fire, they slept in their rugs, keeping watch alternately, in order to guard their horses. During this day's journey they had seen no animals, except some flocks of wild turkeys.

The second day after their departure, they met a party of eight or ten Indians, who were searching for grapes and chinquapins, a small species of chesnuts, superior in taste to those of Europe. As M. Michaux and his friend had only twenty miles to go before they reached West Point, they gave to these men the remainder of their provisions. With the American Indians bread is a great treat; for their usual food consists only of venison and wild-fowl.

The road, which crosses this part of the Indian territory, cuts through the mountains of Cumberland; and, in consequence of the great number of emigrants who travel through it, to settle in the western country, it was, at this time, as broad and commodious as the roads were near Philadelphia. In some places, however, it was very rugged. Little boards painted black and nailed against the trees, every three miles, indicated to travellers the distance they had to go.

In this part of Tenessee the mass of the forests is composed of all the species of trees which belong more particularly to the mountainous regions of North America; such as oaks, maples, hickory-nut trees, and pines.

At *West Point* there was a fort palisadoed round with trees, and built upon a lofty eminence, at the conflux of the *rivers Clinch* and *Holstein*. A company of soldiers was kept here, for the purpose of holding the Indians in check, and also of protecting them against the inhabitants on the frontiers, whose cruelty and illiberal proceedings had frequently excited them to war.

These *Indians* are above the middle size, are well-proportioned, and healthy in appearance, notwithstanding the long fasting they are frequently obliged to endure, whilst in pursuit of animals, the flesh of which forms their chief subsistence. The carbine is the only weapon they use: they are very dexterous with it, and are able to kill animals at a great distance. The usual dress of the men consists of a shirt, which hangs loose, and of a slip of blue cloth, about half a yard in length, which serves them for breeches; they put it between their thighs, and fasten the two ends, before and behind, to a sort of girdle. They wear long gaiters, and shoes made of prepared goat-skins. When full dressed they wear a coat, waistcoat, and hat; but they never have breeches. On the top of their heads they have a tuft of hair, which they form into several tresses, that hang down the sides of their face; and they frequently attach quills or little silver tubes to the extremities. Many of them pierce their noses, in order to put rings through. They also cut holes in their ears, which are made to hang down two or three inches, by pieces of lead, which are fastened to them. They paint their faces red, blue, or black.

A shirt and a short petticoat constitute the chief dress of the women, who also wear gaiters like the men. Their hair, which is of jet-black colour, they suffer to grow to its natural length; but they do not pierce their noses, nor disfigure their ears. In winter both the men and women, in order to guard against cold, wrap themselves in blue rugs, which they always carry with them, and which form an essential part of their luggage.

M. Michaux was informed, at West Point, that the Cherokees had lately begun to cultivate their possessions, and that they had made a rapid progress in agriculture. Some of them had good plantations, and even negro slaves. Several of the women spin cotton and manufacture cotton-stuffs.

The distance from West Point to Knoxville is thirty-five miles. About a mile from West Point the travellers passed through *Kingstown*, a place consisting of thirty or forty log-houses. After that the road extended, upwards of eighteen miles, through a rugged and flinty soil, covered with a kind of grass. The trees that occupied this space, grew within twenty or thirty yards of each other.

Knoxville, the seat of government for the state of Tenessee, is situated on the *river Holstein*, here a hundred and fifty fathoms broad. The houses were, at this time, about two hundred in number, and were built chiefly of wood. Although it had been founded eighteen or twenty years, Knoxville did not yet possess any kind of commercial establishment, or manufactory, except two or three tan-yards. Baltimore and Richmond are the towns with which this part of the country transacts most business. The distance from Knoxville to Baltimore is seven hundred miles, and to Richmond four hundred and twenty. The inhabitants of Knoxville send flour, cotton, and lime, to New Orleans, by the river Tenessee; but the navigation of this river is much interrupted, in two places, by shallows interspersed with rocks.

In the tavern at Knoxville travellers and their horses are accommodated at the rate of about five shillings per day; but this is considered dear for a country where the situation is by no means favourable to the sale of provisions. A newspaper is published at Knoxville twice a week.

On the 17th of September, M. Michaux took leave of Mr. Fisk, and proceeded alone towards Jonesborough, a town about a hundred miles distant; and situated at the foot of the lofty mountains which separate North Carolina from Tenessee. On leaving Knoxville the soil was uneven, stony, and bad; and the forests contained a great number of pine-trees. Before he reached *Macby*, M. Michaux observed, for the space of two miles, a copse extremely full of young trees, the loftiest of which was not more than twenty feet high. The inhabitants of the country informed him that this place had formerly been part of a barren, or meadow, which had clothed itself again with trees, after its timber, about fifteen years before, had been totally destroyed by fire. This appears to prove, that the spacious meadows in Kentucky and Tenessee owe their origin to some great conflagration which has consumed the forests and that they continue as meadows, by the practice, still continued, of annually setting them on fire, for the purpose of clearing the land.

M. Michaux stopped, the first day, at a place where most of the inhabitants were Quakers. One of these, with whom he lodged, had an excellent plantation, and his log-house was divided into two rooms. Around the house were growing some magnificent apple-trees: these, although produced from pips, bore fruit of extraordinary size and excellent flavour, a circumstance which proves how well this country is adapted for the culture of fruit-trees. At this house there were two emigrant families, consisting of ten or twelve persons, who were going to settle in Tenessee. Their clothes were ragged, and their children were barefooted and in their shirts.

Beyond this place the road divided into two branches, both of which led to Jonesborough; and, as M. Michaux was desirous of surveying the banks of the *river Nolachuky*, renowned for their fertility, he took the branch which led him in that direction. As he proceeded he found many small rock crystals, two or three inches long, and beautifully transparent. They were loose, and disseminated upon the road, in a reddish kind of earth.

On the twenty-first he arrived at *Greenville*, a town which contained scarcely forty houses, constructed with square beams, and somewhat in the manner of log-houses. The distance between this place and Jonesborough, is about twenty-five miles: the country was slightly mountainous, the soil was more adapted to the culture of corn than that of Indian wheat; and the plantations were situated near the road, two or three miles distant from each other.

Jonesborough, the last town in Tenessee, consisted, at this time, of about a hundred and fifty houses, built of wood, and disposed on both sides of the road. Four or five respectable shops were established there, and the tradespeople, who kept them, received their goods from Richmond and Baltimore.

On the twenty-first of September, M. Michaux set out from Jonesborough to cross the *Alleghany Mountains*, for North Carolina. In some places the road, or rather the path, was scarcely distinguishable, in consequence of the plants of various kinds that covered its surface. It was also encumbered by forests of rhododendron: shrubs, from eighteen to twenty feet in height, the branches of which, twisted and interwoven with each other, greatly impeded his progress. He had also to cross numerous streams; particularly a large torrent, called Rocky Creek, the winding course of which cut the path in twelve or fifteen directions.

On the twenty-third this gentleman proceeded twenty-two miles, through a hilly country; and, in the evening, arrived at the house of a person named Davenport, the owner of a charming plantation upon *Doe River*. M. Michaux staid here a week, in order to rest himself and recruit his strength, after a journey of six hundred miles which he had just made. On the second of October, he again set out, and proceeded towards Morganton. About four miles from Doe River he passed the chain of the *Blue Ridges*, and afterwards that of the *Linneville Mountains*. From the summit of the latter he observed an immense extent of mountainous country, covered with forests. Only three small places appeared to be cleared, which formed as many plantations, three or four miles distant from each other.

From the Linneville Mountains to Morganton, the distance is about twenty-five miles: in this interval the country was slightly mountainous, and the soil extremely bad.

Morganton, the principal town of the county of Burke, contained about fifty houses built of wood, almost all of which were inhabited by tradesmen. There was only one warehouse, and this was supported by a commercial establishment at Charleston. To it the inhabitants of the country, for twenty miles round, came to purchase English manufactured goods and jewellery; or to exchange, for these, a portion of their own produce, consisting of dried hams, butter, tallow, bear-skins and stag-skins.

From Morganton to Charleston the distance is two hundred and eighty-five miles. There are several roads; but M. Michaux took that which led through Lincolnton, Chester, and Columbia. The distance from Morganton to Lincolnton, is forty-five miles. Through the whole of this space the soil is extremely barren; and the plantations, straggling five or six miles from each other, have an unfavourable appearance. The woods are chiefly composed of different kinds of oaks; and the surface of the ground is covered with grass, intermixed with other plants.

Lincolnton, at this time, consisted of forty houses, and, like all the small towns in the interior of the United States, was surrounded by woods. There were, at Lincolnton, two or three large shops, which transacted the same kind of business as that at Morganton. The tradesmen who kept them sent the produce of the adjacent country to Charleston, but they sometimes stocked themselves with goods from Philadelphia.

At Lincolnton a newspaper was published twice a week. The price of subscription was two dollars per annum, but the printer, who was his own editor, took, by way of payment, flour, rye, wax, or other traffic, at the market-price. As in England, the advertisements were the most important source of profit. The foreign news was almost wholly extracted from papers published at the sea-ports.

The district around Lincolnton was peopled, in a great measure, by Germans from Pennsylvania. Their plantations were kept in excellent order, and their lands were well cultivated. Almost all had negro slaves, and there reigned among them a greater independence than in the families of English origin.

From Lincolnton to Chester, in the state of South Carolina, the distance is about seventy miles. Through the whole of this space the earth is light, and of a quality inferior to that between Morganton and Lincolnton, although the mass of the forests is composed of various species of oaks. In some places, however, pine-trees are in such abundance that, for several miles, the ground is covered with nothing else.

Chester contained about thirty houses, built of wood; and among the number were two inns and two respectable shops.

From Chester the country becomes worse in every respect than before; and the traveller is obliged to put up at inns, where he is badly accommodated both in board and lodging, and at which he pays dearer than in any other part of the United States. The reputation of these inns is esteemed according to the quantity and different kinds of spirits which they sell.

From Chester to Columbia the distance is fifty-five miles. M. Michaux passed through *Winesborough*, containing about a hundred and fifty houses. This place is one of the oldest inhabited towns in Carolina, and several planters of the low country go thither every year to spend the summer and autumn.

[*Columbia*, now the seat of government for the state of South Carolina, is situated below the confluence of the *Broad* and *Saluda Rivers*. It is laid out on a regular plan, the streets intersecting each other at right angles. The buildings are erected at the distance of about three quarters of a mile from the *Cangaree River*, on a ridge of high land, three hundred feet above the level of the water. In 1808, Columbia contained about one hundred and fifty houses. Vineyards, cotton, and hemp-plantations are successfully cultivated in its vicinity; and oil-mills, rope walks, and some other manufactories have been established here.]

The distance from Columbia to Charleston is about a hundred and twenty miles; and, through the whole of this space, the road crosses an even country, sandy and dry during the summer, whilst in the autumn and winter, it is so covered with water that, in several places, for the space of eight or ten miles, the horses are up to their middle. Every two or three miles there were, by the side of the road, miserable log-houses, surrounded by little fields of Indian corn.

The extreme unwholesomeness of the climate is shown by the pale and livid countenances of the inhabitants, who, during the months of September and October, are almost all affected with tertian fevers. Very few persons take any remedy for this complaint: they merely wait the approach of the first frosts, which, if they live so long, generally effect a cure.

M. Michaux arrived at *Charleston* on the eighteenth of October, 1802, three months and a half after his departure from Philadelphia, having, in that time, travelled over a space of nearly eighteen hundred miles.

Eleventh Day's Instruction

UNITED STATES CONTINUED.

A Description of Charleston, and of some places in the adjacent parts of Carolina and Georgia.

Charleston is situated at the conflux of the rivers Ashley and Cooper. The ground that it occupies is about a mile in length. From the middle of the principal street the two rivers might be clearly seen, were it not for a public edifice, built upon the banks of the Cooper, which intercepts the view. The most populous and commercial part of the town is situated along the Ashley. Several ill-constructed *quays* project into the river, to facilitate the trading-vessels taking in their cargoes. These quays are formed of the trunks of palm-trees, fixed together, and laid out in squares, one above another. The *streets* of Charleston are wide, but not paved; consequently, every time the foot slips, from a kind of brick pavement before the doors, it is immersed, nearly ancle deep, in sand. The rapid and almost incessant motion of carriages grinds this moving sand, and pulverizes it in such a manner, that the most gentle wind fills the shops with it, and renders it very disagreeable to foot-passengers. The principal streets extend east and west between the two rivers, and others intersect these nearly at right angles.

From its exposure to the ocean, this place is subject to storms and inundations, which affect the security of its harbour. The town also has suffered much by fires. The last, in 1796, destroyed upwards of five hundred houses, and occasioned damage to the amount of £.300,000 sterling.

The *houses*, in the streets near the water-side, are, for the most part, lofty, and built close together. The bricks are of a peculiar nature, being porous, and capable of resisting weather better than the firm, close, and red bricks of the northern states. They are of a dark brown colour, which gives to the buildings a gloomy appearance. The roofs are tiled or slated. In this part of the town the principal shopkeepers and merchants have their stores and warehouses. Houses here bear a very high rent: those in Broad and Church-streets, which are valuable for shops, let for more than £.300 per annum; and those along the bay, with warehouses, let for £.700 and upwards, according to the size and situation of the buildings. The houses in Meeting-street and the back part of the town, are in general lofty and extensive, and are separated from each other by small gardens or yards, in which are the kitchens and out-offices. Almost every house is furnished with balconies and verandas, some of which occupy the whole side of the building, from top to bottom, having a gallery for each floor. The houses are sometimes shaded with Venetian blinds, and afford to the inhabitants a cool and pleasant retreat, from the scorching rays of the sun. Most of the modern houses are constructed with taste and elegance; but the chief design seems to be, to render them as cool as possible. The town is also crowded with wooden buildings, of an inferior description.

Three of the *public buildings* in Charleston, and the episcopal church of St. Michael, are situated at the corners, formed by the intersection of Broad and Meeting-streets. St. Michael's is a large and substantial edifice, with a lofty steeple and spire. The Branch Bank of the United States occupies one of the corners: this is a substantial, and, compared with others in the town, is a handsome building; but, from an injudicious intermixture of brick, stone, and marble, it has a very motley appearance. Another corner of the street is occupied by the gaol and armory: the fourth corner has a large and substantial brick building, cased with plaster. The ground-floor of this building is appropriated to the courts of law: in the first story are most of the public offices; and the upper story contains the public library and the museum.

A kind of tree, called the "pride of India," (*melia azedarach*,) is planted, in rows, along the foot-paths and the streets of Charleston. It does not grow very high; but its umbrageous leaves and branches afford, to the inhabitants, an excellent shelter from the sun. It has the advantage also of not engendering insects; for, in consequence of its poisonous qualities, no insect can live upon it. When in blossom, the large clusters of its flowers resemble those of the lilac; these are succeeded by bunches of yellow berries, each about the size of a small cherry. It is a deciduous tree; but the berries remain during the winter, and drop off in the following spring.

The health of the *inhabitants* is very much injured, in consequence of their general neglect of cleanliness. The drains that are formed for carrying off the filth and putrid matter, which collect from all parts of the town, are too small for the purpose. This circumstance, added to the effluvia of the numerous swamps and stagnant pools in the neighbourhood, are known to be extremely injurious. Another neglect of health and comfort arises from a filthy practice, which prevails, of dragging dying horses, or the carcasses of dead ones, to a field in the outskirts of the town, near the high road, and there leaving them, to be devoured by troops of ravenous dogs and vultures. The latter, in appearance, are not much unlike turkeys, and thence have obtained the name of turkey buzzards; but, from their carnivorous habits, they have a most offensive smell. These birds hover over Charleston in great numbers; and are useful in destroying putrid substances, which lie in different parts of the city.

At Charleston there is a garden dignified by the name of *Vauxhall*. It is situated in Broad-street, at a short distance from the theatre; but it possesses no decoration worthy of notice. It cannot even be compared with the common tea-gardens in the vicinity of London. On one side of it are warm and cold baths, for the accommodation of the inhabitants. During summer, vocal and instrumental concerts are performed here, and some of the singers from the theatre are engaged for the season. The situation and climate of Charleston are, however, by no means adapted for entertainments of this description.

There are, in this town, four or five *hotels* and coffee-houses; but, except the Planters' Hotel, in Meeting-street, not one of them is superior to an English public-house.

Charleston contains a handsome and commodious *market-place*, which extends from Meeting-street to the water-side, and is as well supplied with *provisions* as the country will permit. Compared, however, with the markets in the towns of the northern states, the supply is very inferior, both in quality and quantity. The beef, mutton, veal, and pork, of South Carolina, are seldom in perfection; and the hot weather renders it impossible to keep meat many hours after it is killed. Though the rivers abound in a great variety of fish, yet very few are brought to market. Oysters, however, are abundant, and are cried about the streets by negroes. They are generally shelled, put into small pails, which the negroes carry on their heads, and are sold, by measure, at the rate of about eight-pence per quart. Vegetables have been cultivated, of late years, with great success; and, of these, there is generally a tolerable supply in the market.

In winter, the markets of Charleston are well supplied with fish, which are brought from the northern parts of the United States, in vessels so constructed as to keep them in a continual supply of water, and alive. The ships, engaged in this traffic, load, in return, with rice and cotton.

At Charleston, wood is extravagantly dear: it costs from forty to fifty shillings a *cord*, notwithstanding forests of almost boundless extent, commence at six miles, and even at a less distance, from the town. Hence a great portion of the inhabitants burn coals that are brought from England.

The pestilential marshes around Charleston yield a great abundance of rice. It is true that no European frame could support the labour of its cultivation; but Africa can produce slaves, and, amid contagion and suffering, both of oppressors and oppressed, Charleston has become a wealthy city.

The road from Charleston towards North Carolina, extends, for some distance, through the districts adjacent to the sea-coast; and much of the country is clad with bright evergreens, whence, in many places, it appears like the shrubbery of a park. In this part of America the trees are covered with a curious kind of vegetable drapery, which hangs from them in long curling tendrils, of gray or pale green colour. It bears a small blue flower, which is succeeded by a plumed seed, that adheres to the bark of the trees. Though the bark of the oak seems to afford the most favourite soil, it suspends itself to trees of every description; and, as it has no tenacity, but hangs like loose drapery, it probably does them no injury.

In the interior of the country the road traverses a desolate tract of swamps and sandy pine-forests, and afterwards a series of granite rocks.

The capital of North Carolina is *Raleigh*, a clean little country town. At one end of the only street stands the governor's brick house; and, at the other, the senate or court-house, surrounded by a grass-plot, neatly laid out. The houses are, in general, small, and built of wood; but some of them have foundations of granite, which is the only kind of stone in the country. The total want of limestone, and the scarcity of brick-earth, render it here extremely difficult and expensive to give to buildings any degree of stability.

Although Raleigh is considered the capital of North Carolina, *Newbern* is the largest town in the state. So long ago as the year 1790, it contained four hundred houses; but these were chiefly built of wood. In September, 1791, about one-third of this town was consumed by fire; but, since that period, more of the houses have been built of brick than before. Newbern is situated on a flat, sandy point of land, near the junction of the two rivers Neus and Trent, and about thirty miles from the sea. It carries on a trade with the West Indies and the interior of Carolina, chiefly in tar, pitch, turpentine, lumber, and corn.

About a hundred miles south-west of Charleston is the town of *Savannah*, situated upon an open, sandy plain, which forms a bluff or cliff, about fifty feet above the level of the river of the same name. It is laid out, in the form of a parallelogram, about a mile and a quarter long, and half a mile wide. The streets are broad, and open into spacious squares, each of which has in the middle a pump, surrounded by trees. There are neither foot-paths nor pavement in this place; and, consequently, every one walking in the streets, sinks, at each step, up to the ancles in sand; and, in windy weather, the eyes, mouth, and nostrils, are filled with sand.

The houses in Savannah are, for the most part, built of wood, and stand at a little distance from each other. In two or three of the streets, however, they are close together, and many of them are built with brick: these contain the shops and stores. The principal street is that called the Bay; and in this there are several good houses, of brick and wood. It extends nearly three quarters of a mile in length; and opposite to it is a beautiful walk, planted with a double row of trees. Similar trees are planted in other parts of the town. This agreeable promenade is near the margin of the height, upon which the town stands; and the merchants' stores, warehouses, and wharfs, for the landing, housing, and shipping of goods, are immediately below. From the height there is a fine view of the Savannah river, as far as the sea; and, in a contrary direction, to the distance of several miles above the town.

About the centre of the walk, and just on the verge of the cliff, stands the Exchange, a large brick building, which contains some public offices; and an assembly-room, where a concert and ball are held every fortnight, during the winter.

The situation of Savannah, and the plan upon which it is laid out, if the town contained better houses, would render it far more agreeable, as a place of residence, than Charleston. Its greater elevation must also be more conducive to the health of the inhabitants, than the low and flat site of the other city. Both, however, are in the neighbourhood of swamps, marshes, and thick woods, which engender diseases, injurious to the constitution of white people. On the swamps, around Savannah, great quantities of rice are grown.

Twelfth Day's Instruction

UNITED STATES CONTINUED.

Narrative of an excursion from Charleston into Georgia and West Florida. From Travels in North America, by William Bartram.

At the request of Dr. Fothergill, an eminent physician in London, Mr. Bartram went to North America, for the purpose, chiefly, of collecting, in Florida, Carolina, and Georgia, some of the rare and useful productions which had been described, by preceding travellers, to abound in those states. He left England in the month of April, 1773, and continued abroad several years.

In 1776, he was at *Charleston*; and on the 22d of April, in that year, he set off on horseback, intending to make an excursion into the country of the Cherokee Indians. He directed his course towards Augusta, a town on the Savannah river.

During his first day's journey he observed a large orchard of mulberry-trees, which were cultivated for the feeding of silkworms. The notes of the mocking-bird enlivened all the woods. He crossed into Georgia, by a ferry over the Savannah; and he thence passed through a range of pine-forests and swamps, about twelve miles in extent. Beyond these, in a forest, on the border of a swamp, and near the river, he reached a cow-pen, the proprietor of which possessed about fifteen hundred head of cattle. He was a man of amiable manners, and treated Mr. Bartram with great hospitality. The chief profits made by this person were obtained from beef, which he sent, by the river, for the supply of distant markets.

About one hundred miles beyond this place is *Augusta*, in one of the most delightful and most eligible situations imaginable. It stands on an extensive plain, near the banks of the river Savannah, which is here navigable for vessels of twenty or thirty tons burden. Augusta, thus seated near the head of an important navigation, commands the trade and commerce of the vast and fertile regions above it; and, from every side, to a great distance. [Since Mr. Bartram was here, this place has become the metropolis of Georgia.]

Below Augusta, and on the Georgia side of the river, the road crosses a ridge of high swelling hills, of uncommon elevation, and sixty or seventy feet higher than the surface of the river. These hills, from three feet below the common vegetative surface, to the depth of twenty or thirty feet, are entirely composed of fossil oyster-shells, which, internally, are of the colour and consistency of white marble. The shells are of immense magnitude; generally fifteen or twenty inches in length, from six to eight wide, and from two to four inches in thickness; and their hollows are sufficiently deep to receive a man's foot.

From Augusta, Mr. Bartram proceeded to Fort James. For thirty miles the road led him near the banks of the Savannah. The surface of the land was uneven, in ridges or chains of swelling hills, and corresponding vales, with level downs. The latter afforded grass and various herbage; and the vales and hills produced forest-trees and shrubs of several kinds. In the rich and humid lands, which bordered the creeks and bases of the hills, Mr. Bartram discovered many species of plants which were entirely new to him.

Fort James enclosed about an acre of ground, and contained barracks for soldiers, and a house for the governor or commandant. It was situated at the extreme point of a promontory, formed by the junction of the *Broad* and *Savannah rivers*; and, at the distance of two miles, there was a place laid out for the construction of a town, which was to have the name of *Dartmouth*.

The surgeon of the garrison conducted Mr. Bartram, about five miles from the fort, to a spot where he showed him some remarkable Indian monuments. These were on a plain, about thirty yards from the river, and they consisted of conical mounds of earth, with square terraces. The principal mount was in the form of a cone, forty or fifty feet high, and two or three hundred yards in circumference at the base. It was flat at the top; a spiral track, leading from the ground to the summit, was still visible; and it was surmounted by a large and spreading cedar-tree. On the sides of the hill, facing the four cardinal points, were niches or centry-boxes, all entered from the winding path. The design of these structures Mr. Bartram was unable to ascertain. The adjacent grounds had been cleared, and were at this time planted with Indian corn.

On the 10th of May, Mr. Bartram set out from Fort James. He rode six or eight miles along the bank of the river, and then crossed it into South Carolina. The road led him over a country, the surface of which was undulated by ridges or chains of hills, and sometimes rough with rocks and stones; yet generally productive of forests, and of a great variety of curious and interesting plants.

The season was unusually wet: showers of rain fell almost daily, and were frequently attended with thunder. Hence travelling was rendered disagreeable, toilsome, and hazardous; particularly in the country through which he had to pass; an uninhabited wilderness, abounding in rivers and brooks.

During his progress, Mr. Bartram was kindly received into the houses of such planters as lived near the road. In his journey betwixt Fort James and the Cherokee town of *Sinica*, he observed an abundance of grape-vines, which ramble and spread themselves over the shrubs and low trees. The grapes, when ripe, are of various colours, and yield excellent juice.

Sinica is a respectable Cherokee settlement, on the east bank of the *Keowe river*; but the greatest number of Indian habitations are on the opposite shore, where also stands the council-house, in a plain, betwixt the river and a range of lofty hills, which rise magnificently, and seem to bend over the green plains and the river. Sinica had not, at this time, been long built. The number of inhabitants was estimated at about five hundred, among whom about a hundred warriors could be mustered.

From Sinica Mr. Bartram went to another Indian town, about sixteen miles distant, called *Keowe*. It stood in a fertile vale, which was now enamelled with scarlet strawberries and blooming plants, of innumerable kinds, through the midst of which the river meandered, in a most pleasing manner. The adjacent heights were so formed and disposed, that, with little, expence of military architecture, they might have been rendered almost unassailable. In the vicinity of Keowe, Mr. Bartram saw several ancient Indian mounts or tumuli, and terraces.

On leaving this place he crossed the river at a ford, and, soon afterwards, began to ascend the steep ridges on the west side of the valley. The prospects of the surrounding country here presented to his view, were, in many instances, peculiarly beautiful. Having reached the summits of the mountains, he afterwards passed through a series of magnificent forests, and then approached an ample meadow, bordered with a high circular amphitheatre of hills, the ridges of which rose magnificently one above another. After this the surface of the land was level, and, in some places exhibited views of grand forests, and dark, detached groves, and in others of fertile vales and meadows.

After having crossed a delightful river, a main branch of the *Tugilo*, Mr. Bartram passed through a mountainous country. Here, being overtaken by a tremendous hurricane, accompanied with torrents of rain, and the most awful thunder imaginable, in the midst of a solitary wilderness, he was glad to obtain shelter in a forsaken Indian dwelling. In this he lighted a fire, dried his clothes, comforted himself with a frugal repast of biscuit and dried beef, and afterwards passed the night.

At some distance beyond this cottage, were the ruins of an Indian town called *Sticoe*. At this place was a vast Indian mount or tumulus, with a great terrace. Here also were old peach and plum-orchards, some of the trees of which still appeared to be thriving and fruitful. From Sticoe, proceeding along a vale, and crossing a delightful brook, which falls into the Tenessee, Mr. Bartram followed its course nearly as far as *Cowe*, an Indian town which stands in a valley on the bank of one of the branches of the *river Tenessee*. He had letters of introduction to a gentleman resident in this place, who had, for many years, been a trader with the Indians, and who was noted for his humanity, his probity, and his equitable dealings with them. By this gentleman he was received with every demonstration of hospitality and friendship.

After having staid two days at Cowe, and, in the mean time, having made some excursions to places in its vicinity, Mr. Bartram proceeded on his journey, and was accompanied, about fifteen miles, by his hospitable friend, the trader. After this gentleman had left him, he was in the midst of solitude, surrounded by dreary and trackless mountains; and, for some time, he was unable to erase from his mind a notion that his present situation in some degree resembled that of Nebuchadnezzar, when expelled from the society of men, and constrained to roam in the wilderness, there to herd and to feed with the beasts of the forest. He, however, proceeded with all the alacrity which prudence would permit. His present object was, at all events, to cross the Jore Mountains, said to be the highest land in the Cherokee country. These he soon afterwards began to ascend; and, at length, he accomplished one part of his arduous task. From the most elevated peak of these mountains, he beheld, with rapture and astonishment, a sublimely awful scene of magnificence, a world of mountains piled upon mountains.

On the ensuing day, still proceeding in his journey westward, Mr. Bartram, on descending from the heights, observed a company of Indians on horseback. They rapidly approached him; and, under an impression that one of them, who was at the head of the troop, was the emperor or grand chief of the Cherokees, Mr. Bartram turned out of the path in token of respect. In this supposition he was correct, and the compliment was accepted, for the chief, with a cheerful smile, came up to him, and placing his hand on his breast, then offered it to Mr. Bartram, and heartily shook hands with him. The chief made enquiry respecting a gentleman of Charleston, with whom he was acquainted, and afterwards welcomed Mr. Bartram into his country, as a friend and brother. Being, at this time, on a journey to Charleston, he shook hands with Mr. Bartram, bade him heartily farewell, and then proceeded.

Describing the *Cherokee* Indians, our traveller says that these people construct their habitations in a square form, each building being only one story high. The materials consist of logs or trunks of trees, stripped of their bark, notched at the ends, fixed one upon another, and afterwards plastered both inside and out, with clay well tempered with dry grass; and the whole covered or roofed with the bark of the chesnut-tree, or with broad shingles or wooden tiles. The principal building is partitioned transversely, so as to form three apartments, which communicate with each other by inside doors. Each habitation has also a little conical house, which is called the winter or hot-house; this stands a few yards from the mansion-house, and opposite to the front door.

The council or town-house at Cowe, is a large rotunda, capable of accommodating several hundred people. It stands on the summit of an ancient artificial mount, about twenty feet high; and the rotunda at the top, being about thirty feet more, gives to the whole fabric an elevation of sixty feet from the ground. But the mount on which the rotunda stands, is of much more ancient date than the building, and perhaps was raised for some other purpose than to support it. The Cherokees themselves are ignorant by what people, or for what purpose, these artificial hills were raised. According to their traditions, they were found in much the same state as they now appear, when their forefathers arrived from the west, and possessed themselves of the country, after vanquishing the nations of red men who then inhabited it, and who themselves found these mounts when they took possession of the country.

Mr. Bartram, in company with some Europeans that were resident here, went one evening to the rotunda, to witness a grand entertainment of music and dancing. This was held principally for the purpose of rehearsing what is called a ball-play dance; the inhabitants of Cowe having received a challenge to play against those of another town.

The people, being assembled and seated, and the musicians having taken their station, the ball was opened, first with a long harangue or oration, spoken by an aged chief, in commendation of the manly exercise of ball-play. This chief recounted the many and brilliant victories which the town of Cowe had gained over the other towns in the nation; not forgetting to recite his own exploits, together with those of other aged men now present, coadjutors in the performance of these athletic games during their youthful days.

This oration ended, the music, both vocal and instrumental, began. Presently a company of girls, hand in hand, dressed in clean white robes, and ornamented with beads, bracelets, and a profusion of gay ribbons, entering the door, sang responses in a gentle, low, and sweet tone of voice; and formed themselves in a semicircular file, or line of two ranks, back to back, facing the spectators, and moving slowly round. This continued about a quarter of an hour, when the strangers were surprised by a sudden loud and shrill whoop, uttered by a company of young men, who came in briskly, after one another, each with a racket or hurl in his hand. These champions likewise were well dressed, painted, and ornamented with silver bracelets, gorgets, and wampum, and having high waving plumes in their diadems: they immediately formed themselves in a semicircular rank in front of the girls; on which these changed their position, and formed a single rank parallel to that of the men. They raised their voices, in responses to the tunes of the young champions, the semicircles continually moving round during the time.

The Cherokees, besides the ball-play dance, have several others, equally entertaining. The men, especially, exercise themselves in a variety of gesticulations and capers, some of which are extremely ludicrous. They have others of a martial kind, and others illustrative of the chase: these seem to be somewhat of a tragical nature, in which they exhibit astonishing feats of military prowess, masculine strength, and activity. Indeed, all their dances and musical entertainments seem to be theatrical exhibitions or plays, varied with comic, and sometimes indecent interludes.

On the ensuing morning, Mr. Bartram set off on his return to Fort James; and, two days afterwards, he again arrived at *Keowe*, where he continued two or three days. In the environs of this place he observed some very singular Indian antiquities. They each consisted of four flat stones, two set on edge for the side, another closed one end, and a very large flat stone was laid horizontally on the top. Mr. Bartram conjectures that they must have been either altars for sacrifices, or sepulchres.

This gentleman accompanied the traders to *Sinica*, where he continued some time, employing himself in observations, and in making collections of such things as were deserving of notice; and, not long afterwards, he once more reached *Fort James*.

From this place he set out with a caravan, consisting of twenty men and sixty horses. Their first day's journey was, for the most part, over high gravelly ridges, and hills of considerable eminence. Many scarce and interesting plants were discovered along the sides of the roads. They passed several considerable creeks, branches of the *Ocone*, and, on the first of July, encamped, on the banks of that river, in a delightful grove. They forded the river at a place where it was about two hundred and fifty yards wide. Subsequently they crossed the *Oakmulge* and *Flint rivers*. In many places they observed that the soil was rich, and admirably adapted to every branch of agriculture and grazing. The country was diversified with hills and dales, savannas, and vast cane-meadows, and watered by innumerable rivulets and brooks. During the day the horses were excessively tormented by flies of several kinds, and the numbers of which were almost incredible. They formed, around the caravan, a vast cloud, so thick as to obscure every distant object. The heads, necks, and shoulders of the leading horses were continually covered with blood, the consequence of the attacks of these tormenting insects. Some of them were horse-flies, as large as humble-bees; and others were different species of gnats and musquitoes. During the day the heat was often intense.

After traversing a very delightful country, the party reached the *Chata Uche* river, which was betwixt three and four hundred yards in width. They crossed it to *Uche* town, situated on a vast plain. This, Mr. Bartram observes, was the most compact and best situated Indian town he had ever seen. The habitations were large and neatly built, having their walls constructed of a wooden frame, then lathed and plastered inside and out with a reddish, well-tempered clay or mortar, which gave them the appearance of brick. Uche appeared to be populous and thriving. The whole number of inhabitants was about fifteen hundred, of whom about five hundred are gun-men or warriors.

Beyond this the travellers arrived at another Indian town called *Apalachucla*, the capital of the Creek Indians. This place is sacred to peace. No captives are here put to death, and no human blood is spilt. And when a general peace is proposed, deputies from all the towns in the confederacy assemble at this capital, in order to deliberate on the subject. On the contrary, the great *Coweta* town; about twelve miles distant, is called the bloody town, for here the micos, chiefs, and warriors assemble, when a general war is proposed; and here captives and state malefactors are executed.

The caravan continued at Apalachucla about a week, for the purpose of recruiting the strength of the horses, by turning them out into the swamps to feed. After this, having repaired their equipage, and replenished themselves with fresh supplies of provisions, on the thirteenth of July they resumed their journey for Mobile.

Beyond *Talasse*, a town on the Tallapoose river, they changed their course to a southerly direction, and, not long afterwards, arrived at *Coloome*, a settlement, where they continued two days. The houses of this place are neat and commodious; each of the buildings consists of a wooden frame with plastered walls, and is roofed with cypress bark or shingles. Every habitation consists of four oblong square houses, of one story, and so arranged as to form an exact square, encompassing an area or court-yard of about a quarter of an acre of ground, and leaving an entrance at each corner. There was a beautiful square, in the centre of the new town; but the stores of the principal trader, and two or three Indian habitations, stood near the banks of the opposite shore, on the side of the old Coloome town. The Tallapoose river is here three hundred yards wide, and fifteen or twenty feet deep.

Having procured a guide, to conduct them into the great trading path of West Florida, they set out for Mobile. Their progress, for about eighteen miles, was through a magnificent forest, which, at intervals, afforded them a view of distant Indian towns. At night, they encamped beneath a grove of oaks; but, shortly afterwards, there fell so extraordinary a shower of rain, that, suddenly, the whole adjacent ground was inundated, and they were obliged to continue standing through the whole of the night. Early in the morning, the guide, having performed his duty, returned home; and the travellers continued their journey, over an extended series of grassy plains, more than twenty miles in length, and eight or nine miles wide. These plains were bounded by high forests, which, in some places, presented magnificent and pleasing sylvan landscapes, of primitive and uncultivated nature. They crossed several rivulets and creeks, branches of the *Alabama*, the eastern arm of the Mobile. These rivulets were adorned with groves of various trees and shrubs. Immediately beyond the plains, the travellers entered a high, and grand forest; and the road, for several miles, led them near the banks of the *Alabama*. The surface of the land was broken into hills and vales; some of them of considerable elevation, and covered with forests of stately trees.

After many miles' travelling, over a varied and interesting country, they arrived at the eastern channel of the *river Mobile*, and, on the same day, reached the city to which they were proceeding. *Mobile* stands on the easy ascent of a rising bank, near the western side of the bay of that name. This place has been nearly a mile in length; but it was now in ruins. Many of the houses were, at this time, unoccupied, and mouldering away; yet there were a few good buildings, inhabited by French, English, Scotch, and Irish, and emigrants from the northern parts of America. The principal French buildings were constructed of brick, and were one story high, but on an extensive scale. They were square, and were built so as to encompass, on three sides, a large area or court-yard. The principal apartment was on the side fronting the street. This plan of habitations seems to have been copied from that of the Creek Indians. The houses of the poorer class of inhabitants were constructed of a strong frame of cypress-timber, filled up with brick; plastered and white-washed inside and out.

On the 5th of August, having procured a light canoe, Mr. Bartram set out on a voyage up the river. He sailed along the eastern channel, and passed several well-cultivated plantations, on fertile islands. Here the native productions exceeded, in luxuriance, any that he had ever seen: the reeds and canes, in particular, grew to an immense height and thickness. On one part of the shore of the river, he was delighted by the appearance of a great number of plants, of a species of oenothera, each plant being covered with hundreds of large golden yellow flowers. Near the ruins of several plantations, were seen peach and fig-trees, richly laden with fruit. Beyond these, were high forests and rich swamps, where canes and cypress-trees grew of astonishing magnitude. The *magnolia grandiflora*, here flourished in the utmost luxuriance; and flowering-trees and shrubs were observed, in great numbers and beauty. Several large alligators were seen basking on the shores, and others were swimming along the river. After having pursued his course for several miles, and made many important botanical discoveries, Mr. Bartram returned to *Mobile*, for the purpose of proceeding thence, in a trading-vessel, westward, to the Pearl river.

Previously, however, to setting out on his voyage westward, he had an opportunity of visiting *Pensacola*, the capital of West Florida, about a hundred miles east of Mobile. This city possesses some natural advantages, superior to those of any other port in this province. It is situated on a gently rising ground, environing a harbour, sufficiently capacious to shelter all the navies of Europe. Several rivers fall into this *harbour*; but none of them are navigable for ships of burden, to any considerable distance. In Pensacola there are several hundred habitations. The governor's palace is a large brick building, ornamented with a tower. The town is defended by a fortress, within which is the council-chamber, houses for the officers, and barracks for the soldiers of the garrison. On the sand-hills, near this place, Mr. Bartram discovered several species of plants, which at that time had not been described.

Having again returned to Mobile, he left that place, in a trading-boat, the property of a Frenchman, who was about to sail to his plantations, on the banks of the Pearl river. Before Mr. Bartram set out on this expedition, he had been attacked by a severe complaint in his eyes, which occasioned extreme pain, and almost deprived him of sight: it did not, however, deter him from proceeding. On his arrival at *Pearl river*, he was, however, so ill, as to be laid up, for several weeks, at the house of an English gentleman, who resided on an island in that river. As soon as he was sufficiently recovered to prosecute his journey, he proceeded, in a boat, to Manchac on the Mississippi.

Having sailed westward for some days, he entered the *river Amite*, and, ascending it, arrived at a landing-place, from which he crossed, by land, to *Manchac*, about nine miles distant. The road was straight, spacious, and level, and extended beneath the shadow of a grand forest. On arriving at the banks of the *Mississippi*, Mr. Bartram stood, for some time, fascinated by the magnificence of this grand river. Its width was nearly a mile, and its depth at least two hundred and forty feet. But it is not merely the expansion of its surface which astonishes and delights: its lofty banks, the steady course of its mighty flood, the trees which overhang its waters, the magnificent forests by which it is bounded; all combine in exhibiting prospects the most sublime that can be imagined. At Manchac, the banks are at least fifty feet in perpendicular height.

After having continued in this place a short time, Mr. Bartram made an excursion several miles up the Mississippi. At his return, he once more set sail for *Mobile*, where, not long afterwards, he safely arrived.

On the 27th of November, he sailed up the river, from Mobile, in a large trading-boat, and the same evening arrived at *Taensa*. Here the merchandise, which the boat had conveyed, was formed into small packages, and placed on horses, for the purpose of being conveyed overland. The party now consisted of between twenty and thirty horses, two drivers, the owner of the goods, and Mr. Bartram; who found this mode of travelling very unpleasant. They seldom set out till the sun had been some hours risen. Each of the men had a whip, made of cow-skin; and, the horses having ranged themselves in a line, the chief drove them by the crack of his whip, and by a whoop or shriek, so loud as to ring through the forests and plains. The pace was a brisk trot, which was incessantly urged, and continued as long as the miserable creatures were able to move forward. Each horse had a bell; and the incessant clattering of the bells, smacking of the whips, and whooping of the men, caused an uproar and confusion which was inexpressibly disagreeable. The time for encamping was generally about the middle of the afternoon; a time which, to Mr. Bartram, would have been the pleasantest for travelling.

After having proceeded on their journey several days, they came to the banks of a large and deep river, a branch of the *Alabama*. The waters ran furiously, being overcharged with the floods of a violent rain, which had fallen the day before. There was no possibility of crossing this river by fording it. With considerable difficulty, a kind of raft was made, of dry canes and pieces of timber, bound together by a species of vines or vegetable cords, which are common in the woods of the tropical districts of America. When this raft was completed, one of the Indians swam over the river, having in his mouth the end of a long vine attached to it; and, by hauling the raft backward and forward, all the goods were safely landed on the opposite side: the men and horses swam across.

In the evening of the day on which they passed this stream, the party arrived at the banks of the great *Tallapoose river*; and encamped, for the night, under the shelter of some Indian cabins. On the ensuing day they were conducted across the river, in the canoes of a party of Indians who were resident in the neighbourhood. Not long afterwards, the travellers arrived at the Indian town of *Alabama*, situated near the junction of two fine rivers, the *Tallapoose* and the *Coosa*. At this place were seen the traces of an ancient French fortress, with a few pieces of cannon, half-buried in the earth. This, says Mr. Bartram, is perhaps one of the most eligible situations in the world for a large town: it is a level plain, at the conflux of two majestic rivers, each navigable for vessels, to the distance of at least five hundred miles above it, and spreading their numerous branches over a great extent of fertile and delightful country.

The travellers continued all night at Alabama, where a grand entertainment was made for them, with music and dancing, in the great square. They then proceeded along the Tallapoose to *Mucclasse*. In their journey they passed through numerous plantations and Indian towns, and were every where treated by the inhabitants with hospitality and friendship.

About three weeks after this, Mr. Bartram joined a company of traders, and proceeded with them to Augusta. They set out in the morning of the 2d of January, 1788, the whole surface of the ground being covered with a white and beautifully sparkling frost. The company, besides Mr. Bartram, consisted of four men, with about thirty horses, twenty of which were laden with leather and furs. In three days they arrived at the *Apalachula* or *Chata Uche* river, and crossed it at the towns of *Chehau* and *Usseta*. These towns nearly join each other, yet the inhabitants speak different languages. Beyond this river nothing of importance occurred, till they arrived at *Oakmulge*. Here they encamped in expansive, ancient Indian fields, and within view of the foaming flood of the river, which now raged over its banks. There were, at this place, two companies of traders from Augusta, each consisting of fifteen or twenty men, with seventy or eighty horses. The traders whom Mr. Bartram accompanied, had with them a portable leather boat, eight feet long. It was made of thick sole-leather, was folded up, and carried on one of the horses. This boat was now put together, and rigged; and in it the party was ferried across the river. They afterwards crossed the *Ocone*, in the same manner; and encamped in fertile fields on the banks of that beautiful river. Proceeding thence, they encamped, the next day, on the banks of the *Ogeche*; and, after two days hard travelling, beyond this river, they arrived at *Augusta*, whence, shortly afterwards, Mr. Bartram proceeded to *Savannah*.

Thirteenth Day's Instruction

UNITED STATES CONTINUED.

Narrative of Mr. Bartram's *Journey from Savannah into East Florida.*

Leaving *Savannah* at the most beautiful season of the year, Mr. Bartram proceeded, on horseback, to *Sunbury*, a sea-port, about forty miles distant; and thence to Fort Barrington. Much of the intervening country was level, and well watered by large streams. The road was straight, spacious, and in excellent repair. For a considerable distance it was bordered on each side by groves, of various kinds of trees and shrubs, entwined with bands and garlands of flowering-plants. Extensive plantations of rice and corn, now in early verdure, were seen, decorated, here and there, with groves of floriferous and fragrant trees and shrubs, through which, at intervals, appeared the neat habitations of the proprietors.

At Fort Barrington, Mr. Bartram crossed the river Alatamaha, here about five hundred yards in width. When safely landed on the opposite side, he mounted his horse, and followed the high road, through an uninhabited wilderness, to the ferry on *St. Ille*. The sudden transition, from rich cultivated settlements, to high pine-forests, and dark grassy savannas, formed, he says, no disagreeable contrast; and the new objects, in the works of nature, which here excited his attention, soon reconciled him to the change. In the midst of the woods he observed great numbers of dens, or caverns, which had been dug in the sand-hills, by the gopher, or great land tortoise.

The next day's progress, presented scenes nearly similar to these; though the land was lower, more level and humid, and the produce was more varied. Mr. Bartram passed some troublesome cane-swamps, in which he saw several herds of horned-cattle, horses, and deer, and noticed many interesting plants.

In the evening, he arrived at *St. Ille's*, where he lodged; and, next morning, having crossed the river in a ferry-boat, he proceeded towards St. Mary's. The appearance of the country, its soil, and productions, between these rivers, were nearly similar to those which he had already passed, except that the savannas were more frequent and extensive.

Mr. Bartram had now passed the utmost frontier of the white settlements, on that border; and the day was drawing towards a close, when, on a sudden, an Indian, armed with a rifle, crossed the path, at a considerable distance before him. This man, turning short round, came up at full gallop. Though his intentions, at first, seemed hostile, he, after some hesitation, shook Mr. Bartram by the hand, directed him on his way, and then proceeded in his former course. Mr. Bartram again set forward, and, after riding eight or ten miles, arrived at the banks of *St. Mary's*, opposite to the stores, and got safely over that river, before dark.

The savannas about St. Mary's displayed a very charming appearance, of flowers and verdure: their more elevated borders were varied with beds of violets, lupines, and amaryllis; and with a new and beautiful species of sensitive plant.

In a subsequent excursion, Mr. Bartram, accompanied by some other gentlemen, passed the mouth of St. Mary's, and entered the *river St. Juan*, or *St. John*.

At *Cowford*, a public ferry over this river, and about thirty miles from its mouth, he procured a neat little sail-boat; and, having stored it with necessaries for his voyage, he proceeded up the river alone, in search of new productions of nature; having his chief happiness centered in tracing and admiring the infinite power, majesty, and perfection of the great Creator, and in the contemplation that, through divine permission, he might be instrumental in introducing into his native country, some productions which might become useful to society. His little vessel, being furnished with a good sail, and with fishing-tackle, a swivel gun, powder, and ball, Mr. Bartram found himself well equipped for his voyage, of about one hundred miles, to the trading houses of the Indians.

Having proceeded about eight miles above Cowford, to a place where the river was nearly three miles broad, he was obliged to land, as his boat had sustained some damage from the wind; and, a thunder-storm coming on, he resolved to continue on shore till the morning. Observing a large oak-tree, which had been thrown down by a hurricane, and which offered him a convenient shelter, as its branches bore up the trunk a sufficient height from the earth, to admit him either to, sit or to lie down beneath it, he spread his sail, slanting from the trunk of the tree to the ground, on the windward side; and, having collected a quantity of wood sufficient to keep up a fire during the night, he kindled one in front. He then spread skins on the ground, and upon these he placed a blanket, one half of which he lay down upon, and the other he turned over him for a covering.

The wind was furious, and the thunder and lightning were tremendous; but, happily, not much-rain fell. Next morning, on reconnoitring the neighbourhood, he was roused by the report of a musket not far off; and, shortly afterwards, an Indian stepped out of a thicket, having a large turkey-cock slung across his shoulders. He saw Mr. Bartram, and, stepping up to him, spoke in English, bidding him good morning. He stated that he lived at an adjacent plantation, and that he was employed as a hunter. Mr. Bartram accompanied him to the house of his master, about half a mile distant, and was there received in the most polite and friendly manner imaginable. The owner of this plantation invited him to stay some days, for the purpose of resting and refreshing himself; and he immediately set his carpenters to work, to repair the damaged vessel.

Mr. Bartram spent one day with this gentleman. The house in which he resided was on an eminence, about one hundred and fifty yards from the river. On the right of it was an orangery, consisting of many hundred trees, natives of the place, and left standing when the ground about it was cleared. Those trees were large, flourishing, in bloom, and, at the same time, loaded with ripe golden fruit. On the other side was a spacious garden, occupying a regular slope of ground, down to the water; and a pleasant lawn lay between. The owner of this plantation having, with great liberality, supplied him with an abundance of ammunition and provision, Mr. Bartram departed on the ensuing morning. He again embarked on board his little vessel, and had a favourable, steady gale. The day was extremely pleasant; the shores of the river were level and shallow; and, in some places, the water was not more than eighteen inches or two feet in depth. At a little distance it appeared like a green meadow; having water-grass, and other amphibious vegetables, growing from its oozy bottom, and floating upon its surface.

Mr. Bartram kept as near the shore as possible; and he was greatly delighted with the prospect of cultivation, and the increase of human industry, which were often visible from the water. In pursuing his voyage, he sometimes slept at plantations that were near the banks of the river; but sometimes he was obliged to pitch his tent upon the shore, or to sleep under the protection of his sail. In the latter case he was, not unfrequently, disturbed at night, by the plunging and roaring of alligators, and the loud croaking of frogs; and, in the morning, by the noise of wild turkeys, hundreds of which roosted around him. During his progress he saw great numbers of alligators, some of them immensely large. He was successful in collecting seeds, and specimens of uncommon trees and plants. In some places he was astonished to see the immense magnitude to which the grape-vines grew. These were not unfrequently from nine to twelve inches in diameter: they twined round the trunks of trees, climbed to their very tops, and then spread along, from tree to tree, almost throughout the forest. The fruit, however, was small and ill-flavoured.

As Mr. Bartram was coasting along the shore, he suddenly saw before him an Indian settlement or village. It was in a fine situation, on the slope of a bank which rose gradually from the water. There were eight or ten habitations, in a row or street, fronting the water, and about fifty yards distant from it. Some of the youths of this settlement were naked, and up to their hips in water, fishing with rods and lines; whilst others, younger, were diverting themselves in shooting frogs with bows and arrows. As Mr. Bartram passed, he observed some elderly people reclining on skins, spread upon the ground, beneath the cool shade of oaks and palm-trees, that were ranged in front of the houses. These persons arose, and eyed him as he passed; but, perceiving that he proceeded without stopping, they resumed their former position.

There was an extensive orange-grove, at the upper end of the village: the trees were large, and had been carefully pruned; and the ground beneath them was clean, open, and airy. Around the village were several acres of cleared land, a considerable portion of which was planted with maize, batatas, beans, pompions, squashes, melons, and tobacco.

After leaving this village, the river became much contracted, and continued so till Mr. Bartram reached *Charlotia* or *Rolle's Town*, where it was not more than half a mile wide. Here he came to an anchor. This town was founded by Denis Rolle, Esq. and is situated on a cliff on the east side of the river.

Having obtained directions for discovering a little remote island, where the traders and their goods were secreted, he set sail again, and, in about an hour and a half, arrived at the desired place. At this island he was received with great politeness; and he was induced to continue there several months, during which he was treated with the utmost hospitality, by the agents of one of the British mercantile houses.

The numerous plains and groves in the vicinity of the island, afforded to Mr. Bartram much gratification in his botanical pursuits; and, at the termination of his residence here, he set out with a party of traders, who were about to proceed to the upper parts of the river. The traders, with their goods in a large boat, went first, and Mr. Bartram, in his little vessel, followed them. The day was pleasant, and the wind fair and moderate. In the evening they arrived at *Mount Royal*, a house belonging to a Mr. Kean. This place was surrounded by magnificent groves of orange-trees, oaks, palms, and magnolias; and commanded a most enchanting view of the great Lake George, about two miles distant.

Lake George is a beautiful piece of water, a dilatation of the river St. John, and about fifteen miles wide. It is ornamented with two or three fertile islands. Mr. Bartram landed, and passed the night on one of them; and he found, growing upon it, many curious flowering shrubs, a new and beautiful species of convolvulus, and some other species of plants, which he had never before seen.

A favourable gale enabled the voyagers, towards the close of the ensuing day, to enter the river at the southern extremity of the lake. Here they found a safe and pleasant harbour, in a most desirable situation. Opposite to them was a vast cypress swamp, environed by a border of grassy marshes; and, around the harbour, was a grove of oaks, palm, magnolia, and orange-trees. The bay was, in some places, almost covered with the leaves of a beautiful water-lily, the large, sweet-scented yellow flowers of which grew two or three feet above the surface of the water. A great number of fine trout were caught, by fishing, with a hook and line, near the edges of the water-lilies; and many wild turkeys and deer were seen in the vicinity of this place.

On the ensuing day the party reached a trading-house, called *Spalding's upper Store*, where Mr. Bartram resided for several weeks. Being afterwards desirous of continuing his travels and observations higher up the river, and, having received an invitation to visit a plantation, the property of an English gentleman, about sixty miles distant, he resolved to pursue his researches to that place. For several miles the left bank of the river had numerous islands of rich swamp land. The opposite coast was a perpendicular cliff ten or twelve feet high: this was crowned by trees and shrubs, which, in some places, rendered the scenery extremely beautiful. The straight trunks of the palm-trees were, in many instances, from sixty to ninety feet high, of a bright ash colour, and were terminated by plumes of leaves, some of them nearly fifteen feet in length.

Mr. Bartram landed, for the night, in a little bay, not far from the entrance to a small lake, another expansion of the river. Near this place there was much low and swampy land, and the islands in the river were numerous. The evening was cool and calm, and he went out in his canoe, to fish for trout. As the evening closed, alligators appeared in great numbers along the shores and in the river. Mr. Bartram states that he was witness to a combat between these dreadful animals, which inspired him with horror, especially as his little harbour was surrounded by them. In endeavouring to paddle his canoe through a line of alligators, he was pursued by several large ones; and, before he could reach the shore, he was assailed on every side. His situation became extremely precarious. Two very large alligators attacked him closely, rushing with their heads and part of their bodies above the water, roaring terribly, and, from their mouths, throwing floods of water over him. They struck their jaws together so close to his ears as almost to stun him; and he, every moment, expected to be dragged out of the boat and devoured by them. He held in his hand a large club, which he used so efficaciously, as to beat them off: he then hastened towards the shore, as the only means of preservation left. Here the water was shallow; and his ferocious opponents, some of which were twelve feet in length, returned into deeper water. After this, as Mr. Bartram was stepping out of his canoe, an alligator rushed up to him, near his feet, and, with its head and shoulders out of the water, lay there for some time. Mr. Bartram ran for his gun, and, having a heavy charge in it, he shot the animal in the head and killed him. While Mr. Bartram was employed in cleansing some fish for his supper, he raised his head, and beheld, through the clear water, another of these animals of large size, moving slowly towards him; and he stepped back, at the instant the beast was preparing to spring upon him. This excessive boldness gave him great uneasiness, as he feared he should be obliged to keep on watch through the whole night. He had made the best preparation, in his power, for passing the night, when he was roused by a tumultuous noise, which seemed to come from the harbour. On going to the water's edge he beheld a scene so astonishing, that it was some time before he could credit the evidence even of his own senses. The river, though of great width, appeared, from shore to shore, to be almost a solid bank of fish. These were of various species, and were pushing along the river, towards the little lake, pursued by alligators in such incredible numbers, and so close together, that, had the animals been harmless, Mr. Bartram imagined it might have been possible to have walked across the water upon their heads. During this extraordinary passage, thousands of fish were caught and swallowed by them. The horrid noise of their closing jaws, their plunging amid the broken banks of fish, and rising with their prey some feet above the water, the floods of water and blood rushing from their mouths, and the clouds of vapour issuing from their nostrils, were truly frightful. This scene continued, at intervals, during the whole night. After it was ended, Mr. Bartram says he found himself more reconciled to his situation than he had before been; as he was convinced that the extraordinary assemblage of alligators at this place had been owing to the annual passage of these shoals of fish; and that they were so well employed in their own element, that he had little occasion to fear they would wander from the banks for the purpose of annoying him.

It being now almost night, he returned to his tent, where he had left his fish broiling, and his kettle of rice stewing; and having, in his packages, oil, pepper, and salt, and, in place of vinegar, excellent oranges hanging in abundance over his head, he sat down and regaled himself cheerfully. Before he retired to rest, he was suddenly roused by a noise behind him, towards the land. He sprang up, seized his gun, and, going cautiously in the direction from which the sound approached, he beheld two large bears, advancing towards him. He waited till they were about thirty yards distant, when he snapped his piece at them. It flashed in the pan, but they both galloped off, and did not return. After this he passed the night without any other molestation than being occasionally awaked by the whooping of owls, the screaming of bitterns, or by wood-rats running among the leaves. When he arose in the morning there was perfect peace: very few alligators were to be seen, and these were asleep near the shore. His mind was not, however, free from alarm. He could not but entertain considerable dread lest, in pursuing his voyage up the river, he should, every evening, encounter difficulties similar to those which he had now experienced.

Having loaded his gun and re-embarked, he set sail cautiously along the shore; and was, not long afterwards, attacked by an alligator, which he beat off with his club; another passed close by his boat, having a brood of young ones, a hundred or more in number, following her, in a long train. On one part of the shore Mr. Bartram beheld a great number of hillocks, or small pyramids, in shape resembling haycocks, and ranged like an encampment. They were on a high marsh, fifteen or twenty yards from the water, and each about four feet in height. He knew them to be the nests of alligators, and now expected a furious and general attack, as he saw several large alligators swimming near them. Notwithstanding this he was determined to land and examine them. Accordingly, he ran his canoe on shore; and, having ascended a sloping bank or road which led to the place, he found that most of the nests were deserted, and thick whitish egg-shells lay broken and scattered upon the ground around them.

These nests were in the form of obtuse cones, and were constructed with mud, grass, and herbage. In the formation of them, the alligators had made a kind of floor of these substances, upon the ground; on this they had deposited a layer of eggs, and upon that a stratum of mortar, seven or eight inches in thickness, and then another layer of eggs; and, in this manner, one stratum upon another, nearly to the top. Mr. Bartram supposes that the eggs are hatched by the heat of the sun; and that the female alligator carefully watches her own nest of eggs until they are all hatched. He says it is certain that the young ones are not left to shift for themselves, for he had frequent opportunities of seeing female alligators leading about the shores their offspring, as a hen does her chickens.

After having gratified his curiosity, he continued his voyage up the river. In his progress he observed several small floating islands. The swamps on the banks of the river were, in general, three or four feet above the level of the water; and the timber upon them was large, but thinly scattered. The black mould of these swamps was covered with a succulent and tender kind of grass, which, when chewed, was sweet and agreeable to the taste, somewhat like young sugar-canes. Alligators were still numerous. Exposed, during the day, to the rays of a vertical sun, Mr. Bartram experienced great inconvenience in rowing his canoe against the stream; and, at night, he was annoyed by the stings of musquitoes, and he was obliged to be constantly on guard against the attacks of alligators. In one instance an alligator, of immense size, came up to his tent, and approached within six feet of him, when he was awakened by the screaming owl. Starting up, he seized his musket, which, during the night, he always kept under his head; and the animal, alarmed by the noise, rushed again into the water.

In many places the banks of the river were ornamented with hanging garlands of various climbing vegetables, both shrubs and plants. One of these had white flowers, each as big as a small funnel, the tube five or six inches in length, and not thicker than a tobacco-pipe. It was curious to observe the wild squash, (a species of cucurbita,) which grew upon the lofty limbs of the trees: its yellow fruit, somewhat of the size and shape of a large orange, pendant over the water. In some parts there were steep cliffs on each side of the river. During the middle of the day the weather was so intensely hot, that Mr. Bartram was obliged to seek for shelter under the shade of the trees which grew upon the banks.

He passed another lake, the eastern shores of which were adorned with dark, high forests: on the north and south were apparently endless plains and meadows, embellished with islets and promontories covered with trees. Whilst he was navigating this lake, he was exposed to the most tremendous storm of thunder and lightning that he had ever witnessed. The lofty forests bent beneath the fury of the blast, and the sturdy limbs of the trees cracked under the weight of the wind. Groves were torn up; and the spreading branches of the trees were rent asunder, and, like leaves or stubble, were whirled aloft in the air. After a while the wind and rain abated. Mr. Bartram then crossed the lake, about a mile in length, and arrived in safety at a plantation near its southern extremity. Here he found that nearly all the buildings had been overturned by the hurricane; and that a hundred acres of indigo plants, almost ripe for cutting, and several acres of sugar-canes, had been ruined.

About four miles beyond this plantation, Mr. Bartram was shown a vast fountain of hot mineral water, which issued from a ridge or bank of the river, in a great cove or bay. The water, though hot and of a disagreeable brassy and vitriolic taste, and very offensive to the smell, was perfectly transparent, and exhibited to view a prodigious number of fish, and alligators, which were lying about the bottom.

Mr. Bartram now returned, in his canoe, to the station called the *Upper Store*. Thence, in company with five persons who had been commissioned to make some commercial arrangements with the Indians, he set out for an Indian town called *Cuscowilla*. For four or five miles they travelled westward, over a level plain, which, before and on each side of them, appeared like a green meadow, thinly planted with low and spreading pine-trees. The whole surface seemed clad with grass, herbage, and low shrubs, and with many kinds of plants, which were rare and highly interesting. Here also many species of birds were seen, the plumage of some of which was extremely beautiful. Snakes, lizards, and insects were also very abundant. Beyond this plain was a hill, ornamented with a great variety of herbaceous plants and grasses, and with a magnificent grove of pines. After the pine-groves were passed, the travellers entered a district called the *Sand-hills*.

They encamped, for the first night, at the *Half-way Pond*. This is a lake, about three miles in circumference, which extends, through an apparently spacious meadow, and beneath a chain of elevated sand-hills. It is inhabited by numerous kinds of fish, by alligators, and by a kind of turtles with soft shells. The latter are so large as to weigh from twenty to thirty, and even forty pounds each. They are extremely fat and delicious; but, if eaten to excess, are unwholesome. Numerous herds of deer, and extensive flocks of turkeys, frequent the vicinity of this place.

From Half-way Pond the travellers proceeded, still westward, through the high forests of Cuscowilla. The country, for five or six miles, presented nearly the same scenery as before. After this the sand-ridges became higher, and their bases proportionally more extensive. The savannahs and ponds were larger; the summits of the ridges more gravelly; and here and there rocks, formed of a sort of concrete of sand and shells, were seen above the sand and gravel.

Having passed an extensive and fruitful orange-grove, through a pine-forest, and crossed two or three streams that were tributary to the river St. John, the travellers at length came within sight of the great and beautiful *Lake of Cuscowilla*. Their course now lay through a magnificent forest, about nine miles in extent, and consisting of orange-groves, overtopped by grand magnolias, palm-trees, oaks, beech, and other trees. This forest bounded one edge of the lake; and, beyond it, lay the town of *Cuscowilla*, the place of their destination. This place is situated on the banks of a brook, which, at a little distance, falls into the lake.

They were welcomed to the town, and conducted, by a party of young men and maidens, to the house of the chief. This stood on an eminence, and was distinguished from the other dwellings by its superior magnitude, and by having a flag hoisted, on a high staff, at one corner. The chief, attended by several old men, came to them, and shook them by their hands, or rather their arms, (a form of salutation peculiar to the American Indians,) saying at the same time, "You are come." They followed him into an apartment prepared for their reception.

The following customs are practised towards their guests, by the Indians in this part of America. The pipe being filled, it is handed round to each. After this a large bowl, containing what is called "thin drink," is brought, and is set down on a low table. In the bowl is a great wooden ladle: each person takes up in the ladle as much of the liquor as he pleases; and, after drinking until he is satisfied, he returns it into the bowl, pushing the handle towards the next person in the circle; and so it goes round.

On the present occasion, after the usual compliments had passed, the principal trader informed the Indian chief, in the presence of his council or attendants, respecting the purport of their business; and with this the chief expressed his satisfaction. When the latter was informed concerning the object of Mr. Bartram's journey, he received him with complaisance; giving him unlimited permission to travel over his country, for the purpose of collecting plants, and saluting him by the name of *Pug Puggy*, or "Flower-hunter."

This chief was a tall, well-formed man, very affable and cheerful, about sixty years of age. His eyes were lively and full of lustre, his countenance was manly and placid, yet ferocious; his nose aquiline, and his dress extremely simple; but his head was ornamented in the manner of the Creek Indians. He had been a great warrior, and had now, attending him as slaves, many captives, which had been taken by himself when young. They were dressed better than he, and served and waited upon him with signs of the most abject humility. The manners and customs of these Indians, who are called *Alachuas*, and of most of the lower *Creeks* or *Siminoles*, appear evidently tinctured with Spanish civilization. There are several Christians among them, many of whom wear little silver crucifixes, affixed to a collar round their necks, or suspended by a small chain upon their breasts.

Mr. Bartram and his party had not long been here, before the repast was brought in. This consisted of venison stewed in bear's oil, of fresh corn-cakes, milk, and a dish called homony; and the drink was honey and water, very cool and agreeable.

A few days after this some negotiations took place between the traders and the Indians, in the public square or council-house. These having terminated to the satisfaction of both parties, a banquet succeeded; the ribs and choicest fat pieces of bullocks, well barbecued, were brought into an apartment of the square: bowls and kettles of stewed flesh and broth constituted the next course; and with these was brought in a dish, made of the belly or paunch of an ox, not over-cleansed of its contents, cut and minced tolerably fine, and then made into a thin kind of soup, and seasoned with salt and aromatic herbs; but the seasoning was not quite strong enough to overpower the original taste and smell. This is a favourite dish with the Indians.

Cuscowilla is the capital of the Alachua Indians; and it, at this time, contained about thirty habitations, each of which consisted of two houses, nearly of the same size, about thirty feet in length, twelve feet wide, and twelve high. Of these, one is divided into two apartments; the cook-room, or common hall, and the lodging-room. The other house is nearly of the same dimensions, and stands about twenty yards from the dwelling-house. This building is two stories high, and is constructed in a different manner from the former. Like that, it is divided across; but the end next the dwelling-house is open on three sides, and is supported by posts or columns. It has an open loft or platform, the ascent to which is by a portable stair or ladder: this is pleasant, cool, and airy; and here the master or chief of the family retires to repose, in the hot seasons, and receives his guests or visitors. The other half of this building is closed on all sides: the lowest or ground part is a potatoe-house; and the upper story a granary, for corn and other provisions.

The town of Cuscowilla stands in an extremely pleasant situation, upon a high, swelling ridge of sand-hills, within three or four hundred yards of a large and beautiful lake, which continually washes a sandy beach, under a moderately high, sloping bank; terminated on one side by extensive forests of orange-groves, and overtopped with magnolias, palms, poplars, limes, live oaks, and other trees. The ground, between the town and the lake, is adorned by an open grove of tall pine-trees, which, standing at a considerable distance from each other, admit a delightful prospect of the sparkling waters. The lake abounds with various kinds of excellent fish and wild fowl.

The inhabitants of Cuscowilla have each a small garden attached to their dwellings, for the purpose of producing corn, beans, tobacco, and other useful articles; but the plantation which supplies them with their chief vegetable provisions, is near the great Alachua savannah, and about two miles distant. This plantation has one common enclosure, and is worked and tended by the whole community: yet every family has its particular part, marked off when planted; and this portion receives the common labour and assistance, until the corn, or other articles cultivated upon it, are ripe. Each family then gathers and deposits in its store-house its own proper share, setting apart a small gift or contribution for a public granary, which stands near the centre of the plantation.

Mr. Bartram made several excursions to places in the vicinity of Cuscowilla and the Alachua Swamp. In one of these, he came to a little clump of shrubs, where he observed several large snakes, entwined together. They were each about four feet in length, and as thick as a man's wrist. Mr. Bartram approached, and endeavoured to irritate them, but they appeared perfectly harmless. Numerous herds of cattle and deer, and many troops of horses were seen peacefully browsing on the grass of the savannah, or strolling through the groves on the surrounding heights. Large flocks of wild turkeys were also observed in the woods.

At some distance from Cuscowilla, is an Indian town called *Talahasochte*, which Mr. Bartram some time afterwards visited. It is delightfully situated on the elevated east bank of a river called *Little St. John's*. The habitations were, at this time, about thirty in number, and constructed like those of Cuscowilla; but the council-house was neater and more spacious.

The Indians of this town have large and handsome canoes, which they form out of the trunks of cypress-trees: some of them are sufficiently commodious to accommodate twenty or thirty persons. In these canoes they descend the river, on trading and hunting excursions, as far as the sea-coast, to the neighbouring islands and shores; and they sometimes even cross the Gulf of Florida to the West India Islands.

In this neighbourhood are seen many singular and unaccountable cavities. These are funnel-shaped; and some of them are from twenty to forty yards across at the rim. Their perpendicular depth is, in many instances, upwards of twenty feet.

At this time, nearly the whole of East Florida, and a great portion of West Florida, were in the possession of Indians; and these chiefly a tribe called *Siminoles*, an apparently contented and happy race of people, who enjoyed, in superabundance, the necessaries and the conveniences of life. With the skins of deer, bears, tigers, and wolves, together with honey, wax, and other productions of their country, this people purchased, from

Europeans, clothing, equipage, and domestic utensils. They seemed to be free from want or desires: they had no enemy to dread; and, apparently, nothing to occasion disquietude, except the gradual encroachments of the white people.

Mr. Bartram returned to the trading-store, on the bank of the river St. John; and, about the end of September, he reached the place from which he had commenced his voyage.

We must now proceed, across the southern states, to the mouth of the Mississippi, for the purpose of tracing the course of that astonishing river, and describing the most important places in its vicinity.

Fourteen Day's Instruction

UNITED STATES CONTINUED.

The River Mississippi.

The Mississippi has its source in about forty-six degrees thirty minutes of north latitude; and terminates in the Gulf of Mexico, at some distance below the town of New Orleans. Its length, in a direct line, exceeds one thousand seven hundred miles; and it falls into the sea, by many mouths, most of which, like those of the Nile, are too shallow to be navigable. For a considerable distance, its banks are low, marshy, and covered with reeds; and are annually overflowed, from the melting of the snows in the interior of the country. The inundation usually commences in March, and continues about three months; and the slime which it deposits on the adjacent lands, tends, in a very important degree, to fertilize the soil. This river is navigable to a great distance; but, at spring-tides, the navigation is difficult, on account of the strength of the currents, and the innumerable islands, shoals, and sand-banks, with which it is interspersed. Vessels of three hundred tons burden can ascend it as high as Natchez, four hundred miles from the sea; and those of lighter burden can pass upward, as far as the Falls of St. Anthony, in latitude forty-four degrees fifty minutes.

New Orleans, the capital of the state of Louisiana, is situated on the northern bank of the Mississippi, and is a place of great commercial importance. It was founded in the year 1717, and now contains near thirty thousand inhabitants. In 1787, it had eleven hundred houses, but, nine hundred of these having been consumed by fire, it has since been rebuilt on a regular plan, and a more enlarged scale. Most of the houses are constructed with wooden frames, raised about eight feet from the ground, and have galleries round them, and cellars under the floors: almost every house has a garden.

Louisiana having, till lately, been a French colony, the French language is still predominant at New Orleans. The appearance of the people too is French; and even the negroes, by their antics and ludicrous gestures, exhibit their previous connexion with that nation. Their general manners and habits are very relaxed. Though New Orleans is now a city belonging to the United

States, the markets, shops, theatre, circus, and public ball-rooms, are open on Sundays, in the same manner as they are in the catholic countries of the old continent. Gambling-houses, too, are numerous; and the coffee-houses and the Exchange are occupied, from morning till night, by gamesters. The general stile of living is luxurious. The houses are elegantly furnished; and the ladies dress in an expensive manner.

Provisions are here of bad quality, and enormously dear. Hams and cheese, from England; potatoes, butter, and beef from Ireland, are common articles of import. The rents of houses, also, are very extravagant.

The country around New Orleans is level, rich, and healthy, and has many extensive sugar-plantations. And, for the space of five leagues below, and ten above the town, the river has been embanked, to defend the adjacent fields from those inundations of the Mississippi which take place every spring. The land, adjacent to the town, yields abundant crops of rice, Indian corn, and vegetables.

There is a regular communication, by means of steam-boats and other vessels, between New Orleans and the towns on the banks of the Mississippi, the Ohio, and other rivers, in the distant parts of North America.

The scenery of the Mississippi, to the distance of one hundred and fifty miles and upwards, from New Orleans, is very uninteresting. The country is a dead flat; so that the banks of the river, and most of the adjacent grounds, are annually overflowed. In the vicinity of Natchez it becomes more varied and pleasing.

Natchez is a town in the state of Mississippi, near the banks of the river, and about four hundred miles from its mouth. It contains about thirty dwellings, most of which are whiskey-shops, gambling, and other houses, where an excess of profligacy prevails, which is not usual in the United States.

Mr. Fearon visited Natchez in the year 1817; and in the port there were twenty-five flats, seven keels, and one steam-vessel. The flats are square covered vessels, of considerable capacity, used for carrying freight from Pittsburgh, on the Ohio, and other places below that town, down to New Orleans. Their construction is temporary and of slight materials; for they are broken up at New Orleans, as not sufficiently strong to be freighted up the river. The keel is a substantial, well-built boat, of considerable length; and, in form, somewhat resembles the floating-bath at Blackfriars' Bridge.

Observing a great many coloured people in these boats, Mr. Fearon concluded that they were emigrants, who had proceeded thus far on their route towards a settlement. The fact, however, proved to be, that fourteen of the flats were freighted with human beings intended for sale. They had been collected in the United States, by slave-dealers, and shipped, up the Mississippi, to Kentucky for a market.

There are, at Natchez, numerous stores, and three-fourths of the goods at every store are articles of British manufacture. Shopkeeping is here profitable, and mechanics are highly paid. Lotteries are very prevalent at Natchez. When Mr. Fearon was here, there was a lottery for *building a Presbyterian church*; and the scheme was preceded by a long address, on the advantages of religion, and the necessity of all citizens supporting Christianity, by purchasing tickets in this lottery!

The streets of Natchez were literally crammed with bales of cotton for the Liverpool market. These are carried to the water-side in carts, each drawn by two mules, horses being here little used. During Mr. Fearon's residence at this town, he twice visited the State legislature, which was composed of men who appeared any thing but legislators. Their place of meeting was in a superior kind of hay-loft; and the imitation of the forms of the British parliament were perfectly ludicrous.

Between Natchez, and the mouth of the Ohio, there is not one spot which could be recommended as a place for an Englishman to settle in. Throughout the whole of this space, the white population are the victims of demoralizing habits. The native Indians present, of course, nothing but a picture of mere savage life; and the negro slaves suffer even more misery than commonly falls to the lot of their oppressed and degraded condition. What a foul stain is it upon the American republic, professing, as they do, the principles of liberty and of equal rights, that, out of twenty states, there should be eleven in which slavery is an avowed part of the political constitution; and that, in those called free, New England excepted, the condition of blacks who are indentured, for terms of years, should practically amount to slavery!

Beyond the state of Louisiana, the Mississippi divides the Missouri territory from the territory of Mississippi; and, north of that, from the states of Tenessee and Kentucky. About the 37th degree of north latitude, and on the western bank of the river, is a town called *New Madrid*. This place, from the advantages of its situation, about forty-five miles from the mouth of the Ohio, may at some future time become of considerable importance. The *Ohio*, at the place of its junction with the Mississippi, is about a mile in width, and is navigable, for vessels of considerable burden, to a distance of more than a thousand miles.

Beyond the Ohio commences the *Illinois territory*. Here the general face of the country is flat; but, in some parts, the land is high and craggy. It abounds in deer, wolves, bears, squirrels, racoons, and foxes; in wild turkeys and quails; geese and ducks, partially; and hawks, buzzards, and pigeons in tolerable abundance; and the rivers contain several species of fish. In the prairies there are rattlesnakes. The woods supply grapes, pecan nuts, (similar to our walnut,) and hickory nuts. Hops, raspberries, and strawberries, here grow wild. Limestone abounds; and salt, copper, and coal have all been found in this district.

The seat of the territorial government is *Kaskaski*, a town which stands on a plain, near the western bank of the Mississippi, and contains about one hundred and fifty houses. This place has been settled somewhat more than a century, and its inhabitants are chiefly French. Some parts of the district of Illinois are occupied by Indians. The other inhabitants are, first, what are here termed "squatters," persons half civilized and half savage; and who, both in character and habits, are extremely wretched: second, a medley of land-jobbers, lawyers, doctors, and farmers, a portion of those who traverse this immense continent, founding settlements, and engaging in all kinds of speculation: and third, some old French settlers, who are possessed of considerable property, and who live in ease and comfort.

About seventy miles north of Kaskaski, and on the opposite side of the river, is a town or large village, called *St. Louis*. It stands on a rock or bank of considerable height, in a beautiful and healthy situation, and is surrounded by a country of exuberant fertility. The inhabitants of this place are chiefly employed in the fur-trade, and seldom occupy themselves in agriculture.

Narrative of a Voyage from St. Louis to the source of the Mississippi.
By Zebulon Montgomery Pike.

Major Pike, at that time a lieutenant in the American army, was employed by the government of the United States, to make a survey of the Mississippi, from the town of *St. Louis*, upwards, to its source. In pursuance of his instructions, he embarked, in a keel-boat, at this place, on the afternoon of Friday the 9th of August, 1805; and was accompanied by a serjeant and seventeen private soldiers of the American army.

As far as the mouth of the river Missouri, he says, the eastern shore of the Mississippi consists of a sandy soil, and is covered with timber-trees of various kinds. The western shore is, for a little distance, composed of high land, bordered by prairie or natural meadow-ground; after which bottom-land occurs, with timber similar to that on the eastern shore. The current is rapid, and, at low water, the navigation is obstructed by sand-banks.

Beyond the entrance of the Missouri, the stream is gentle, as far as the mouth of the *Illinois*; but there, owing to extensive sand-bars, and many islands, it becomes extremely rapid. From the Illinois to the *Buffalo River*, the eastern shore exhibits a series of gentle eminences; but, on the west, the land is a continued prairie. Timber is found on both sides; generally hackberry, cotton-wood, and ash. The Buffalo river enters from the west, and is about a hundred yards wide at its mouth.

On the 14th of August the voyagers passed a camp of the *Sac Indians*, consisting of three men, with their families. The men were employed in spearing and landing a large fish. Mr. Pike gave them a small quantity of whiskey and biscuit; and they, in return, presented him with some fish. The Sacs are a tribe of Indians which hunt on the Mississippi, and its confluent streams, from the Illinois to the river Jowa; and on the plains west of them, which border upon the Missouri. They are much dreaded by other Indians, for their propensity to deceit, and their disposition to commit injury by stratagem.

On the ensuing day, the voyagers reached the mouth of *Salt river*, a considerable stream, which, at high water, is navigable for at least two hundred miles. From the Illinois to this river, the western shore is either immediately bordered by beautiful cedar-cliffs, or the ridges of these cliffs may be seen at a distance. On the east the land is low, and the soil rich.

On the 16th of August they passed the house of a Frenchman, on the western side of the river. The cattle belonging to this person appeared to be in fine order, but his corn-land was in a bad state of cultivation. Three days afterwards their boat was damaged by striking against a vessel carrying timber and planks down the stream. While they were engaged in repairing it, three canoes, with Indians, passed on the opposite side of the river. The men in the canoes called out, in English, "How do you do?" wishing for an invitation to come over; but this was not given, and they proceeded on their voyage.

Beyond Salt river the western shore of the Mississippi is hilly, but the eastern side consists of lowland, timbered with hickory, oak, ash, maple, and other trees. The navigation here is easy, and the soil on both sides tolerably good.

On the 20th of August the voyagers, with great difficulty, passed the *Rapids des Moines*. These are eleven miles in extent; and, with successive ledges and shoals, reach from shore to shore, across the bed of the river. Mr. Pike had here an interview with four chiefs, and fifteen men of the Sac nation, accompanied by a French interpreter, and an agent who had been sent from the United States to teach them agriculture. These men assisted him in his progress up the Rapids; and, in recompense for the service, they were presented with some tobacco, knives, and whiskey.

At some distance beyond the Rapids the voyagers had a beautiful prospect, at least forty miles in extent, down the river. Their average daily progress appears to have been betwixt twenty and thirty miles.

Above the *river Jowa*, which is one hundred and fifty yards wide at its mouth, the shore of the Mississippi consists of high prairie, with yellow clay-banks, and, in some places, banks of red sand: the western shore also is prairie, but bounded by wood. About ten miles up the Jowa is a village of *Jowa Indians*. This people subsist chiefly by hunting, but they cultivate some corn-land. Their chief residence is on the small streams in the rear of the Mississippi. From the Jowa to *Rock river*, there are, on the west, beautiful prairies, and, in some places, rich land, with black walnut and hickory timber.

On the 28th of August the vessel was much injured in passing up a series of rapids nearly eighteen miles in extent, and, in some places, reaching from shore to shore. Four days after this they arrived in the vicinity of some extensive lead-mines, which belonged to a Frenchman named Dubuque. The only animals they had hitherto seen were a few wild turkeys and some deer.

From the lead-mines to *Turkey river*, the Mississippi continues nearly of the same width, and the banks, soil, and productions appear precisely similar. On the bank of the Turkey river is a village of *Reynard Indians*, who raise there a considerable quantity of corn. The Reynards reside in three villages on the Mississippi, two of which Mr. Pike had already past. They grow corn, beans, and melons; and they annually sell many hundred bushels of corn to the inhabitants of the United States.

On the 2d of September, Mr. Pike and some of his men landed for the purpose of shooting pigeons; but the guns were no sooner fired, than a party of Indians, who were on shore at a little distance, ran to the water, and escaped in their pirogues or canoes, with great precipitation. After this the voyagers passed the mouth of the *Ouisconsin river*, which enters the Mississippi in latitude 43 degrees 44 minutes, and is nearly half a mile wide. This river is an important source of communication with the great American lakes, and is the route by which all the traders of Michillimackinac convey their goods to the Mississippi.

On the 6th of September, a council was held with a party of *Puant* or *Winebagoe Indians*, and one of the *Sioux* chiefs. The former occupy seven villages, and are supposed to be a nation who originally emigrated from Mexico, to avoid the oppression of the Spaniards. They are reputed to be brave; but their bravery resembles the ferocity of tigers, rather than the deliberate resolution of men. They are so treacherous that, it is said, a white man should never lie down to sleep in their villages, without adopting the utmost caution to preserve himself from injury. The *Sioux* are a powerful nation, the dread of whom is extended over all the adjacent country. They are divided into numerous bands, headed by celebrated chiefs. Few of them cultivate land; but they chiefly live on the production of the chase, and on a kind of bread which they make from wild oats. This species of grain is here produced in such abundance, that a sufficiency for their subsistence is easily collected in the autumn, without any trouble whatever in cultivating the land.

Not long after their interview with these Indians, the voyagers reached the *Prairie des Chiens*. The houses of this village, about eighteen in number, are arranged in two streets, along the front of a marsh. They are chiefly built of wood; are daubed on the outside with clay, and white-washed within. The furniture in most of them is decent, and, in those of the most wealthy inhabitants, displays a considerable degree of taste. The Prairie des Chiens was first settled under the protection of the English government, in the year 1783; and derives its name from a family of Reynards, who formerly lived there, and were distinguished by the appellation of Dog Indians. It is a place of resort for Indian traders and others, who reside in the interior. Mr. Pike here engaged two interpreters to accompany him; one of whom was to perform the whole voyage, and the other to sail with him as high as the falls of St. Anthony.

On the 9th of September he had an interview with a party of *Sioux Indians*. When he went towards the shore to meet them, they saluted him by firing three rounds from their muskets, loaded with ball. On landing, Mr. Pike was met by the chief, and invited to his lodge. This invitation he complied with, having first stationed some of his men as guards, to protect him in case of danger. In the lodge he found a clean mat and a pillow arranged for him to sit upon; and the complimentary pipe of peace was placed before him, on a pair of small crutches. The chief sate at his right hand, and the interpreter at his left. After they had satisfied each other of their mutual good wishes, and Mr. Pike had accepted the pipe, dinner was prepared. This consisted of wild rye and venison.

Mr. Pike was afterwards conducted by the chief to a dance, the performance of which was accompanied by many curious gestures. Men and women danced indiscriminately. They were all dressed in the gayest manner imaginable. Each had, in his hand, a small skin of some kind of animal. They frequently ran up, pointed their skin, and gave a puff with their breath; on which the person blown at fell, and either appeared lifeless, or in great agony; but afterwards slowly recovered, rose, and joined in the dance. This was understood to be of a religious description; and the Indians believed that they actually puffed, into each others bodies, something which occasioned them to fall. For persons to be permitted to take a part in these dances, it was requisite that they should make valuable presents to the society, give a feast, and be admitted with great ceremony. When Mr. Pike returned to his boat, he sent for the chief, and presented him with a quantity of tobacco, four knives, half a pound of vermilion, a quart of salt, and several gallons of spirits.

At some distance beyond this place, Mr. Pike was shewn several holes, which had been dug in the ground by the Sioux Indians. These were, in general, of circular shape, and about ten feet in diameter; but some of them were in the form of half moons. When this people apprehend an attack from their enemies, or discover an enemy near them, they dig into the ground, with their knives, tomahawks, and wooden ladles; and, in an incredibly short space of time, sink holes that are sufficiently capacious to protect both themselves and their families from the balls or arrows of their foe.

Though the part of the river which the voyagers were now traversing was nearly two thousand miles distant from the sea, the width of the stream was supposed to be at least two miles.

The wet season had commenced, and rain fell, in considerable quantity almost every day. In this part of his voyage, Mr. Pike was accompanied by a Mr. Frazer and two other persons, with three birch canoes. On the 16th of September, they passed the mouth of the *Sauteaux* or *Chippeway river*, a deep and majestic stream, which has a communication, by a short passage, with the Montreal river, and, by this river, with Lake Superior. The shores of the Mississippi were here, in many places, bold and precipitous, forming a succession of high perpendicular cliffs and low valleys; and they exhibited some of the most romantic and picturesque views imaginable. But this irregular scenery was sometimes interrupted by wide and extensive plains, which brought to the minds of the voyagers the verdant lawns of civilized countries, and almost induced them to imagine themselves in the midst of a highly-cultivated plantation. The timber of this part of the country was generally birch, elm, and cotton-wood; and all the cliffs were bordered with cedars. The prevailing species of game were deer and bears.

On the 21st of September, the voyagers breakfasted at a Sioux village, on the eastern side of the river. It consisted of eleven lodges, and was situated at the head of an island, just below a ledge of rocks; but the inhabitants had all left it. About two miles beyond this village, they saw three bears, swimming over the river, but beyond the reach of gun-shot.

In a camp of Sioux, which they afterwards passed, Mr. Pike was astonished by the garrulity of the women. At the other camps the women had not opened their lips; but here they flocked around the strangers, and talked without cessation. The cause of this freedom is supposed to have been the absence of their husbands. In a spot at which the voyagers arrived this day, the Mississippi was so narrow that Mr. Pike crossed it, in a boat, with forty strokes of his oars.

From the *Canoe river* to the *St. Croix*, it becomes still narrower, and the navigation is less obstructed by islands, than below. From the *Cannon river* it is bounded on the east, by high ridges; but the left shore consists of low ground. The timber is generally ash and maple; except the cedars of the cliffs, the sugar-tree, and ash. Mr. Pike this day observed, on the shore, a white flag, and, on landing, he discovered it to be of silk. It was suspended over a scaffold, on which were laid four dead bodies; two enclosed between boards, and two between pieces of bark. They were wrapped in blankets, which appeared quite new; and were the bodies of two Sioux women, a child, and a relative. This is the manner in which the Sioux Indians bury such of their people as die a natural death: such as are killed, they suffer to lie unburied.

On the 23d, the voyagers arrived at the *Falls of St. Anthony*. These are about seventeen feet in height, and the approach to them is through rapids, which vessels have great difficulty in passing. At the foot of the falls, the voyagers unloaded their boats, which they carried up the hill, and placed and reloaded in the river above. While this process was going on, a small party of Indians, painted black, and prepared for war, appeared on the heights. They were armed with guns, bows and arrows, clubs, and spears; and some of them had cases of pistols. Mr. Pike was desirous of purchasing from them a set of bows and arrows, and one of their war-clubs, made of elk-horn, and decorated with inlaid work; but they took offence at something which occurred, and suddenly went away.

The weather was now so rainy, and the men had been so much fatigued with conveying the vessels and their lading, to the upper part of the falls, that seven of the twenty-two, who accompanied Mr. Pike, were taken ill. It is impossible for vessels of any description, or in any state of the river, to pass up these falls. The width of the river, immediately below them, is two hundred and nine yards, and above them, six hundred and twenty-seven yards. At high-water, the appearance is extremely sublime; as then, the quantity of water falling throws up a spray, which, in clear weather, reflects, from some positions, the colours of the rainbow; and, when the sky is overcast, this spray covers the falls in gloom and chaotic majesty.

On Tuesday, the 1st of October, Mr. Pike and his men again embarked, to proceed on their voyage above the falls. At first the river was sufficiently deep for the easy passage of the boats; but, at the distance of about four miles, the shoals commenced, and there was much difficulty in proceeding. Nearly from the Falls of St. Anthony to the *Rum river*, the Mississippi is a continued chain of rapids, with eddies, formed by winding channels. The land, on both sides, consists of Prairie, with scarcely any timber, except small groves of scrubby oaks. Not far from this spot is *Red Cedar lake*, the grounds in the vicinity of which are considered, by the Indians, extremely valuable for hunting.

In some parts of the river it was requisite for the men to wade for many successive hours, in order to force the boats over the shoals, and draw them through the rapids. The weather was now cold and rainy. On the 10th of October, in the course of four miles, the voyagers passed a cluster of more than twenty islands, which Mr. Pike called *Beaver islands*, from numerous dams and paths which had been made by these animals upon them. The passage up the river was still much impeded by rocks and shoals.

About the beginning of October, the voyagers began to look out for a station in which they could pass the winter. Mr. Pike was determined, if possible, to reach the *Corbeau* or *Raven river*, the highest point that had ever been reached by traders, in bark canoes. But he was not able to accomplish his intention; for, on the seventeenth, many of his men were so benumbed with cold, that their limbs became useless, and others were laid up with illness. He consequently fixed on a station near *Pine Creek*, where the borders of the Mississippi consisted of prairie, with groves of pine at the edge of the banks; and, in some places, with oak, ash, maple, and lime-trees. The banks of *Lake Clear*, a small and beautiful lake, about three miles distant, are the resort of immense herds of elks and buffaloes; and *Clear river*, which unites this lake with the Mississippi, is a delightful little stream, about eighty yards wide.

On the seventeenth, snow fell during the whole day: Mr. Pike killed four bears, and his hunter three deer. Several ensuing days were occupied in cutting down trees, for the formation of winter-huts; and in constructing the huts, and forming a fence round them. When the latter was completed, the two boats were hauled out of the water, and turned over, on each side of the gateways, so as to form a defence against any Indians who might be inclined to attack the encampment.

At this place, and in its vicinity, the voyagers continued several weeks, during which they suffered great hardships. Much of their time was occupied in hunting. They occasionally saw large herds of elks, some of them of immense size; the horns of the bucks measuring four feet and upwards in width. Many droves of buffaloes were also seen, and deer of various kinds: bears, wolves, racoons, and otters, were occasionally shot.

On the 7th of November the Mississippi was nearly filled with snow; and, on the land, the snow was knee deep. Before the end of the month, the river was frozen over.

During his residence at this place, Mr. Pike did not see many Indians. On one occasion he visited the tent or hut of an Indian chief, whom he found sitting amidst his children, and grand-children, ten in number. The hut was constructed of rushes, platted into mats.

In the month of December, Mr. Pike and some of his men proceeded, in sledges, up the Mississippi. On the twenty-fourth, they reached *Corbeau river*; which, at its mouth, was nearly as wide as the Mississippi. For a considerable distance, the Mississippi was interrupted by a continued succession of rapids, shoals, and falls. One of the latter, called the *Falls of the Painted Rock*, formed the third important obstacle to the navigation of the river, which Mr. Pike had encountered. Most of the timber, now observed near the banks, consisted of pine-trees.

On the thirty-first, Mr. Pike passed *Pine river*. For many miles, the Mississippi had been much narrower, and more free from islands, than in the lower parts of the stream. The shores, in general, presented a dreary prospect of high barren knobs, covered with dead and fallen pine-timber; and most of the adjacent country was interspersed with small lakes. Deer of various kinds, were plentiful; but no buffaloes, nor elks, had been seen.

Near the mouth of the Pine river, an encampment of *Chippeway Indians* was observed. This had been occupied in the summer, but it was now vacant. By certain marks which had been left, the voyagers understood that these Indians had marched a party of fifty warriors against the Sioux, and had killed four men and four women, who were here represented by figures carved in wood. The figures of the men were painted, and put into the ground, to the middle; and, by their sides, were four painted poles, sharpened at the end, to represent the women. Near this spot were poles with deer-skins, plumes, silk-handkerchiefs, &c. and a circular hoop of cedar, with something attached to it which resembled a scalp.

Beyond this place, Mr. Pike observed, on the bank of the river, six elegant bark-canoes, which had been laid up by the Chippeways, and a camp, which appeared to have been evacuated about ten days before. After having endured considerable hardship and much fatigue for some weeks longer, he accomplished the object of his expedition, by arriving, on the 1st of February, at *Leech Lake*, from which issues the main source of the Mississippi. He crossed this lake, (about twelve miles in width,) to an

English fort, an establishment belonging to the North West Company, and was there received, with great hospitality, by a Mr. Hugh Mac Gillis. His men reached the fort on the sixth; but, in traversing the lake, some of them had their ears, some their noses, and others their chins frozen.

Near this place, Mr. Pike effected some arrangements with the Indians, which were considered advantageous to the American government; and, not long afterwards, having examined the adjacent country, as well as the severity of the weather would permit, he set out on his return, accompanied by a deputation of Indian chiefs. The river still continued frozen, and the party travelled chiefly in sledges, drawn by dogs. On the 5th of March, they again reached the encampment near *Pine Creek*.

About a fortnight after this, Mr. Pike visited a plantation of sugar maple-trees, at a little distance from the creek, one of the finest he had ever seen. He was conducted to the lodge of the chief, who received him in a truly patriarchal style. This person assisted him in taking off his clothes, conducted him to the best part of his lodge, and offered him dry clothes. He then presented him with syrup of the maple-tree, to drink, and asked whether he preferred eating beaver, swan, elk, or deer? Preference being given to the first, a large kettle was filled with beavers' flesh, for the purpose of its being made into soup. This was afterwards served up; and when the repast was ended, Mr. Pike visited other lodges, at each of which he was presented with something to eat. He continued here all night; and, on the ensuing day, having purchased two baskets filled with sugar, he departed, and returned to his camp.

Some Indians, whom Mr. Pike and his men visited not long after this, were extremely well-formed and elegant people. They were about the middle size; and their complexions, for savages, were, in general, fair: their teeth were good: their eyes were large and somewhat languishing; and they had a mild but independent expression of countenance.

In the evening, these Indians entertained their visitors with the calumet and dog-dance; and with another dance, in which some of the men struck a post, and related their war exploits. After the dance, was a feast of the dead. At this, every two or three persons had a pan or vessel full of meat set before him; a prayer was then said, and the eating commenced. Each was expected to devour his whole portion, and not to drop even a bone; for all the bones were carefully collected and put into a dish. When the eating was finished, the chief gave an exhortation, which concluded the ceremony.

About the end of March, Mr. Pike ordered the boats to be prepared for the voyage, in return, down the river. The ice had not, indeed, yet broken up; but he was every day in anxious expectation of seeing it begin to move. On the 6th of April, the river was found sufficiently clear of ice, to permit the party to re-embark. They accordingly loaded the boats, and, on the ensuing morning, experienced inexpressible joy, in leaving the savage wilderness, in which they had been so long imprisoned. On the 10th, they again reached the *Falls of St. Anthony.* The appearance of this cataract was much more tremendous than it had been when they ascended; and the great increase of the water occasioned the spray to rise much higher than it had done before. The river was still nearly covered with floating-ice; and much snow continued to fall.

After his arrival at the *Prairie des Chiens,* Mr. Pike held a council, with the Puant chiefs, respecting some murders which had been committed by the men of their nation; and, in the afternoon, he was entertained with a game of "the cross," between the Sioux on one side, and the Puants and the Reynards on the other. The ball used in this game is made of a hard substance, and covered with leather. When the parties are ready, and the bets have been agreed upon, (and these are sometimes to the amount of several thousand dollars,) the goals are erected on the prairie, about half a mile asunder. The ball is then thrown up, in the middle, and each party, with a kind of racket, strives to beat it to the opposite goal. After the first rubber is gained, which is done by the ball being driven round one of the posts, it is again taken to the centre, the ground is changed, and the contest is renewed; and this is continued until one of the parties has been four times victorious, on which the bets are decided.

It is an interesting sight, says Mr. Pike, to behold two or three hundred naked savages contending, on the plain, who shall bear off the palm of victory; for the man who drives the ball round the goal, receives the shouts of his companions, in congratulation of his success. It sometimes happens, that one of them catches the ball in his racket, and, depending on his speed, endeavours to carry it to the goal; but if he finds himself too closely pursued, he hurls it, with great force and dexterity, to an amazing distance, where there are always flankers, of both parties, ready to receive it. The ball seldom touches the ground; but it is sometimes kept in the air, for hours, before either party can gain the victory.

About ten miles above *Salt river,* the voyagers, on the 28th of April, stopped at some islands where there were numerous roosts of passenger pigeons; and, in about fifteen minutes, they knocked on the head, and brought on board the boat, about three hundred. Mr. Pike, though he had frequently heard of the fecundity of these birds, had never given credit to it; but, he says, that the most fervid imagination cannot conceive their numbers. The noise, which they made in the woods, was like the continued roaring of the wind. The young ones were still in their nests: these consisted only of small bunches of sticks; and their number was such, that all the small trees were covered with them.

On the 30th of April, after an absence of eight months and twenty-two days, Mr. Pike once more reached St. Louis in safety.

Fifteenth Day's Instruction

WESTERN TERRITORY OF AMERICA.

The river Missouri.

Previously to the commencement of the expedition commanded by Mr. Pike, the government of the United States had directed arrangements to be made for examining the Missouri, from its mouth to its source; thence exploring the vast and dreary range of mountains, which form the highest land in the centre of that part of the American continent; and afterwards, of descending, by some one of the rivers which flow westward, to the Pacific ocean. This formidable undertaking was committed to captains Lewis and Clarke, two officers, in the American army, who were, in every respect, qualified for the arduous duties which it required; and who had, under their command, a party of forty-two soldiers and boatmen. Its professed object was to ascertain the possibility of opening an inland communication, between the Atlantic and Pacific oceans; but the American government had also in view the obtaining of information, respecting the country of Louisiana, which they were desirous of possessing, and which has since been ceded to them by France.

Narrative of a voyage from St. Louis to the source of the Missouri.
From the travels of Captains Lewis and Clarke.

The party having embarked in three boats, set out from St. Louis, on the 14th of May, 1804; and, for several days, they proceeded without interruption. Early in the morning of the twenty-fourth, they ascended a difficult rapid, called the *Devil's Race-ground*, and narrowly escaped having one of their boats upset. Beyond this place, they met two canoes, laden with furs, which had been eight weeks on their voyage from the Mahar nation, about seven hundred miles distant. On the banks of the river was much timber, consisting of cotton-wood, sycamore, hickory, and white walnut.

On the 1st of June, they passed the mouth of the *Osage river*, which falls into the Missouri, at the distance of a hundred and thirty-three miles from its junction with the Mississippi. This stream gives name to a nation of Indians which inhabit its banks. The *Osage Indians* are, in their persons, well formed: they reside in villages, and, having made considerable progress in agriculture, they seem less addicted to war than their northern neighbours.

Beyond the Osage river, the southern bank of the Missouri was low, and covered with rushes; and occasionally with oak, ash, and walnut-trees. On the north, the land was, in some places, rich, and well adapted to agriculture. Near the mouth of *Big Manitou Creek*, the voyagers met a raft, formed of two canoes joined together. On this, two French traders were descending, from the river Kanzes: it was laden with beaver-skins, which they had collected during the winter. Not long afterwards, captains Lewis and Clarke landed, to examine a singular limestone rock, which was nearly covered with inscriptions and uncouth paintings of animals; but they found the place occupied by a nest of rattlesnakes, and left it. In several parts of their voyage, they passed canoes, boats, and rafts laden with furs.

In many places the river was bordered with prairies or swampy meadows, on which grew several kinds of fruit, such as mulberries, plums, wild apples, raspberries, and strawberries. Numerous herds of deer were seen, pasturing in the plains, or feeding on the young willows of the river.

Near the mouth of the *Kanzes*, the Missouri is about five hundred yards wide. On the south, the hills or highlands approach within a mile and half of the shore; but, on the north, they are several miles distant; and the country, on all sides, is fine. In some places the navigation was interrupted by sand-banks, and in others, by the remains of trees which had fallen into the water. On the second of July, the whole surface of the stream, for a considerable distance, was covered with drift wood. This had probably been occasioned by the giving way of some sand-bank, which had before detained the wood, as it floated down the stream.

The weather was now so hot that some of the men experienced from it great inconvenience; but the air was occasionally cooled by showers. In the evenings the voyagers often landed and encamped, for the purpose of passing the night on shore. In that part of the river at which they arrived on the 16th, the width, from bank to bank, was about a mile; but the water was so shallow that they could perceive the remains of fallen timber scattered quite across the bottom. The Missouri is here wider than it is below, where the timber, which grows on its banks, resists the power of the current.

On the 21st of July the voyagers reached the mouth of the great *river Platte*. Captains Lewis and Clarke ascended it for about a mile, and found the current very rapid; rolling over sands, and divided into several channels, none of which, however, appeared to be more than five or six feet deep.

At this place they encamped for several days, in order to dry their provisions, make some oars, prepare an account and make maps of the country through which they had passed. The game they saw here were chiefly deer, turkeys, and grouse; and they obtained an abundance of ripe grapes. During the nights they were much annoyed by wolves. The country behind their camp was a plain, about five miles in extent, one half covered with wood, and the other dry and elevated.

Not far from this place was a settlement of the *Pawnee Indians*; a race which had once been extremely numerous, but which now consisted of only four bands, comprising, in the whole, about one thousand four hundred persons.

On the 30th of July, the commanders of the expedition directed an encampment to be formed on the southern bank of the river, for the purpose of their waiting the arrival of the chiefs of the Ottoe Indians, with whom an interview had been appointed to take place. From an elevated station near the camp, they had a beautiful view of the river and of the adjoining country. The hunters abundantly supplied them with deer, turkeys, geese, and beavers; and they were well supplied with fish.

A party of fourteen *Ottoe* and *Missouri Indians*, came, at sunset, on the 2d of August, accompanied by a Frenchman who had resided among them and acted as an interpreter. The next morning an awning was formed with the mainsail of the largest vessel; and, under this, Captains Lewis and Clarke received them. A speech was made to these Indians, announcing that the territory which they inhabited had been ceded to the American government, and advising them respecting their future conduct towards the Americans. They promised obedience, requested permission to trade with the Americans, asked for a supply of arms, and solicited the mediation of the voyagers, between them and the Mahars, with whom they were then at war. The chiefs were each presented with a medal, to be worn round his neck, some paint, garters, and cloth ornaments of dress: to these were added a canister of gunpowder, a bottle of whiskey, and a few other articles.

Not long after the ceremonies of the council had concluded, the voyagers again embarked. The hills which now extended along the river, were nearly fifteen miles asunder: those on the north were clad with a considerable quantity of timber; but those on the south had only some scattered trees in the ravines or narrow valleys.

On the 5th of August they passed round a peninsula; and, having encamped on the north side of it, Captain Clarke, in pursuing some game, about three hundred and seventy yards from the camp, found himself at a point of the river which they had already passed, and which, by water, was distant nearly twelve miles. Some miles beyond this, on traversing a part of the country, to reach one of the Indian villages, the vegetation was so luxuriant, that the men, who had been sent to explore it, were forced to break their way through grass, sunflowers, thistles, and other plants, more than ten feet high. This village had once consisted of three hundred huts; but, about four years before the voyagers were here, it had been burnt, in consequence of the small-pox having destroyed four hundred of the men, and a great number of women and children. On a hill behind the village were seen the graves of the nation.

The accounts which the voyagers received of the effects of the small-pox among these Indians, were most distressing. They had been a military and a powerful people; but, when they saw their strength wasting before a malady which they were unable to resist, their phrensy was extreme. They burnt their village; and many of them put to death their wives and children, in order to save them from so cruel an affliction, and that they might all go together to the unknown and better country.

A party of *Ottoe* and *Missouri Indians* with whom the voyagers had an interview after this, were almost naked, having no covering, except a cloth round their middle, and a loose blanket or buffalo robe thrown over their shoulders.

In one place Captain Lewis noticed that the hills which extended to the edge of the river on the south side, contained alum, copperas, cobalt, (having the appearance of soft isinglass,) pyrites, and sand-stone: the two first very pure. In another cliff, seven miles distant, he observed an alum rock, of dark brown colour, containing, in its crevices, great quantities of cobalt, cemented shells, and red earth. The appearance of these mineral substances enabled him to account for some disorders of the stomach with which his men had of late been much afflicted. They had been in the habit of dipping up the water of the river inadvertently, and drinking it; and he had now no doubt but the sickness was occasioned by a scum which covered its surface along the southern shore. Always after this the men agitated the water, so as to disperse the scum, before they drank of it, and these disorders ceased.

The soil of a plain over which the two commanders and some of the men walked, on the 25th, was exceedingly fine; and was encumbered with but little timber, except immediately on the banks of the Missouri. They found delicious plums, grapes, and blue currants. The musquitoes, and other insects which here abounded, seem, however, to have occasioned them some inconvenience.

On the 29th they were joined by five chiefs and seventy men of the *Yanktons*, a tribe belonging to the Sioux Indians. The camps or huts of this people are of a conical form: they are covered with buffalo robes, painted with various figures and colours, and have an aperture at the top for the smoke to pass through. Each hut is calculated to contain from ten to fifteen persons, and the interior arrangement is compact and handsome: the kitchen or place for cooking is always detached. Captain Lewis delivered to these people a speech containing, as he says, the usual advice and counsel with regard to their future conduct towards the government and the "great father" (as the Indians are taught to call the president) of the United States. He gave to the grand chief a flag, a medal, a certificate, a laced uniform coat of the United States artillery corps, a cocked hat and a red feather; and to the other chiefs medals, tobacco, and clothing. Among the inferior men were distributed knives, tobacco, bells, tape, binding, and other articles of trifling value. After this the Indian chiefs, and Captains Lewis and Clarke, smoked together the pipes of peace. These chiefs begged the strangers to have pity on them, as they were very poor; to send traders to them, as they wanted powder and ball: they were also anxious to be supplied with some of "the great father's milk," by which they meant rum, or other ardent spirits. This people are stout and well proportioned, and have a peculiar air of dignity and boldness: they are fond of decorations, and use, for this purpose, paint, porcupine-quills, and feathers. Some of them wear a kind of necklace of white bear's claws, three inches long, and closely strung together round their necks. They had among them a few fowling-pieces, but they were, in general, armed with bows and arrows.

Beyond the village of the Yanktons the country, on both sides of the river, was low, and, for the most part, destitute of timber; but, in some places, it was covered with cotton-wood, elm, and oak. The weather had been intensely hot; but, in the beginning of September, the wind was violent, and the weather cold and rainy. On the second of this month, the hunters killed four elks, and the whole party was supplied with an abundance of grapes and plums, which grew wild near the river. They this day observed, on the south side of the Missouri, the remains of an ancient Indian fortification, formed chiefly of walls of earth.

On the 7th of September the weather was very cold. The voyagers, this evening, encamped at the foot of a round mountain, about three hundred feet in height, which, at a distance, had the appearance of a dome. In this part of the country the hunters chiefly killed elks, deer, and squirrels: and they occasionally brought in beavers, porcupines, and foxes. On the 12th they passed an island covered with timber; and they had great difficulty in struggling through the sand-bars, the water being both rapid and shallow. The weather was now becoming so cold, that it was requisite to give out flannel-shirts to the men; and several animals were killed, for the sake of their skins to cover the boats. In many places the strong current of the river had worn away the banks, to considerable extent.

An interview took place, on the 25th, with some chiefs of the *Tetons*, a tribe of the Sioux Indians: nearly the same ceremonies and agreements were used and entered into, as with the preceding tribes; and similar presents were made. They promised obedience to the "great father," but they soon showed how little dependance could be placed on the promises of uncivilized nations. As they were going away, a party of them endeavoured to seize one of the boats, declaring that they had not received presents enough. On being told they should receive no more, they drew their arrows from their quivers, and were bending their bows, when the swivel-gun in one of the boats was levelled at them. Perceiving from this that the most determined resistance would be made, they at length ceased from their claims.

On the ensuing day these Indians approached the banks of the river, accompanied by their wives and children, and by a great number of their friends. Their disposition now seemed friendly, and the voyagers accepted an invitation to remain, during the night, on shore, to witness a dance which was preparing for their entertainment.

When Captains Lewis and Clarke landed, they were met by ten young men, who took each of them up in a robe highly decorated, and carried him to a large council-house, where he was placed on a dressed buffalo-skin, by the side of the grand chief. The hall or council-room was in the shape of three quarters of a circle, and covered, at the top and sides, with skins sewed together. Under this sate about seventy men, forming a circle round the chief. In the vacant part of the circle, between these men and the chief, the pipe of peace was raised, on two forked sticks, six or eight inches from the ground, and having the down of the swan scattered beneath it. At a little distance was a fire, at which some of the attendants were employed in cooking provisions. As soon as Captains Lewis and Clarke were seated, an old man rose up, and stating that he approved of what they had done, begged of their visitors to take pity on them. Satisfactory assurances of amity were made by both parties; and the chief, after some previous ceremony, held up the pipe of peace, first pointed it toward the heavens, then to the four quarters of the globe, and then to the earth, made a short speech, lighted it, and presented it to the strangers. They smoked it, and he harangued his people, after which the repast was served up. It consisted of the body of a dog, a favourite dish among the Sioux; to this was added a dish made of buffalo-meat dried, pounded, and mixed raw with grease, and a kind of potatoe. Of this the strangers ate freely, but they could not relish the roasted dog. The party ate and smoked till it was dark, when every thing was cleared away for the dance. A large fire was lighted in the centre of the room, for the purpose of giving, at the same time, light and warmth. The music was partly vocal and partly instrumental. The instruments consisted chiefly of a sort of tambourine, formed of skin stretched across a hoop; and a small skin bag with pebbles in it. The women then came forward, highly decorated: some with poles in their hands, on which were hung the scalps of their enemies; and others with guns, spears, or different trophies, taken in war by their husbands, brothers, or connexions. Having arranged themselves in two columns, one on each side of the fire, they danced towards each other till they met in the centre, when the rattles were shaken, and they all shouted and returned to their places. They had no step, but shuffled along the ground. The music appeared to be nothing more than a confusion of noises, distinguished only by hard or gentle blows upon the skin; and the song was extemporaneous. In the pauses of the dance, any man in the company, who chose it, came forward and recited, in a sort of low guttural tone, some story or incident: this was taken up by the orchestra and the dancers, who repeated it in a higher strain, and danced to it. These amusements continued till midnight, when the voyagers retired on board their vessels, accompanied by four of the chiefs.

In their persons these Indians were rather ugly and ill made, their legs and arms being peculiarly slender, their cheek-bones high, and their eyes projecting. The females, with the same character of form, were somewhat more handsome. Both sexes appeared cheerful and sprightly, but afforded many indications of being both cunning and vicious. The men shave the hair off their heads, except a small tuft on the top, which they suffer to grow, so as to wear it in plats over the shoulders. In full dress, the principal chiefs wear a hawk's feather, worked with porcupine-quills, and fastened to the top of the head. Their face and body are generally painted with a mixture of grease and coal. The hair of the women is suffered to grow long, and is parted from the forehead, across the head; at the back of which it is either collected into a kind of bag, or hangs down over the shoulders. This people seem fond of finery. Their lodges are very neatly constructed: they consist of about one hundred cabins, made of white buffalo hides, supported on poles fifteen or twenty feet high; and, having a larger cabin in the centre, for councils and for dances. These lodges may be taken to pieces, packed up, and carried from place to place. The beasts of burden are dogs. Some of these Indians had their heads shaved, and others had arrows stuck through their flesh above and below the elbow: these were indications of mourning.

On Friday the 28th of September, Captains Lewis and Clarke pursued their voyage up the river; and on the ensuing day, they passed a spot where a band of *Ricara Indians* had had a village, about five years before: but there were now no remains of it, except a mound which encircled the town.

Beyond this, the country, on the north side of the river, presented an extensive range of low prairie, covered with timber: on the south were high and barren hills; but, afterwards, the land assumed the same character as that on the opposite side. A great number of Indians were discovered on the hills at a distance: they approached the river, and proved to be *Tetons*, belonging to the band which the voyagers had just left. In the course of this day the navigation was much impeded by logs and sand-bars. The weather was now very cold. The voyagers next passed the *Chayenne river*, which flowed from the south-west, and the mouth of which was four hundred yards wide. On both sides of the Missouri, near this river, are richly timbered lowlands, with naked hills behind them. In this part of the country the hunters observed a great numbers of goats, white bears, prairie-cocks or grouse; and a species of quadrupeds described to resemble a small elk, but to have large, circular horns.

For many successive days Indians were observed on the shores; and, if they had been more numerous, some of them seemed inclined to molest the voyagers. On the sand-bars, which here very much obstructed the course of the river, great number of geese, swans, brants, and ducks of different kinds were seen.

On the 9th of October, the voyagers received visits from three chiefs of the *Ricara Indians*; and, though the wind was violent, and the waves ran very high, two or three squaws or females rowed off to them, in little canoes, each made of a single buffalo-skin, stretched over a frame of boughs, interwoven like a basket. These Indians did not use spirituous liquors; and had even rejected, with disgust, all attempts which the traders had hitherto made to introduce them: they said they were surprised that their "father," meaning the president of the United States, should present to them a liquor which would make them fools. Captains Lewis and Clarke visited two of the villages, where they were presented with corn and beans boiled; and also with bread made of corn and beans. The Ricara Indians are tall and well proportioned. The men wear skins round their legs, a cloth round their middle, and they occasionally have a buffalo robe thrown over their shoulders: their hair, arms, and ears, are decorated with ornaments of different kinds. The women, who are handsome and lively, wear long shirts made of goats' skin, generally white and fringed, and tied round the waist; and, in addition to these, they have a buffalo robe dressed without the hair. The lodges of the Ricara Indians are of a circular or octagonal form, and generally thirty or forty feet in diameter. They are made by placing forked posts, each about six feet high, round the circumference of a circle; joining these, by poles lying upon the forks; forming a sloping roof; interweaving the whole with branches and grass, and covering it with mud or clay.

Before the door there is a sort of entrance about ten feet from the lodge. This people cultivate maize or Indian corn, beans, pumpkins, water-melons, and a species of tobacco which is peculiar to themselves. They are well armed with guns, and carry on a considerable traffic in furs.

For many successive days the voyagers continued to see Indians every day. They had occasionally wet and unpleasant weather. In one place they saw, on the bank of the river, a great number of goats; and, soon afterwards, large flocks of these animals were driven into the river by a party of Indians, who gradually lined the shore, so as to prevent their escape, and fired on them, and beat them down with clubs, with so much success, that, in a short time, they killed more than fifty. Many buffaloes, elks, and deer were seen; and a great number of snakes.

On Thursday the 18th, they passed the mouth of *Le Boulet*, or *Cannon-ball river*, the channel of which is about one hundred and forty yards wide. This stream, (which is indebted for its name to a great number of large stones, that are perfectly round and lie scattered about the shore and on the eminences above,) rises in the Black Mountains, and falls into the Missouri on the south. Great numbers of goats were observed to cross the river, and direct their course towards the west. The country, in general, was level and fine, with broken, short, high grounds, low timbered mounds near the river, and a range of rugged hills at a distance. The low grounds had here much more timber than had been observed lower down the river. So numerous are wild animals in this part of the country, that the voyagers counted, at a single view, fifty-two herds of buffaloes, and three of elks.

On the 20th the weather was so cold, that the rain which fell froze on the ground; and, in the course of the night, the ground was covered with snow. A Ricara chief told Captain Lewis that, at some distance up one of the rivers, there was a large rock which was held in great veneration by the Indians, and was often consulted by them, as to their own, or their nations' destinies; all of which they imagine they are able to discern, in some rude figures or paintings, with which it is covered.

The voyagers passed, on each side of the river, the ruins of several villages of *Mandan Indians*; and, on an island of the river, they found a Mandan chief, who, with some of his men, was on a hunting excursion. As they proceeded, several parties of Mandans, both on foot and on horseback, approached the shore to view them. The vessels here got aground several times, among the sand-bars and rocks. In this part of their voyage they saw two Europeans, belonging to the Hudson's Bay company. These men had arrived about nine days before, to trade for horses and buffalo robes.

From one of the villages of the Mandans, a crowd of men, women, and children, came to see the strangers. Some of the chiefs had lost the two joints of their little fingers; for, with this people, it is customary to express grief for the death of relations, by some corporeal suffering, and the usual mode is to cut off the joints of the little fingers.

There were, in this part of the country, many Indian villages, and Captains Lewis and Clarke held, with the chiefs, a council, similar in its nature to those already mentioned; and afterwards presented them with flags, medals, uniform-coats, and other articles.

Sixteenth Day's Instruction

WESTERN TERRITORY CONTINUED.

Conclusion of Lewis *and* Clarke's *Voyage from*
St. Louis to the Source of the Missouri.

As the winter was now fast approaching, the commanders of the expedition considered it requisite to look out for some convenient place, where they might pass those months, during which the river would be frozen and unnavigable. Accordingly, on the 2d of November, they fixed upon a place, not far distant from the Indian villages. They cut down a considerable quantity of timber for the formation of huts; and constructed tolerably comfortable habitations. Food could here be procured in such abundance, that, in the course of two days, a Mandan Indian killed as many as two hundred goats.

In the night of the 5th they were awaked by the man on guard, who called them to witness a peculiarly beautiful appearance of the aurora borealis, or northern lights. Along the sky, towards the north, a large space was occupied by a light of brilliant white colour, which rose from the horizon, and extended itself to nearly twenty degrees above it. After glittering for some time, its colours were occasionally overcast and obscured; but again it would burst out with renewed beauty. The uniform colour was pale; but its shapes were various and fantastic. At times the sky was lined with light-coloured streaks, rising perpendicularly from the horizon, and gradually expanding into a body of light, in which could be seen the trace of floating columns, sometimes advancing, sometimes retreating, and shaping into an infinite variety of forms.

Before the middle of November a store-house was completed, in which the contents of the boats were laid up for the winter. On the 13th, ice began to float down the river for the first time; and, on the ensuing day, the ground was covered with snow. In some traps which had been set, twenty beavers were caught. On the 16th the men moved into the huts, although they were not finished. Three days after this the hunters brought in a supply of thirty-two deer, eleven elks, and five buffaloes, all of which were hung up to be smoked, for future subsistence.

The huts were ranged in two rows, each row containing four rooms, fourteen feet square, and seven feet high. The place in which they were erected was called *Fort Mandan*, and was a point of low ground, on the north side of the Missouri, covered with tall and heavy cotton-wood. The computed distance from the mouth of the Missouri was sixteen hundred miles.

In the vicinity of this place were five villages of three distinct nations: *Mandans, Ahanaways,* and *Minnetarees.* Not many years ago the Mandans were a very numerous race, occupying, in the whole, eighteen villages; but their numbers had been so much reduced, by the small-pox and by their wars with the Sioux, that they were compelled to emigrate in a body, and unite themselves with the Ricara nation; and they now occupy only two villages, on opposite sides of the Missouri, and about three miles asunder. Each of these contains forty or fifty lodges, built in the same manner as those of the Ricaras. The whole force of the Ahanaways is not, at present, more than fifty men. Their residence is on an elevated plain, near the mouth of the *Knife river.* On the south side of the same river, and about half a mile distant from this people, is a village of the *Minnetarees;* and there are four other villages of these Indians at a little distance.

The religion of the Mandans consists in the belief that one great Spirit presides over their destinies; but they also believe that various beings, some imaginary and some existing in the form of animals, have the power of interceding for them with the great spirit. To these they pay their devotion. They believe in a future state; and that, after death, they shall go to the original seats of their forefathers, which they suppose to be underground, immediately beneath a spot on the banks of the Missouri, where they formerly had nine villages.

On the 7th of December, the Missouri was frozen over, and the ice was an inch and half in thickness. The cold was so intense, that the air was filled with icy particles resembling a fog; and the snow was several inches deep. Notwithstanding this, one of the commanders, accompanied by some of the men, went out almost every day to hunt. On the tenth, Captain Clarke and his hunters, after having killed nine buffaloes, were obliged to spend a wretched night on the snow: having no other covering than a small blanket and the hides of the buffaloes they had killed. The next day the wind blew from the north; and the ice in the atmosphere was so thick, as to render the weather hazy, and to give the appearance of two suns reflecting each other. On the seventeenth, the mercury in the thermometer fell to seventy-four degrees below the freezing point. The fort was completed on the day before Christmas.

The Indians, inured to the severity of the climate, are able to support the rigours of the season, in a way which Captains Lewis and Clarke had hitherto considered impossible. Many parts of their bodies were exposed; and one of the Indians, in particular, although his dress was very thin, was known to have passed the night on the snow, without a fire; and yet he did not suffer the slightest inconvenience.

After having spent nearly five months in this dreary abode, the ice broke up, the boats were repaired and once more got into the river; and other preparations were made for the voyagers to pursue their course towards the sources of the Missouri.

In the afternoon of Sunday, the 7th of April, the arrangements being all completed, the party, consisting of thirty-two persons, once more embarked. They now occupied six small canoes and two large pirogues. The barge was sent down the river, to the United States, with presents of natural curiosities, which had been collected, and with dispatches to the president.

At some distance from Fort Mandan, the land, on each side of the Missouri, after ascending the hills near the water, exhibits the appearance of one fertile and unbroken plain, which extends as far as the eye can reach, without a solitary tree or shrub, except in moist situations, or in the steep declivities of hills. In some parts the plains were on fire; for, every spring, as soon as the ice breaks up in the river, these plains are set on fire by the Indians, for the purpose of driving out and attacking the buffaloes, and other wild animals which inhabit them. Beavers were here very abundant. A herd of antelopes, and the track of a large white bear, were seen in the plain: geese and swans were observed, in great numbers. The musquitoes now began to be very troublesome.

Before the middle of April, the weather became so warm, that, in the day-time, the men worked with no clothes on, except round their waist. On the twelfth, the voyagers reached the mouth of the *Little Missouri*, where they remained during the day, for the purpose of making celestial observations. This river falls into the Missouri, on its south side, and at the distance of sixteen hundred and ninety-three miles above its confluence with the Mississippi. Its current is strong, and its width a hundred and thirty-four yards; but its greatest depth is only two feet and half. The adjacent country is hilly and irregular; and the soil is, for the most part, a rich dark-coloured loam, intermixed with a small proportion of sand.

On the thirteenth, the voyagers passed the remains of forty-three temporary lodges, which were supposed to have belonged to the Assiniboin Indians. The waters of many of the creeks were found to be so strongly impregnated with mineral salts, that they were not fit to be drunk. On each bank of the Missouri the country presented the appearance of low plains and meadows; bounded, at the distance of a few miles, by broken hills, which end in high, level, and fertile lands: the quantity of timber was increasing. In the timbered-grounds, higher up the river, the voyagers observed a great quantity of old hornets' nests. Many of the hills exhibited a volcanic appearance, furnishing great quantities of lava and pumice stone: of the latter, several pieces were observed floating down the river. In all the copses there were remains of Assiniboin encampments.

On the twentieth, near an Indian camp, the voyagers observed a scaffold, about seven feet high, on which were two sleds, with their harness; and under the scaffold was the body of a female, carefully wrapped in several dressed buffalo-skins. Near it lay a bag, made of buffalo-skin, and containing some articles of apparel, scrapers for dressing hides, some dried roots, plats of sweet grass, and a small quantity of tobacco. These, as well as the body, had probably fallen down by accident, as it is customary to place the dead bodies on scaffolds. At a little distance was the body of a dog, not yet decayed: he had, no doubt, been employed in dragging, in the sled, the body of his mistress, and, according to the Indian usage, had been sacrificed to her.

From the sand-bars in the river, the wind sometimes blew such vast quantities of sand into the air, as to appear like clouds, and even to conceal the opposite bank from view. These clouds of sand floated, like columns of thick smoke, to the distance of many miles; and the particles were so penetrating, that nothing could be kept free from them.

Near the junction of *Yellow-stone river* with the Missouri, the country was much more woody than it had been in any other part, since the voyagers had passed the Chayenne; and the trees were chiefly of cotton-wood, elm, ash, box, and alder. In the low grounds were rose-bushes, the red-berry, service-berry, red-wood, and other shrubs; and among the bushes on the higher plains, were observed willows, gooseberry-trees, purple currant-trees, and honeysuckles. The sources of Yellow-stone river are said to be in the Rocky Mountains, near those of the Missouri and the Platte; and this river is navigable, in canoes, almost to its head.

Near the junction of the Yellow-stone and Missouri rivers, there is a high plain, which extends three miles in width, and seven or eight miles in length; and which Captain Lewis says might be rendered a very advantageous station for a trading establishment.

Beyond this place, the hills were rough and high, and almost overhung the river. As the voyagers advanced, the low grounds were fertile and extensive, with but little timber, and that cotton-wood. On the 3d of May, they reached the mouth of a river, which; from the unusual number of porcupines that were seen near it, they called *Porcupine river*. For several days after this, they continued their progress without much interruption. In many places the river was, at least, half a mile wide. During their excursions on the shore, in pursuit of food, they encountered many perils in shooting at bears. Some of these were of vast size and strength: one of them weighed nearly six hundred pounds, and measured eight feet seven inches and a half, from the nose to the extremity of the hind feet.

Beyond the *Muscle-shell river*, which the voyagers reached on the 21st, the shores of the Missouri were abrupt and bold, and composed of a black and yellow clay.

After a navigation of two months, and a progress of more than a thousand miles from their winter camp, the party became considerably embarrassed, at the conflux of two rivers, which were, apparently, of equal magnitude. It was important for them to decide which of the streams in question was the true Missouri; because the river, which it was their object to ascend, was described to be at no great distance from the head waters, running, from the opposite side of the Rocky Mountains, towards the Pacific ocean. Two canoes, with three men, were consequently dispatched, to survey each of these doubtful streams; and parties were sent out by land, to discover, if possible, from the rising grounds, the distant bearings of the lofty ranges of mountains, which were conspicuous in the west; and some of which, though it was now the month of June, were covered with snow. Hence, there was no doubt of their vicinity to the great central ridge of American mountains; but the direction of the rivers just mentioned, could not be distinguished to any considerable distance. Of the two, the one coming from the north, had the brown colour and thick appearance of the Missouri; while the southern river had a rapid current, a pebbly bed, and transparent water, as if it issued from a mountainous country. The resemblance of the former to the river already navigated, led nearly all the privates of the party to consider it as the Missouri; but the clearness of the other stream induced the two captains to the conclusion that it proceeded from those central mountains, which were the grand objects of their search. After a further investigation, they resolved to pursue the course of the latter.

It was, however, requisite to make a deposit of all the heavy baggage, that could possibly be spared, as the increasing shallowness of the water would soon render the navigation much more laborious than it had hitherto been. They accordingly adopted a plan, common among traders who bring merchandise into the country of Indians of doubtful integrity, that of digging a hole in the ground, small at the top, but widened in the descent, somewhat like the shape of a kettle. Choice was made of a dry situation; and the sod, being carefully removed, the excavation was completed, a flooring of wood and hides was laid at the bottom, and the goods were covered with skins: the earth was then thrown into the river, and the sod laid on again with so much care, that not the slightest appearance remained of the surface having been disturbed.

These arrangements being completed, Captain Clarke took charge of the canoes; while Captain Lewis, with four men, proceeded by land, in hopes of soon putting it beyond a doubt that the river which they were now ascending was the Missouri. The decisive proof was to be sought in its falls, which the Indians had described as not remote from the Rocky Mountains, and as of remarkable grandeur. Captain Lewis passed along the direction of the river, during two days, and, on the next day, found himself in a position which overlooked a most beautiful plain.

Finding that the river here bore considerably to the south; and fearful of passing the falls before he reached the Rocky Mountains, he now changed, his course towards the south, and, leaving these hills to the right, proceeded across the plain. In this direction he had gone about two miles, when his ears were saluted with the agreeable sound of a fall of water; and, as he advanced, a spray, which seemed to be driven by the high south-west wind, arose above the plain, like a column of smoke, and vanished in an instant. Towards this point he directed his steps; and the noise, increasing as he approached, soon became too tremendous to be mistaken for any thing but the *Great Falls of the Missouri*. Having travelled seven miles after he first heard the sound, he at length reached the falls.

The hills became difficult of access, and were two hundred feet high. Down these he hurried with impatience; and, seating himself on some rocks under the centre of the falls, he enjoyed the sublime spectacle of this stupendous object; which, since the creation of the world, had been lavishing its magnificence on the desert, unknown to civilization. For ninety or a hundred yards from the left cliff, the water falls in one smooth, even sheet, over a precipice of at least eighty feet. The remaining part of the river precipitates itself with a more rapid current; but, being received, as it falls, by the irregular and somewhat projecting rocks below, it forms a splendid prospect of perfectly white foam, two hundred yards in length, and eighty yards in perpendicular elevation. This spray is dissipated into a thousand shapes, sometimes flying up in columns fifteen or twenty feet high; and then being oppressed by larger masses of white foam, which exhibit all the brilliant colours of the rainbow.

On the 14th of June, one of the men was sent to Captain Clarke, with an account of the discovery of the falls; and Captain Lewis proceeded to examine the rapids above. From the falls, he directed his course, south-west, up the river. After passing one continued rapid, and three small cascades, each three or four feet high, he reached, at the distance of five miles, a second fall. Above this, the river bends suddenly towards the north. Here captain Lewis heard a loud roar above him; and, crossing the point of a hill, for a few hundred yards, he saw one of the most beautiful objects in nature: the whole Missouri is suddenly stopped by one shelving rock, which, without a single niche, and with an edge as straight and regular as if formed by art, stretches from one side of the river to the other, for at least a quarter of a mile. Over this, the water precipitates itself, in an even, uninterrupted sheet, to the perpendicular depth of fifty feet; whence, dashing against the rocky bottom, it rushes rapidly down, leaving behind it a spray of the purest foam.

The scene here presented was indeed singularly beautiful; since, without any of the wild, irregular, sublimity of the lower falls, it combined all the regular elegancies which the fancy of a painter would select to form a beautiful cataract. Captain Lewis now ascended the hill which was behind him, and saw, from its top, a delightful plain, extending from the river to the base of the Snowy Mountains. Along this wide, level country, the Missouri pursued its winding course, filled with water, to its even and grassy banks; while, about four miles above, it was joined by a large river, flowing from the north-west, through a valley three miles in width, and distinguished by the timber which adorned its shores: the Missouri itself stretched to the south, in one unruffled stream of water; and bearing on its bosom, vast flocks of geese, while numerous herds of buffaloes were feeding on the plains which surround it.

Captain Lewis then descended the hills, and directed his course towards the river. Here he met a herd of at least a thousand buffaloes; and, being desirous of providing for his supper, he shot one of them. The animal immediately began to bleed; and the captain, having forgot to reload his rifle, was intently watching to see him fall, when he beheld a large brown bear, cautiously approaching him, and already within twenty yards. In the first moment of surprise, he lifted his rifle; but, recollecting that it was not charged, and that he had no time to reload, he felt that there was no safety but in flight. He was in an open, level plain; not a bush nor a tree was within three hundred yards of him; and the bank of the river was sloping, and not more than three feet high, so that there was no possible mode of concealment. Captain Lewis therefore thought of retreating, in a quick walk. He did so, but the bear approached, open mouth and at full speed, upon him. He ran about eighty yards; but finding that the animal gained on him fast, he plunged into the river, about waist deep, and, then facing about, presented the point of an espontoon or kind of spear, which he had carried in his hand. The bear arrived at the water's edge, within twenty feet of him; but, as soon as the captain put himself in this posture of defence, the animal seemed frightened, and, wheeling about, retreated with as much precipitation as he had pursued.

With respect to Captain Clarke, he and his canoes advanced up the river, but they proceeded very slowly; for the rapidity of the current, the number of large stones, and the numerous shoals and islands, greatly impeded their progress. After they had passed a stream, to which he gave the name of *Maria's river*, they redoubled their exertions. It, however, soon became necessary for them once more to lighten the canoes. They did so, and filled another hole, with a portion of their provisions and ammunition.

On the 29th of June, Captain Clarke left the canoes, and went on to the falls, accompanied by a black servant, named York, an Indian and his wife, with her young child. On arriving there, they observed a very dark cloud rising in the west, which threatened rain. They therefore looked around for shelter, but could find no place where they would be secure from being blown into the river, if the wind should prove as violent as it sometimes does in the plains. At length, about a quarter of a mile above the falls, they found a deep ravine, where there were some shelving rocks; and under these they took refuge. Being now perfectly safe from the rain, they laid down their guns and compass, and the other articles which they had brought with them. The shower was, at first, moderate; but it increased to a heavy rain, the effects of which they did not feel: soon afterwards, a torrent of intermingled hail and rain was poured from the clouds: the rain seemed to fall in a solid mass; and, collecting in the ravine, it came rolling down, like a cataract, carrying along with it mud and rocks, and every thing that opposed it. Captain Clarke saw the torrent a moment before it reached them; and, springing up, with his gun and shot-pouch in his left hand, he, with his right, clambered up the steep cliff, pushing on before him the Indian woman, with her child in her arms. Her husband, too, had seized her hand, and was dragging her up the hill; but he was so terrified at the danger, that, but for Captain Clarke, himself and his wife and child would have been lost. So instantaneous was the rise of the water, that before Captain Clarke had reached his gun, and had begun to ascend the bank, the water was up to his waist; and he could scarcely get up faster than it rose, till it reached the height of fifteen feet. Had they waited a moment longer, it would have swept them all into the river, just above the great cataract, down which they must inevitably have been precipitated. They had been obliged to escape so rapidly, that Captain Clarke lost his compass and umbrella: the Indian left his gun, shot-pouch, and tomahawk; and the Indian woman had just time to grasp her child, before the net, in which it had lain at her feet, was carried down the current.

After the storm was over, they proceeded to a fountain, perhaps the largest in America. It is situated in a pleasant, level plain, and about twenty-five yards from the river, into which it falls over some steep, irregular rocks.

In this part of the country a remarkable phenomenon was noticed. A loud report, precisely resembling the sound of a cannon, was repeatedly heard from the mountains, at different times, both of the day and night; sometimes in one stroke; at others, in five or six successive discharges. This report was occasionally heard when the air was perfectly still and without a cloud; and it was supposed to be occasioned by the bursting of rocks.

The party, continuing indefatigable in their exertions, dragged the canoes, or pushed them along with poles, up the current of the Missouri. This they did, day after day, until the 27th of June, when they arrived at the *Three forks of the river*; that is, at the point at which three rivers, each of considerable size, flow together, and form the great stream. As it was difficult to determine the largest of the three, Captains Lewis and Clarke decided on discontinuing here the appellation of Missouri; and named the streams, respectively, Jefferson's, Madison's, and Gallatin's river. As the first of these flowed from the west, they ascended it in preference to the others; but they continued to experience great difficulty with the canoes, in consequence of the rapidity of the current.

They were now approaching the termination of the first great division of their journey. The river continued to lessen as they proceeded: its width, in the part at which they arrived on the 8th of July, was not more than forty yards; and, on the 11th, it was diminished to twelve, so as to admit of being waded over without hazard. They had now proceeded, by computation, three thousand miles from the mouth of the Missouri; and they, not long afterwards, reached its extreme navigable point, in latitude 43 degrees 30 minutes, and nearly in longitude 112 degrees west from Greenwich.

Here they laid up their canoes, until they should return from the Pacific ocean; and, proceeding by land, had the gratification of tracing the current to its *fountain head*, in the midst of the Rocky Mountains.

Seventeenth Day's Instruction

WESTERN TERRITORY CONTINUED.

*Narrative of Lewis and Clarke's Travels from the
Source of the Missouri to the Pacific Ocean.*

From the source of the Missouri, we will now accompany these gentlemen in their journey across the Rocky Mountains, and in their subsequent navigation of the Oregan or Columbia to the Pacific Ocean.

They had reached the highest ground in the *Rocky Mountains*, or that elevated part of the continent which constitutes the boundary between the streams flowing to the Atlantic on the one side, and the Pacific on the other. Their next object was to prosecute their journey westward, through this cold and barren track, until they should come to a navigable stream flowing into the Columbia, the great channel of access to the western ocean.

They had been told, by Indians in the Mandan country, that, immediately on crossing the central ridge, they would discover copious rivers running in a direction towards the Columbia. Captain Lewis accordingly found a clear stream forty yards wide, and three feet deep, which ran towards the west. It was bounded on each side by a range of high mountains, and was so closely confined between them, as not only to be unnavigable, but to be impassable along its banks. A still more discouraging circumstance was the total want, in this wintry region, of timber fit for building canoes.

An old Indian, being consulted respecting these mountains, stated them to be so inaccessible, that neither he nor any of his nation had ever attempted to cross them; and another Indian, a native of the south-west mountains, described them in terms scarcely less terrific. The course to the Pacific lay, he said, along rocky steeps, inhabited by savages, who lived in holes, like bears, and fed on roots and on horse-flesh. On descending from the mountainous ridge, he stated that the traveller would find himself in a parched desert of sand, where no animals, of a nature to afford subsistence, could be discovered; and, although this plain was crossed by a large river running towards the Columbia, its banks had no timber for the construction of canoes.

After all these mortifying communications, there appeared to be left, to the present travellers, only one route, that by which some individuals of the Chopunnish Indians, living to the west of the mountains, find means to make their way to this elevated region; and the accounts that had been given of this road, were very discouraging; the Indians being obliged to subsist for many days on berries, and suffering greatly from hunger. The commanders of the expedition were not, however, disheartened; for they were convinced that their men could accomplish a passage without enduring so much hardship as Indians, who are generally accompanied by women and children.

Having ascertained that the accounts of the impractibility of navigating the river were well founded, it became indispensable to take measures for proceeding on horseback. The men had already begun to suffer from want of food, for the country afforded very little except berries, and a few river-fish.

Captain Lewis describes the ravenous propensities of the Indians who reside in this part of America, to be very extraordinary. While some of them were with the travellers, a deer was killed. They all hastened to the spot, like so many beasts of prey, and actually tumbled over each other, to reach the intestines which had been thrown aside. Each tore away whatever part he could seize, and instantly began to devour it. Some had the liver, some the kidneys; in short, no part was left, on which we are accustomed to look with disgust. One of them, who had seized about nine feet of the entrails, was chewing, at one end, while, with his hand, he was diligently clearing his way by discharging the contents at the other. Yet, though suffering from excessive hunger, they did not attempt, as they might have done, to take by force the whole deer, but contented themselves with what had been thrown away by the hunters. After this, Captain Lewis gave one quarter of the body of the deer to the Indians; and they immediately devoured it raw. A second deer was killed, and nearly the whole of it was given to the Indians. This they also devoured, even to the soft parts of the hoofs; and they shortly afterwards ate nearly three quarters of a third.

It happened fortunately for the travellers, in the prosecution of their journey by land, that the horses of the country were good, and that there was no difficulty in purchasing as many as were necessary, for the conveyance of themselves and their baggage. They were thus enabled to set out about the end of August, under the guidance of an old man, who, notwithstanding the dissuasion of his countrymen, undertook to conduct them to the Indians who live westward of the mountains.

Arriving, soon afterwards, in a district where no tract could be discovered, they were obliged to cut their way through thickets of trees and brushwood, along the sides of hills. Here their horses suffered great fatigue; and the season was still so little advanced, that the ground was covered with snow. On the 9th of September they reached the road or path commonly taken by the Indians in crossing from the Columbia to the Missouri; and here they learned that they might have lessened the hardships of the mountain journey, had they laid up their canoes and struck off to the west, before they navigated the latter river to its furthest-point. A small creek at this station received the name of *Traveller's Rest-creek*.

From this spot the party proceeded nearly due west, along the Indian path; but they still experienced considerable inconvenience, from a deficiency of provisions. On some days they killed only a few birds; and, being obliged to turn their horses loose at night to feed, the morning hours were frequently passed in finding and catching them. On the 15th of August, they reached the upper parts of the river *Koos-koos-kee*, which affords one of the most direct channels of communication with the Columbia; but there is no timber, in its neighbourhood, of size large enough for canoes; nor did its channel promise an easy navigation. The travellers were consequently obliged to continue their journey by land; and on the 19th they were cheered with the prospect, towards the south-west, of an extensive plain, which, though still distant, assured them of an outlet from the barren region which they were traversing. By this time they had suffered so much from hunger, that horse-flesh was deemed a luxury.

At last, on the 22d, having reached the plain, they found themselves once more in an inhabited country. They explained their pacific intentions to the people, who were Indians of a tribe called *Chopunnish*. The removal, however, from a cold to a warm district, and, still more, the sudden change from scarcity to an abundance of food, proved very detrimental to the health of the men; and it was fortunate that the most laborious part of their task was now, for a time at least, at an end.

The river Koos-koos-kee being navigable in the place which the party had now reached, it remained only to build the requisite canoes. The wood was soon obtained; and such of the men as had sufficient strength for the undertaking, worked at the canoes, during the intervals of cool weather, and were not very long in completing them. In this part of the country the weather was cool during an easterly wind; exactly as, on the opposite side of the mountains, it had been in a westerly one. Their horses, to the number of thirty-eight, they consigned to the care of three Indian chiefs, to be kept till their return; and the saddles, with a small supply of ammunition, they buried in a hole, dug for the purpose, near the river.

On the 8th of October, the travellers once more proceeded by water; and they now occupied five canoes. Exertion was still requisite, in the shoals and other difficult places; but the change was, on the whole, extremely favourable to them, and their progress down the current was proportionally rapid.

This part of the country is inhabited by the *Shoshonees*, a tribe of *Snake Indians*, which, at present, consists of about a hundred warriors, and thrice as many women and children. Within their own recollection these Indians had lived in the plains; but they had been driven thence by the Pawkees and other powerful tribes, and they now live a wandering and precarious life. From the middle of May till the beginning of September they reside on the western waters; but, when the salmon, on which they chiefly subsist there, disappear, they cross the ridge and descend, slowly and cautiously, till they are joined, near the Three Forks, by other bands, either of their own nation, or of the Flat-heads, who make common cause with them. They then venture to hunt buffaloes in the plains eastward; but such is their dread of the Pawkees, that, so long as they can obtain the scantiest subsistence, they do not leave the interior of the mountains; and, as soon as they collect a large stock of dried meat, they again retreat: thus they alternately obtain food at the hazard of their lives, and hide themselves to consume it. Two-thirds of the year they are forced to live in the mountains, passing whole weeks with no other subsistence than a few fish and roots. The salmon were, at this time, fast retiring; roots were becoming scarce, they had not yet attained strength to hazard a meeting with their enemies, and nothing could be imagined more wretched than their condition.

Notwithstanding their miseries they were cheerful, and, in many important points of character, were superior to any other tribes whom the travellers had seen. They never begged: they were not tempted to a single act of dishonesty by the sight of the treasures which their visitors displayed; and they were ready to share with their guests, the little which they themselves possessed. They were also a high-spirited people. The Spaniards, the only white men with whom they had hitherto had any intercourse, would not supply them with fire-arms, alleging that, if they were possessed of such weapons, they would only be the more induced to kill one another. The Shoshonees, perhaps, do not perceive that policy is the real motive of the Spaniards; but they clearly see that the plea of humanity is fallacious, and they complain that they are thus left to the mercy of their enemies the Minnetarees, who, having fire-arms, plunder them of their horses, and slay them at pleasure.

Though many of their stock had lately been stolen, the Shoshonees possessed, at this time, not fewer than seven hundred horses, of good size, vigorous, and patient of fatigue, as well as of hunger. They had also a few mules, which had been purchased or stolen from the Spaniards, by the frontier Indians. These were the finest animals of the kind, that Captain Clarke had ever seen; even the worst of them was considered worth the price of two horses.

The horse is a favourite animal with this people. His main and tail, which are never mutilated, they decorate with feathers, and his ears they cut into various patterns. A favourite horse, also, is sometimes painted; and a warrior will suspend, at the breast of his horse, the finest ornaments which he possesses.

The Shoshonees always fight on horseback. They have a few bad guns among them, which are reserved, exclusively, for war; but their common weapons are bows and arrows. The bows that are chiefly prized, are made of the argali's horn, flat pieces of which are cemented together with glue. They have also lances, and a formidable sort of club, consisting of a round stone, about two pounds in weight, fastened, by a short thong, to a wooden handle. Their defensive armour is a shield of buffalo's hide, manufactured with equal ingenuity and superstition. The skin must be the whole hide of a male buffalo, two years old, and never suffered to dry, since it was flayed off. A feast is held, to which all the warriors, old men, and jugglers, are invited. After the repast, a hole is dug in the ground, about eighteen inches deep, and of the same diameter as the intended shield. Red hot stones are thrown into this hole; and water is poured upon them, to produce a strong steam. Over this, the skin is laid, with the fleshy side to the ground; and stretched, in every direction, by as many persons as can take hold of it. As it becomes heated, the hair separates, and is taken off; and the skin is, at last, contracted into the compass designed for the shield. It is then removed, placed on a dry hide; and, during the remainder of the festival, is pounded by the bare heels of the guests. This operation sometimes continues for several days. The shield is then actually proof against any arrow; and, if the old men and the jugglers have been satisfied with the feast, they pronounce it impenetrable by bullets also, which many of the warriors believe. It is ornamented with feathers, with a fringe of dressed leather, and with paintings of strange figures. This people have also a sort of arrow-proof mail, with which they cover themselves and their horses. It is made of dressed antelope-skins, in many folds, united by a mixture of glue and sand.

The Shoshonees are a diminutive and ill-formed race; with flat feet, thick ancles, and crooked legs. The hair of both sexes is usually worn loose over the face and shoulders; some of the men, however, divide it, by leather thongs, into two equal queues, which they allow to hang over the ears. Their tippet, or rheno, as it is called, is described to have been the most elegant article of Indian dress, that the travellers had ever seen. It is of otter-skin, tasselled with ermine; and not fewer than an hundred ermine-skins are required for each.

The inhabitants of the plains, to the west of the Rocky Mountains, appear to differ considerably from their neighbours on the higher grounds. The *Chopunnish* or *Pierced Nose nation*, who reside on the Kooskooskee, and the river now called Lewis's river, are, in person, stout, portly, and, good-looking men. The women are small, with regular features; and are generally handsome, though dark. Their chief ornaments are a buffalo or elk-skin robe, decorated with beads; and sea-shells, or mother-of-pearl, attached to an otter-skin collar, and hung in the hair, which falls in front in two queues. They likewise ornament themselves with feathers and paints of different kinds; principally white, green, and light blue, all of which they find in their own country. In winter, they wear a shirt of dressed skins, long painted leggings and moccasins, and a plat of twisted grass round the neck.

The dress of the women is more simple: it consists of a long shirt of argali-skin, which reaches down to the ankles, and is without a girdle: to this are tied shells, little pieces of brass, and other small articles; but their head is not at all ornamented.

The Chopunnish Indians have very few ornaments; for their life is painful and laborious; and all their exertions are necessary to earn their subsistence. During the summer and autumn they are busily occupied in fishing for salmon, and collecting their winter store of roots. In the winter, with snow-shoes on their feet, they hunt deer over the plains; and, towards the spring, they cross the mountains to the Missouri, for the purpose of trafficking for buffalo-robes.

In descending the *Kooskooskee*, the travellers had many opportunities of observing the arrangements of the Indians for preserving fish, particularly salmon, which are here very abundant. In some places, especially in the Columbia, the water was so clear, that these fish were seen at the depth of fifteen or twenty feet. During the autumn, they float down the stream in such numbers, that the Indians have only to collect, split, and dry them. Scaffolds and wooden houses, piled up against each other, for the purpose of fishing, were frequently observed. Indeed fish are here so abundant, that, in a scarcity of wood, dried salmon are often used as fuel.

A considerable trade is carried on in dried fish, which is thus prepared. The salmon, having been opened, and exposed some time to the sun, is pounded between two stones; then packed in baskets, neatly made of grass and rushes, which are lined and covered with salmon-skins, stretched and dried for that purpose. In these baskets, the pounded salmon is pressed down as hard as possible. Each basket contains from ninety to one hundred pounds; seven baskets are placed side by side, and five on the top. They are then covered with mats, and corded; and then again matted, thus forming a stack. In this manner the fish is kept sweet and sound for many years.

The Koo-koos-kee is greatly augmented by the junction of Lewis's river from the south; and the united streams, after flowing a considerable distance, fall into the still larger flood of the Columbia. At their junction, the width of the Columbia is nine hundred and sixty yards.

The Indians, in this part of America, are called *Solkuks*; and seem to be of a mild and peaceable disposition, and to live in a state of comparative happiness. Each man is contented with a single wife, with whom he shares the labours of procuring subsistence, much more than is usual among savages. What may be considered as an unequivocal proof of their good disposition, is the great respect which is shown to old age. Among other instances of it, the travellers observed, in one of the houses, an old woman perfectly blind; and who, as they were informed, had lived more than a hundred winters. In this state of decrepitude she occupied the best position in the house, seemed to be treated with great kindness, and whatever was said by her, was listened to with much attention.

The fisheries supply the *Solkuks* with a competent, if not an abundant subsistence. Fish is, indeed, their chief food; except roots, and the casual supplies of the antelope, which, to those who have only bows and arrows, must be very scanty. Most of the Solkuks have sore eyes, and many of them are blind of one or both eyes; and decayed teeth are very common among them.

The party proceeded down the Columbia. Fish was here so abundant, that in one day's voyage, they counted no fewer than twenty stacks of dried salmon.

They passed the falls of this river. These are not great; but, at a little distance below them, a very remarkable scene is presented to the view. At a place where the river is about four hundred yards wide, and where the stream flows with a current more rapid than usual, it widens into a large bend or basin, at the extremity of which a black rock, rising perpendicularly from the right shore, seems to run wholly across. So completely did it appear to block up the passage, that the travellers could not, as they approached, see where the water escaped; except that the current appeared to be drawn with peculiar velocity towards the left of the rock, where there was a great roaring. On landing, to survey it, they found that, for about half a mile, the river was confined within a channel only forty-five yards wide, whirling, swelling, and boiling, the whole way, with the wildest agitation imaginable.

Tremendous as the pass was, they attempted it; and, to the astonishment of the Indians, they accomplished it in safety.

In the vicinity of this place, a tribe of Indians, called *Echeloots*, were settled. Here the travellers, for the first time, since they had left the Illinois country, observed wooden buildings. The floors were sunk about six feet in the ground, a custom implying at the same time a cold and dry climate.

Proceeding on their way, they saw an Indian, dressed in a round hat and a sailor's jacket, with his hair tied. Jackets, brass kettles, and other European or American articles, were observed to be common. These Indians are fond of ornamenting their boats and houses with rude sculptures and paintings. One of the chiefs exhibited, from what was called his great medicine-bag, fourteen fore-fingers, the trophies taken from as many enemies, whom he had killed in war. This was the first time that the travellers had known any other trophy preserved than the scalp. The great medicine-bag, among these Indians, is an useful invention; for, as it is deemed sacrilegious for any person, except the owner, to touch it, this bag serves the purpose of a strong-box, in which the most valuable articles may safely be deposited.

The Echeloots in their mode of sepulture, differ much from the generality of North American Indians. They have common cemeteries, where the dead, carefully wrapt in skins, are laid on mats, in a direction east and west. The vaults, or rather chambers, in which the bodies are deposited, are about eighty feet square, and six in height. The whole of the sides are covered with strange figures, cut and painted; and wooden images are placed against them. At the top of these sepulchral chambers, and on poles attached to them, brass-kettles are hung, old frying-pans, shells, skins, and baskets, pieces of cloth, hair, and other similar offerings. Among some of the tribes, the body is laid in one canoe and covered with another. Every where the dead are carefully deposited, and with like marks of respect. Captain Clarke says it is obvious, from the different articles which are placed by the dead, that these people believe in a future state of existence.

On the 2d of November, the travellers perceived the first tide-water; four days afterwards, they had the pleasure of hearing a few words of English, spoken by an Indian, who talked of a Mr. Haley, as the principal trader on the coast; and, on the 7th, a fog clearing off, gave them a sight of the *Pacific Ocean*.

They suffered great hardships near the mouth of the river. At one place, where they were detained two nights by the violence of the wind, the waves broke over them, and large trees, which the stream had carried along with it, were drifted upon them, so that, with their utmost vigilance, they could scarcely save the canoes from being dashed to pieces. Their next haven was still more perilous: the hills rose steep over their heads, to the height of five hundred feet; and, as the rain fell in torrents, the stones, upon their crumbling sides, loosened, and came rolling down upon them. The canoes, in one place, were at the mercy of the waves; the baggage was in another place; and the men were scattered upon floating logs, or were sheltering themselves in the crevices of the rocks.

The travellers, having now reached the farthest limits of their journey, once more began to look out for winter-quarters. But it was not till after a long search, that they discovered, at some distance from the shore, and near the banks of the Columbia, a situation in all respects convenient. But so incessant was the rain, that they were unable to complete their arrangements, till about the middle of December. Here, in latitude 46 degrees, 19 minutes, they passed three months, without experiencing any thing like the cold of the interior; but they were, in other respects, exposed to numerous inconveniences. The supply of food was precarious; being confined to the fish caught along the sea-coasts, and to a few elks and other animals, which were killed in the adjacent country.

The Indians, in this part of America, had been accustomed to traffic, along the shore, with European vessels, and had learned to ask exorbitant prices for their commodities. Their circulating money consisted of blue beads; but with these, as well as with other merchandise, their visitors were, at this time, very scantily supplied. These Indians were unacquainted with the use of ardent spirits, but they were no strangers to the vice of gaming.

During the winter, Captains Lewis and Clarke occupied much of their time in acquiring information concerning the country; and obtained some account of the number of tribes, languages, and population of the inhabitants, for about three hundred and sixty miles southward, along the coast; but of those in an opposite direction, they were unable to learn any thing more than their names.

The people of the four nations with whom they had the most intercourse; the *Killamucks*, *Clatsops*, *Chinnoocks*, and *Cathlamahs*, were diminutive and ill-made. Their complexions were somewhat lighter than those of the other North American Indians: their mouths were wide, their lips thick, and their noses broad, and generally flat between the eyes.

All the tribes who were seen west of the Rocky Mountain, have their foreheads flattened. The child, in order to be thus beautified, has its head placed in a kind of machine, where it is kept for ten or twelve months; the females longer than the males. The operation is gradual, and seems to give but little pain; but if it produces headache, the poor infant has no means of making its sufferings known. The head, when released from its bandage,

Captain Clarke says, is not more than two inches thick, about the upper part of the forehead; and still thinner above. Nothing can appear more wonderful, than that the brain should have its shape thus altered, without any apparent injury to its functions.

There is an extensive trade carried on upon the Columbia, which must have existed before the coast was frequented by foreign traders; but to which the foreign trade has given a new impulse. The great emporium of this trade is at the falls, the *Shilloots* being the carriers between the inhabitants above and below. The Indians of the Rocky Mountains bring down bear's-grease, horses, and a few skins, which they exchange for beads, pounded fish, and the roots of a kind of water-plant, which are produced, in great abundance, in a tract of land between the Multomah and a branch of the Columbia. The mode of obtaining these roots is curious. A woman carries a canoe, large enough to contain herself, and several bushels of them, to one of the ponds where the plants grow; she goes into the water breast high, feels out the roots with her feet, and separates the bulbs from them with her toes. These, on being freed from the mud, float. The women often continue in the water at this employment for many successive hours, even in the depth of winter. The bulbs are about the size of a small potato, and, when roasted in wood ashes, constitute a palatable food.

These Indians are a very ingenious race. Even with their own imperfect tools, they make, in a few weeks, a canoe, which, with such implements, might be thought the work of years. A canoe, however, is very highly prized: it is considered of equal value with a wife, and is what the lover generally gives a father in exchange for his daughter. The bow and stern are ornamented with a sort of comb, and with grotesque figures of men or animals, sometimes five feet high, composed of small pieces of wood, skilfully inlaid and morticed, without a spike of any kind. Their bowls or troughs are scooped out of a block of wood; in these they boil their food. Their best manufacture is a sort of basket, of straw-work or cedar bark, and bear-grass, so closely interwoven as to be water-tight. Further south the natives roast their corn and pulse over a slow charcoal-fire, in baskets of this description, moving the basket about in such manner that it is not injured, though every grain within it is completely browned.

Among these Indians the women are well treated, and enjoy an extraordinary degree of influence. On many subjects their opinions are consulted: in matters of trade, their advice is generally asked and pursued. Sometimes they even take upon themselves a tone of authority; and the labours of the family are almost equally divided. No account is given by Captain Lewis of the superstitions of these people; and no inquiry seems to have been made concerning their religious belief.

Narrative of the return of Captains Lewis *and* Clarke,
from the Pacific Ocean to St. Louis.

The commanders of the expedition were desirous of remaining on the coast of the Pacific till the arrival of the annual trading ships, hoping from them to be able to recruit their almost exhausted stores of merchandise; but, though these were expected in April, it was found impossible to wait. The elks, on which they chiefly depended for subsistence, had retreated to the mountains; and, if the Indians could have sold them food, they were too poor to purchase it. The whole stock of goods, on which they had to depend, for the purchase of horses and food, during a journey homeward, of nearly four thousand miles, was so much diminished, that it might all have been tied in two pocket-handkerchiefs. Their muskets, however, were in excellent order, and they had plenty of powder and shot.

On the 23d of March, 1806, the canoes were loaded, and they took a final leave of their encampment. Previously to their departure, they deposited, in the hands of the Indian chiefs, some papers specifying the dates of the arrival and departure of the expedition. This was done in a hope that at least some one of them might find its way into a civilized country. The course homeward was, during the first month, by water; the canoes being dragged, or carried overland, in places where the current of the Columbia was too strong to be navigated. On these occasions, the travellers were exposed to much annoyance from the pilfering habits of the Indians; and their provisions were so scanty that they were obliged to subsist on dog's-flesh: a diet which, at first, was extremely loathsome to them, but to which they in time became reconciled.

The difficulties of the navigation made it expedient for them to leave the canoes at some distance below the junction of the *Columbia* with *Lewis's river*, after which they prosecuted their journey on horseback. Proceeding in an easterly direction, they arrived, on the seventh of May, within sight of the *Rocky Mountains*, and saw the tops of these mountains completely covered with snow. Anxious, however, to cross them as early as they could, they lost no time in recovering their horses from the Chopunnish Indians, and in extracting their stores from the hiding places in the ground. Still it was necessary for them to encamp for a few weeks, that they might occupy themselves in hunting, and that the health of the invalids might be reinstated.

Here Captains Lewis and Clarke practised physic among the natives, as one means of supplying themselves with provisions. Their stock of merchandise was reduced so low, that they were obliged to cut off the buttons from their clothes, and to present them, with phials and small tin boxes, as articles of barter with the Indians; and, by means of these humble commodities, they were enabled to procure some roots and bread, as provision during their passage over the Rocky Mountains, which they commenced on the tenth of June.

Towards the middle of June the fall of the rivers showed that the great body of snow on the mountains was at last melted; and they ventured to leave their encampment, against the advice of several of the Indians. They, however, soon found that they had been premature in their motions; for, on the higher grounds, there was no appearance whatever of vegetation. The snow, which covered the whole country, was indeed sufficiently hard to bear the horses, but it was still ten or twelve feet deep; so that a further prosecution of their journey was, at present, impossible; and the travellers, after having deposited, in this upper region, their baggage, and such provisions as they could spare, reluctantly traced back their steps to the plain. There they remained ten days; and, on the 26th, they again began to ascend the lofty ridge; the snow on which had, in the interval, melted nearly four feet, leaving still a depth of six or seven. They now implicitly followed the steps of their guides, who traversed this trackless region with a kind of instinctive sagacity: these men never hesitated respecting the path, and were never embarrassed. In three days they once more reached the stream which, in their former journey, they had named *Traveller's Rest Creek.*

Here Captains Lewis and Clarke agreed to separate, for the purpose of taking a more comprehensive survey of the country in their journey homeward. It was considered desirable to acquire a further knowledge of the Yellow-stone, a large river which flows from the south-west, more than one thousand miles before it reaches the Missouri; and it was of importance to ascertain, more accurately than they had hitherto done, the course of Maria's river.

The separation took place on the 3d of July; and Captain Lewis, holding on an eastern course, crossed a large stream which flowed towards the Columbia, and which had already been named *Clarke's river.* On the 18th of July he came to *Maria's river,* the object of his search; and he continued for several days, his route along its northern bank. After having ascertained the course of this river, he again set out on his journey homeward, that he might not lose the opportunity of returning before the winter.

He and his companions were only four in number; and, in one part of their journey, they had an alarming intercourse with a party of Indians. Not very long after this they embarked on the *Missouri*; and, with the aid of their oars and the current, they proceeded at the rate of between sixty and eighty miles a day. On the 7th of August they reached the mouth of the *Yellow-stone river*, the place of rendezvous, appointed with Captain Clarke. Here, by a note stuck upon a pole, they were informed that he had accomplished his voyage along that river, and would wait for them lower down the Missouri.

Captain Clarke, on quitting the central encampment at *Traveller's Rest Creek,* had marched in a southerly direction, and had traversed a distance of one hundred and sixty-four miles, to the head of *Jefferson's river.* This journey was performed, on horseback, and in six days, over a country by no means difficult; so that, in future, the passage of this elevated region will be divested of a considerable portion of its terrors. He also discovered that the communication between the *Upper Missouri* and the *Yellow-stone river*, was attended with little trouble; for Gallatin's river, one of the tributary streams of the Missouri, approaches within eighteen miles of the Yellow-stone, and, at a place, where the latter is completely navigable.

Being unable to find wood of sufficient magnitude for the formation of canoes, Captain Clarke and his men were obliged to proceed on horseback, about one hundred miles down the side of this river. At length they succeeded in constructing boats, and sailed down the remainder of this stream with great rapidity. On the 27th, at the distance of two hundred miles from the Rocky Mountains, they beheld that elevated region for the last time. The Yellow-stone being easy of navigation, they reached the place of rendezvous earlier than they had expected.

The whole party being now assembled below the conflux of the Yellow-stone and Missouri rivers, they prosecuted the remainder of their voyage together; experiencing, in the prospect of home, and in the ease with which they descended the river, a compensation for all their fatigues; and receiving the visits of various tribes of Indians who resided upon its banks.

The greatest change which was experienced by them, in their southward progress, was that of climate. They had passed nearly two years, in a cool, open country, and they were now descending into wooded plains, eight or ten degrees further to the south, but differing in heat much more than is usual in a correspondent distance in Europe. They were likewise greatly tormented by musquitoes.

On landing at *La Charrette*, the first village on this side of the United States, they were joyfully received by the inhabitants, who had long abandoned all hopes of their return. On the 23d of September they descended the Mississippi to *St. Louis*, which place they reached about noon; having, in two years and nine months, completed a journey of nearly nine thousand miles.

At St. Louis we shall resume the narrative of Mr. Pike, who, in the month of July, 1806, set out from that place on an expedition westward, through the immense territory of Louisiana, towards New Spain. The chief objects of this expedition were to arrange an amicable treaty between the Americans and Indians of this quarter; and to ascertain the direction, extent, and navigation, of two great rivers, known by the names of Arkansaw and Red River.

Eighteenth Day's Instruction

WESTERN TERRITORY CONCLUDED.

Narrative of Mr. Pike's Journey from St. Louis,
through Louisiana, to Santa Fé, New Spain.

The party engaged in this expedition, were Mr. Pike and another lieutenant, a surgeon, a serjeant, two corporals, sixteen private soldiers, and one interpreter. They had, under their charge, some chiefs of the Osage and Pawnee nations, who, with several women and children, had been redeemed from captivity, and now, to the number of fifty-one, were about to be restored to their friends.

They set out from *St. Louis* on the 15th of July, 1806, and proceeded, in two boats, up the *Missouri*. About six miles from the village of *St. Charles*, they passed a hill of solid coal, so extensive that it would probably afford fuel sufficient for the whole population of Louisiana.

Mr. Pike says that, every morning, he was awaked by the lamentations of the savages who accompanied him. These invariably began to cry about day-light, and continued to do so for an hour. On enquiry respecting this practice, he was informed that it was customary, not only with persons who had recently lost their friends; but also with others who called to mind the loss of some friend, dead long before. They seemed to be extremely affected: tears ran down their cheeks, and they sobbed bitterly; but, when the hour was expired, they, in a moment, ceased their cries, and dried their cheeks.

In their progress up the river, the Indians walked along the banks, and, every night, encamped near the boats. On the 28th the boats reached the mouth of the *Osage river*. For some distance the southern shore of the Missouri had been hilly, and covered with trees; and on the north were low bottoms and heavy timber. The soil was rich, and well adapted for cultivation.

They entered the Osage, and encountered few difficulties in their voyage up that river. From the shores, the hunters amply supplied the whole party with provisions; deer, turkeys, geese, and game of different kinds.

From the mouth of the Osage to that of the *Gravel river*, a distance of one hundred and eighteen miles, the banks of the former are covered with timber, which grows in a rich soil. Low hills, with rocks, alternately border the eastern and western shores: the lower grounds have excellent soil, and the whole adjacent country abounds in game. From the Gravel-river to to the *Yungar*, the Osage continues to exhibit the appearance of a fertile and well-timbered country.

The Indians joined their friends on the 15th, after which Mr. Pike and his party proceeded alone. On the ensuing day they passed the mouth of the *Grand Fork*, which was nearly as wide as the Osage; and, soon afterwards, reached the villages of the Osage Indians. The country adjacent to these villages is extremely beautiful. Three branches of the river wind round them, giving to their vicinity the advantages of wood and water, and, at the same time, those of an extensive prairie, crowned with rich and luxuriant grass and flowers, diversified by rising swells and sloping lawns.

The *Osage Indians*, in language, habits, and many of their customs, differ little from other tribes which inhabit the country near the Missouri and Mississippi. They raise great quantities of corn, beans, and pumpkins; and all the agricultural labour is performed by women. The government is vested in a few of the chiefs, whose office is, in most instances, hereditary; but these never undertake any affair of importance, without first assembling the warriors, and proposing the subject for discussion in council. The Osage Indians are divided into classes: those of the principal class are warriors and hunters; and the others are cooks and doctors. The last exercise the function of priests or magicians; and, by pretended divinations, interpretations of dreams, and magical performances, they have great influence in the councils of the nation: they also exercise the office of town-criers. Many old warriors assume the profession of cooks: these do not carry arms, and are supported by the public, or by particular families to which they are attached.

When a stranger enters the Osage village, he is received, in a patriarchal style, at the lodge of the chief. He is then invited, by all the great men of the village, to a feast. The cooks proclaim the feast, in different parts of the village, "Come and eat: such a one gives a feast, come and partake of his bounty." The dishes are generally boiled sweet corn, served up in buffalo grease; or boiled meat and pumpkins.

From the Osage villages, Mr. Pike, and his men, accompanied by several Indians, proceeded, on horseback, in a somewhat westerly direction, towards the river Arkansaw. In some places the country was hilly, and commanded beautiful prospects. The wild animals were so numerous, that Mr. Pike, standing on one of the hills, beheld, at a single view, buffaloes, elks, deer, and panthers. Beyond this they passed through numerous herds of buffaloes, elks, and other animals. In many places the country was very deficient in water.

On the 17th of September they reached a branch of the *Kanzes river*, the water of which was strongly impregnated with salt, as was that of many of the creeks. At some distance beyond this river, they were met by a party of Pawnee Indians; one of whom wore a scarlet coat, and had two medals: each of the others had a buffalo robe thrown over his naked body.

From the eastern branch of the Kanzes river, to the village of the Pawnee Indians, the prairies are low, the grass is high, the country abounds in saline places, and the soil appears to be impregnated with particles of nitre and of common salt. The immediate borders of the river near the village, consist of lofty ridges; but this is an exception to the general appearance of the country.

The *Pawnees* reside on the rivers Platte and Kanzes. They are divided into three tribes. Their form is slender, and their cheeks bones are high. They are neither so brave nor so honest as their more northern neighbours. Their government, like that of the Osage Indians, is an hereditary aristocracy; but the power of the chiefs is extremely limited. They cultivate the soil and raise corn and pumpkins: they also breed horses, and have vast numbers of excellent animals. The houses or huts of the Pawnees are circular, except at the part where the door is placed; and, from this part, there is a projection of about fifteen feet. The roofs are thatched with grass and earth, and have, at the top, an aperture for the smoke to pass out: the fire is always made on the ground, in the middle of the hut. In the interior there are, round the walls, many small and neat apartments, constructed of wicker-work: these are the sleeping places of the different members of the family. The Pawnees are extremely addicted to gaming, and have, for that purpose, a smooth piece of ground, about one hundred and fifty yards in length, cleared at each end of their village.

On Monday, the 29th of September, Mr. Pike held a grand council with the Pawnees; at which were present not fewer than four hundred warriors. Some attempts were made, by the chief, to prevent the further progress of the travellers; but Mr. Pike says, that they were not to be deterred by any impediments that could be opposed to them by a band of savages.

Proceeding onward they came to several places which had evidently been occupied by Spanish troops; and they were desirous of tracing the course along which these troops had marched; but the marks of their footsteps had been effaced by the numerous herds of buffaloes, which abound in this part of the country.

On the 18th of October, the travellers crossed the *Arkansaw*. From the Pawnee town, on the Kanzes river, to the Arkansaw, the country may be termed mountainous; and it contains a vast number of buffaloes. In the vicinity of this river it is, in many places, low and swampy.

The travellers were occupied several days in cutting down trees and constructing canoes. During this time the hunters killed several buffaloes, elks, and other animals. When the canoes were completed, Mr. Pike dispatched Lieutenant Wilkinson, and three men, down the river, with letters to the United States; and himself and the rest of his men proceeded, on horseback, up the side of the river. On the 29th of October, a considerable quantity of snow fell, and ice floated along the current. Three days after this, they observed a numerous herd of wild horses. When within about a quarter of a mile of them, the animals approached, making the earth tremble, as if under a charge of cavalry. They stopped; and, among them, were seen some beautiful bays, blacks, and greys, and, indeed, horses of all colours. The next day the party endeavoured to catch some of them, by riding up, and throwing nooses over them. The horses stood, neighing and whinnying, till the assailants approached within thirty or forty yards; but all attempts to ensnare them were vain.

Buffaloes were so numerous, that Mr. Pike says he is confident there were, at one time, more than three thousand within view. Through all the region which the party had hitherto traversed, they had not seen more than one cow-buffalo; but now the whole face of the country appeared to be covered with cows. Numerous herds of them were seen nearly every day.

The course of the travellers still lay along the banks of the river; which, in this part of the country, were covered with wood on both sides; but no other species of trees were observed than cotton-wood. On the 15th of November, a range of mountains was seen, at a great distance, towards the right: they appeared like a small blue cloud; and the party, with one accord, gave three cheers, to what they considered to be the Mexican mountains.

On the 22d, a great number of Indians were seen in the act of running from the woods, towards the strangers. Mr. Pike and his men advanced to meet them; and observing that those in front, extended their hands, and appeared to be unarmed, he alighted from his horse. But he had no sooner done this, than one of the savages mounted the horse, and rode off with it. Two other horses were taken away in a similar manner; but, when tranquillity was restored, these were all afterwards recovered. This was a war-party of the *Grand Pawnees*, who had been in search of an Indian nation called Jetans; but, not finding them, they were now on their return. They were about sixty in number, armed partly with guns, and partly with bows, arrows, and lances. An attempt was made to tranquillize them, by assembling them in a circle, offering to smoke with them the pipe of peace, and presenting them with tobacco, knives, fire-steels, and flints. With some difficulty they were induced to accept these presents, for they had demanded many more; and, when the travellers began to load their horses, they stole whatever they could carry away.

A few days after this, Mr. Pike and his men reached the Blue Mountain, which they had seen on the 15th; and, with great difficulty, some of them ascended it. Along the sides, which were, in many places, rocky, and difficult of ascent, grew yellow and pitch pine-trees, and the summit was several feet deep in snow.

From the entrance of the *Arkansaw* into the mountains, to its source, it is alternately bounded by perpendicular precipices, and small, narrow prairies. In many places, the river precipitates itself over rocks, so as to be at one moment visible only in the foaming and boiling of its waters, and at the next disappearing in the chasms of the overhanging precipices. The length of this river is one thousand nine hundred and eighty-one miles, from its junction with the Mississippi to the mountains; and thence to its source one hundred and ninety-two; making its total length two thousand one hundred and seventy-three miles. With light boats it is navigable all the way to the mountains. Its borders may be termed the terrestrial paradise of the wandering savages. Of all the countries ever visited by civilized man, there probably never was one that produced game in greater abundance than this.

By the route of the Arkansaw and the *Rio Colorado* of California, Mr. Pike is of opinion that a communication might be established betwixt the Atlantic and Pacific oceans. The land-carriage, at the utmost, would not exceed two hundred miles; and this might be rendered as easy as along the public highways over the Alleghany Mountains. The Rio Colorado is, to the great Gulf of California, what the Mississippi is to the Gulf of Mexico; and is navigable for ships of considerable burden.

The travellers left the vicinity of the Arkansaw on the 30th of November; and, though the ground was covered with snow, and they suffered excessively from the cold, they still persevered in their journey, and in their labour of examining and ascertaining the courses of the rivers. They killed a great number of buffaloes and turkeys. Steering their course in a south-westerly direction, for the head of the Red river, one of the party found a camp which had been occupied by at least three thousand Indians: it had a large cross in the middle. They subsequently found many evacuated camps of Indians.

On the 18th of December, they came to a stream, about twenty-five yards in width, which they erroneously supposed to be a branch of the Red river. Its current flowed with great rapidity, and its bed was full of rocks. On ascending this river, to examine its source, it was found to run close to the mountains, in a narrow and rocky channel; and to have its banks bordered with pine-trees, cedar, and other kinds of timber. The whole party suffered extremely from cold; their clothing being frozen stiff, and their limbs considerably benumbed.

Their situation, on Christmas-day, was not very enviable. All the food they possessed, was buffalo-flesh, without salt. Before this time, they had been accustomed to some degree of comfort, and had experienced even some enjoyments: but now, at the most inclement season of the year, and eight hundred miles distant from the frontiers of the United States, not one person was properly clad for the winter; many were even without blankets, having cut them up for socks and other articles; and all were obliged to lie down at night, upon the snow or wet ground, one side burning and the other frozen. For shoes and clothing they were obliged to adopt a miserable substitute in raw buffalo hides.

In their further progress, they suffered excessive hardships for several days. Food became so scarce, that they were obliged to separate into eight different parties, in order to procure subsistence. The roads were so mountainous, stony, and slippery, that it was with the greatest difficulty the horses could be prevented from stumbling; and many of them fell. In one instance, the whole party were four days without food; and some of them had their feet frozen. At length, they were obliged to leave the horses; and each man had to carry a heavy load, and, at the same time, to march through snow two feet and half deep. Several of the men, unable to keep pace with the rest, were left behind.

On the 27th of January, Mr. Pike observed, at a distance, a large river, which he imagined to be the Red river; and, on the 30th, he reached its banks. This, afterwards, proved to be the *Rio del Norte*. They proceeded along its banks, for about eighteen miles; and, at length, came to a spot, where they established a temporary residence, whilst they sent men to assist, and collect together the unfortunate stragglers who had been left in the rear.

The region they had traversed betwixt the Arkansaw and the Rio del Norte, was covered with mountains and small prairies. From the Missouri to the head of the Osage river, a distance of about three hundred miles, Mr. Pike says that the country will admit of a numerous, extensive, and compact population. From the Osage to the rivers Kanzes, La Platte, and Arkansaw, the country could sustain only a limited population; but the inhabitants might, with advantage, rear cattle, horses, sheep, and goats.

On the 16th of February, whilst Mr. Pike and one of his men were hunting, in the vicinity of their residence, they observed, at a distance, two horsemen, armed with lances. They proved to be a Spanish dragoon and an Indian, who had been sent from Santa Fé, a town of New Spain, about four days before. On the 17th, some of the stragglers arrived: several of them had lost the joints of their toes, by the intensity of the frost, and were rendered cripples for life.

The Spanish dragoon and Indian had returned to Santa Fé; and the report which they made of the appearance of the strangers, induced the governor to send out fifty dragoons, and fifty mounted militia, for the purpose of ascertaining their state and numbers. In an interview which took place with the commanders of these troops, Mr. Pike learnt that the river, on the bank of which he had encamped, was the Rio del Norte, and not the Red river, as he had imagined. The officers stated to him that a hundred mules and horses had been sent to convey him, his men, and baggage, to Santa Fé; and that the governor was anxious to see them in that town, to receive an explanation respecting their business on his frontiers.

Mr. Pike and some of his men accompanied the officers to Santa Fé, while others were left behind, to wait the arrival of those who had not yet come up.

In their progress, they were treated, in all the villages, with the utmost hospitality. On their march, they were frequently stopped by women, who invited them into their houses to eat; and, in every place where they halted, there was a contest who should be their hosts. Those that had suffered by having their limbs frozen, were conducted home by old men, who caused their daughters to dress the sores, and to provide for them victuals and drink; and, at night, they gave them the best bed in the house.

In the evening of the 3d of March, Mr. Pike reached *Santa Fé*. This city, the capital of New Mexico, is situated along the banks of a small creek, which issues from the mountains, and runs westward to the Rio del Norte. It is about a mile in length, and not more than three streets in width. The houses are, generally, only one story high, and have flat roofs. There are, in Santa Fé, two churches, the magnificence of whose steeples forms an extraordinary contrast to the miserable appearance of the other buildings. On the north side of the town is a square, constructed for soldiers' houses, each flank of which contains from a hundred and twenty to a hundred and forty. The public square is in the centre of the town. On one side of it is the palace or government-house, with the quarters for the guards; and the other sides are occupied by the houses of the clergy, and public officers. Most of the houses have sheds before them, which occasion the streets to be very narrow. The number of inhabitants in Santa Fé, is supposed to be about four thousand five hundred.

On Mr. Pike and his men entering this town, the crowd assembled to view them was excessively great: and, indeed, their extremely miserable appearance seems to have excited much curiosity. This may easily be accounted for. After they had left the Arkansaw, they had been obliged to carry all their baggage on their backs; and, consequently, the useful were preferred to the ornamental articles. The ammunition, tools, leather-leggings, boots, and moccasins, had been considered absolutely requisite. They had left behind their uniform clothing; and, when they entered Santa Fé, Mr. Pike was dressed in a pair of blue trowsers, moccasins, a blanket-coat, and a red cap. His men had leggings, cloths round their waists, and leather coats: there was not a hat among the whole party. This appearance was extremely mortifying to them all, especially as soldiers; and it made no very favourable impression on the people of Santa Fé. They were asked, by many of the common people, whether they had lived in houses, or in camps, like the Indians; or whether, in their country, the people wore hats.

They were conducted to the government-house, where they dismounted. On entering it they were conducted through various rooms, the floors of all which were covered with the skins of buffaloes, bears, or other animals. Here they underwent an examination, by the governor, respecting their objects and number. The conference terminated amicably; but the governor informed Mr. Pike that he must be conducted to Chihuahua, a town in the province of New Biscay, and upwards of three hundred leagues distant.

Nineteenth Day's Instruction

MEXICO or NEW SPAIN.

The Spanish possessions in North America, extend from the isthmus of Darien, along the coast of the Pacific Ocean, to the distance of more than two thousand two hundred miles. One half of them is situated under the burning sky of the tropics, and the other belongs to the temperate zone. Their whole interior forms an immense plain, elevated from six to eight thousand feet above the level of the adjacent seas. The chain of *mountains* which constitutes this vast plain, is a continuation of that which, under the name Andes, runs through South America. They are, in general, little interrupted by valleys, and, for the most part, their declivity is very gentle. In consequence of this elevation, the Mexican provinces, situated under the torrid zone, enjoy a cold rather than a temperate *climate*. The interior provinces, in the temperate zone, have, like the rest of North America, a climate essentially different from that of the same parallels in the European continent. A remarkable inequality prevails between the temperature of the different seasons: German winters succeed to Neapolitan and Sicilian summers.

This country suffers many inconveniences from a want of water, and particularly of navigable rivers. The Rio del Norte and the Rio Colorado are almost the only *rivers* of any importance. The *lakes* with which Mexico abounds, are merely the remains of immense basins of water, which appear to have formerly existed on the high and extensive plains of the Cordilleras. The largest of these, the *Lake of Chapala*, contains nearly one hundred and sixty square leagues, and is about twice as large as the lake of Constance.

A great portion of high land, in the interior of New Spain, is destitute of vegetation; and some of the loftiest summits are clad with perpetual snow. This country is not so much disturbed by earthquakes as several parts of South America; for, in the whole of New Spain there are only five *volcanos*; Orizaba, Popocatepetl, Tuxtla, Jorullo, and Colima.

The *volcano of Jorullo*, in the province of Valladolid, was formed during the night of the 29th of September, 1759. The great catastrophe, in which this mountain rose from the earth, and by which a considerable space of ground changed its appearance, is, perhaps, one of the most extraordinary physical revolutions in the history of the earth. Geology points out parts of the ocean, where, at recent periods, near the Azores, in the Egean Sea, and to the south of Iceland, small volcanic islands have arisen above the surface of the water; but it gives no example of the formation, amidst a thousand small burning cones, of a mountain of scoria, near seventeen hundred feet in height, above the adjoining plain. Till the middle of the year 1759, fields cultivated with sugar-canes and indigo occupied the extent of ground between the two brooks called Cultamba and San Pedro. In the month of June, a subterraneous noise was heard. Hollow sounds of most alarming description, were accompanied by frequent earthquakes, which succeeded one another for fifty or sixty days, to the great consternation of the inhabitants. From the beginning of September every thing seemed to announce the complete re-establishment of tranquillity; when, in the night between the 28th and 29th, the subterraneous noises recommenced. The affrighted Indians fled to the mountains; and a tract of ground, from three to four square miles in extent, which goes by the name of *Malpays*, rose up in the shape of a bladder. The bounds of this convulsion are still distinguishable in the fractured strata. The Malpays, near its edges, is only about forty feet above the old level of the plain; but the convexity of the ground thus thrown up, increases progressively, towards the centre, to an elevation of more than five hundred and twenty feet.

The persons who witnessed this astonishing catastrophe, assert that flames were seen to issue forth, for an extent of more than half a square league; that fragments of burning rocks were thrown up to prodigious heights; and that, through a thick cloud of ashes, illumined by the volcanic fire, the softened surface of the earth was seen to swell up like an agitated sea. The rivers of Cultamba and San Pedro precipitated themselves into the burning chasms. The decomposition of the water contributed to invigorate the flames, which were distinguishable at a vast distance. Eruptions of mud, and other substances, indicated that subterraneous water had no small share in producing this extraordinary revolution. Thousands of small cones, from six to nine feet in height, called by the Indians "hornitos," or ovens, issued forth from the Malpays. Each small cone is a "fumorola," from which a thick vapour ascends; and in many of them a subterraneous noise is heard, which appears to announce the proximity of a fluid in ebullition. In the midst of the ovens six large masses, elevated from one thousand three hundred to one thousand six hundred and forty feet above the old level of the plains, sprung up from a chasm. The most elevated of these is the great volcano of Jorullo. It is continually burning, and has thrown up an immense quantity of scorified and basaltic lavas, containing fragments of primitive rocks. These great eruptions of the central volcano continued till the month of February,

1760. In the following year they became gradually less frequent. The Indians, frightened at the horrible noises of the new volcano, had abandoned all the villages, within seven or eight leagues of it. They, however, gradually became accustomed to them, and returned to their cottages. So violent were the eruptions of this mountain, that the roofs of houses in Queretaro, though at a distance of more than forty-eight leagues, in a straight line from the scene of explosion, were sometimes covered with ashes.

The Mexican *population* consists of seven races, 1. Individuals born in Europe; 2. Creoles, or Whites of European extraction, born in America; 3. Mesti zos, or descendants of whites and Indians; 4. Mulattoes, descendants of whites and negroes; 5. Zambos, descendants of negroes and Indians; 6. Indians, or the copper-coloured indigenous race; and, 7. African negroes.

The number of *Indians*, including those only who have no mixture of European or African blood, are more than two millions and a half in number; and these appear to constitute about two-fifths of the whole population of Mexico. They bear a general resemblance to the Indians of Canada, Florida, Peru, and Brazil: they have a similar swarthy and copper-coloured skin, smooth hair, little beard, squat body, long eyes, with the corners directed upward towards the temples, prominent cheek bones, and thick lips. There is a great diversity in their language, but they appear to have been all descendants from the same original stock.

It is probable that these Indians would live to a great age, did they not often injure their constitution by drunkenness. Their intoxicating liquors are rum, a fermentation of maize, and the root of the jatropha; and especially a wine which is made from the juice of the great American aloe. The police, in the city of Mexico, sends round tumbrils, to collect such drunkards as are found lying in the streets. These are treated like dead bodies, and are carried to the principal guard-house. The next morning an iron ring is put round each of their ancles, and, as a punishment, they are made to cleanse the streets for three days.

The Mexican Indian, when not under the influence of intoxicating liquors, is grave, melancholic, and silent. The most violent passions are never depicted in his features; and it is sometimes frightful to see him pass, at once, from a state of apparent repose, to the most violent and unrestrained agitation. It is stated that these Indians have preserved, from their ancestors, a particular relish for carving in wood and stone; and that it is astonishing to see what they are able to execute with a bad knife, on the hardest wood. Many Indian children, educated in the college of the capital, or instructed at the academy of painting, founded by the king of Spain, have considerably distinguished themselves, but without leaving the beaten track pursued by their forefathers; they chiefly display great aptitude in the arts of imitation; and in the purely mechanical arts.

The *Spanish inhabitants* and the *Creoles* are noted for hospitality, generosity, and sobriety; but they are extremely deficient in energy, patriotism, enterprise, and independence of character. The women have black eyes and hair, and fine teeth: they are of dark colour, full habit of body, and have, in general, bad figures. They usually wear short jackets and petticoats, high-heeled shoes, and no head-dress. As an upper garment they have a silk wrapper, which, when they are in the presence of men, they affect to bring over their faces. In the towns on the frontiers and adjacent to the sea-coast, many of the ladies wear gowns, like those of our country-women. The lower classes of men are generally dressed in broad-brimmed hats, short coats, large waistcoats, smallclothes open at the knees, and a kind of boot or leather wrapper bound round the leg, and gartered at the knee. The spurs of the gentlemen are clumsy: they are ornamented with raised work; and the straps are embroidered with gold and silver thread. The Spanish Americans are always ready to mount their horses; and the inhabitants of the interior provinces pass nearly half their day on horseback. In the towns, and among the higher ranks, the men dress in the European style.

The *amusements* of this people are music, singing, dancing, and gambling: the latter is, indeed, officially prohibited; but the prohibition is not much attended to. At every large town there is a public walk, where the ladies and gentlemen meet and sing songs. The females have fine voices, and sing French, Italian, and Spanish music, the whole company joining in chorus. In their houses the ladies play on the guitar, and accompany this instrument with their voices. They either sit on the carpet cross-legged, or loll on a sofa: to sit upright, on a chair, appears to put them to great inconvenience.

Both in *eating* and *drinking* the Spanish Americans are remarkably temperate. Early in the morning those of the higher class have chocolate. At twelve they dine on meat, fowls, and fish; after which different kinds of confectionary are placed on the table; they drink a few glasses of wine, sing a few songs, and then retire to take their *siesta* or afternoon nap. The latter is a practice common both to rich and poor: the consequence of it is that, about two o'clock, every day, the windows and doors of the town are all closed, the streets are deserted, and the stillness of midnight reigns throughout. At four they rise, wash and dress, and prepare for the dissipation of the evening. About eleven o'clock refreshments are offered; but few take any thing except a little wine and water and candied sugar.

The *commerce* of New Spain, with Europe and the United States, is carried on through the port of Vera Cruz only; and with the East Indies and South America, through that of Acapulco. But all the commercial transactions, and all the productions and manufactures, are subjected to such severe restrictions, that they are at present of little importance to the prosperity of the country. Were the various bays and harbours of Mexico and California to be opened to the trade of the world; and were correct regulations to be adopted, New Spain might become both wealthy and powerful. Many parts of the country abound in iron ore, yet iron and steel articles, of every description, are brought from Europe; for the manufacturing or working of iron is here strictly prohibited. This occasions the requisite utensils of husbandry, arms, and tools, to be enormously dear; and forms a great check to the progress of agriculture, and to improvements in manufactures.

The *ancient Mexicans* preserved the memory of events by figures painted on skins, cloth, or the bark of trees. These hieroglyphical and symbolical characters, being considered by the ignorant and bigoted Spaniards to be monuments of idolatry, the first bishop of Mexico destroyed as many of them as could be collected. In consequence of this barbarous procedure, the knowledge of remote events was lost, except what could be derived from tradition, and from some fragments of those paintings which eluded the search of the monks.

With regard to the *public edifices* of the Mexicans: their temples were merely mounds of earth faced with stone; and it is probable that their other public buildings were equally rude. The ancient natives bestowed little attention on agriculture, and were strangers to the use of money; but their ornaments of gold and silver indicated considerable ingenuity. They were acquainted with the manufacture of paper, of coarse cotton-cloth, glass, and earthenware; and they possessed the arts of casting metals, of making mosaic work with shells and feathers, of spinning and weaving the hair of animals, and of dying with indelible colours.

The *religion* of the ancient Mexicans, like that of all unenlightened nations, seems to have been founded chiefly on fear; and consisted of a system of gloomy rites and practices, the object of which was to avert the evils that they suffered or dreaded. They had some notion of an invisible supreme Being; but their chief anxiety was to deprecate the wrath of certain imaginary malignant spirits, whom they regarded as the enemies of mankind. They worshipped idols, formed of wood and stone; and decorated their temples with the figures of serpents, tigers, and other destructive animals. They believed in the immortality of the soul; but their notions of a future state may be collected from their funeral rites: the bodies, or the ashes of the deceased, were generally buried with whatever was judged necessary for their accommodation or comfort in the other world, where it was believed they would experience the same desires, and be engaged in the same occupations, as in this. The religion established by the Spaniards is the Roman Catholic; and it is computed that one-fifth part of the Spanish inhabitants are ecclesiastics, monks, and nuns.

The *Spanish government* in America is vested in officers called viceroys, who represent the person of their sovereign; and who possess his royal prerogatives, within the precincts of their own territories. In its present state, New Spain is divided into twelve intendancies, and three districts, which are called provinces[2].

FOOTNOTES:

[2] For particulars respecting the conquest of Mexico by the Spaniards, see "Biographical Conversations on Eminent Voyagers," p. 59 to 73.

Twentieth Day's Instruction

MEXICO CONTINUED.

Narrative of Mr. Pike's Journey from Santa Fé to Montelovez.

Mr. Pike and his men were escorted from Santa Fé by a Spanish officer, and a troop of soldiers. On Thursday, the 5th of March, they arrived at a village called *St. Domingo*. The inhabitants of this place were about a thousand in number; and the chiefs were distinguished by canes, with silver heads and black tassels. Mr. Pike was permitted to visit the church; and he was much astonished to find, enclosed in mud-brick walls, many rich paintings, and a statue of the patron saint, as large as life, and elegantly ornamented with gold and silver.

On the ensuing day, the party marched down the eastern side of the Rio del Norte, the snow being still a foot deep. Near the village of *Albuquerque*, they observed that the inhabitants were beginning to open the canals, for the purpose of letting in the water of the river, to fertilize the lands. They saw men, women, and children engaged in the joyful labour, which was to crown, with rich abundance, their future harvest, and to ensure them plenty for the ensuing year. A little below Albuquerque, the Rio del Norte was four hundred yards wide, but not more than three feet deep.

In their journey southward, they passed through several villages. One of these, called *Sibilleta*, was in the form of a regular square, appearing, on the outside, like an immense mud-wall. All the doors and windows faced the interior of the square; and it was the neatest and most regular village Mr. Pike had ever seen.

Beyond this village, the party met a caravan, consisting of three hundred men, escorted by an officer and thirty-five or forty troops, who were proceeding, with about fifteen thousand sheep, to the different provinces. They afterwards met a caravan of fifty men, and about two hundred horses, laden with traffic, for New Mexico. On the 21st of March they arrived at the *Passo del Norte*: the road now led them through a rough and mountainous country; and passing through *Carracal*, and some other villages, they reached *Chihuahua* on the 2d of April.

They were conducted into the presence of the commanding-officer of the place, before whom Mr. Pike underwent an examination, as he had previously done at Santa Fé. He was treated with great apparent respect, and was offered both assistance and money. He afterwards visited in the houses of some of the principal inhabitants. At the house of the governor, when wine was put on the table, after dinner, the company was entertained with songs in the French, Italian, Spanish, and English languages.

There are, at Chihuahua, and in its vicinity, fifteen mines; thirteen of silver, one of gold, and one of copper; the furnaces for all of which are in the suburbs of the town, and present, except on Sundays, volumes of smoke, rising in every direction. Chihuahua is surrounded by piles of cinders, from ten to fifteen feet in height. In the public square, stand the church, the royal treasury, the town-house, and the richest shops; and, at the western extremity of the town, are two other churches, an hospital, and the military academy. About a mile south of the town, is a large aqueduct. The principal church of Chihuahua is a most superb edifice: its whole front is covered with statues of saints; figures of different saints are set in niches of the wall; and the windows, doors, &c. are ornamented with sculpture. The decorations in the interior are said to be immensely rich. On the south of the town is a public walk, formed by three rows of trees, the branches of which nearly form a junction over the heads of the passengers below. At different distances, there are seats for persons to repose themselves upon; and at each end of the walks, are circular seats, on, which, in the evenings, the inhabitants amuse themselves in singing to the music of guitars. This city contains about eleven thousand inhabitants.

After a residence, in Chihuahua, of somewhat more than three weeks, Mr. Pike received an intimation that he and his men would be escorted out of the country. Accordingly, on the 28th of April, he was accompanied, towards the frontier, by a Spanish officer. Near Chihuahua they passed a small ridge of mountains, and then encamped in a hollow. At the distance of about fifty miles they reached the river *Florida*; on the banks of which are many important settlements, and well-timbered lands. One of the plantations on this river, extended thirty leagues; and had been valued at three hundred thousand dollars.

The country through which they now passed was mountainous. On the 11th of May, they reached *Mauperne*, a village situated at the foot of the mountains, and near which eight or nine valuable copper-mines were worked; but the mass of the people were in a starving and wretched state. The proprietor of the mines, however, gave the travellers an elegant repast.

They pursued their march three miles further, to a station, on a little stream, which flowed through gardens, and formed a terrestrial paradise. Here they remained all day, and at night slept under the shade of the fig-trees. In the morning, Mr. Pike was awakened by the singing of the birds, and the perfume of the trees around. This place, however, was no doubt rendered the more interesting to the travellers, in consequence of their having previously suffered much inconvenience from want of water.

On the 20th, they arrived at the *Hacienda of Polloss*, a handsome place, at which the Marquis de San Miguel, a wealthy nobleman, who possessed extensive property in this part of New Spain, usually passed the summer. The Hacienda of Polloss is a square enclosure of about three hundred feet: the building is no more than one story high; but some of the apartments are very elegantly furnished. In the centre of the square is a fountain, which throws out water from eight spouts. There is also, at this place, a handsome church, which, with its ornaments, is said to have cost at least twenty thousand dollars. The inhabitants are about two thousand in number.

Montelovez, situated on the banks of a small stream, is about a mile in length. It has two public squares, seven churches, some powder-magazines, mills, a royal hospital, and barracks. The number of inhabitants is about three thousand five hundred. This city is ornamented with public walks, columns, and fountains; and is one of the handsomest places in New Spain [3] .

South-west from Montelovez stands *Durango*, the chief city of the province of Biscay. In the vicinity of this place are many rich and valuable mines; and the soil is so fertile as to produce abundant crops of wheat, maize, and fruit. The climate is mild and healthy. Durango contains about twelve thousand inhabitants; and has four convents and three churches.

A Description of the City of Mexico.

This magnificent city is the capital of New Spain, and the residence of the viceroy. In its *situation* it possesses many important advantages. Standing on an isthmus, which is washed on one side by the Atlantic Ocean, and on the other by the South-sea, it might possess a powerful influence over the political events which agitate the world. A king of Spain, resident at this capital, might, in six weeks, transmit his orders to Europe, and, in three weeks, to the Philippine islands in Asia. There are, however, difficulties to be encountered, arising from the unfavourable state of the coasts, and the want of secure harbours. During several months in the year, these coasts are visited by tempests. The hurricanes, also, which occur in the months of September, October, and March, and which sometimes last for three or four successive days, are very tremendous.

Mexico was originally founded in the lake of Tezcuco; and, at the time when the Spaniards first invaded America, it was a magnificent capital. Cortez, describing it in the year 1520, says, that it was in the midst of a salt-water lake, which had its tides, like the ocean; and that, from the city to the continent, there was a distance of two leagues. Four dikes or embankments, each two lances broad, led to the city. The principal streets were narrow: some of them had navigable canals running along them, furnished with bridges, wide enough for ten men on horseback, to pass at the same time. The market-place was surrounded with an immense portico, under which were sold all sorts of merchandise, eatables, ornaments made of gold, silver, lead, pewter, precious stones, bones, shells, and feathers; earthenware, leather, and spun cotton. In some places were exposed to sale hewn stone, tiles, and timber for building; in others game; and, in others, roots, garden-stuff, and fruit. There were houses where barbers shaved the head, with razors made of obsidian, a volcanic substance not much unlike bottle-glass; and there were others, resembling our apothecary-shops, where prepared medicines, unguents, and plasters were sold. The market abounded with so many things, that Cortez was unable to name them all. To avoid confusion, every species of merchandise was sold in a separate place. In the middle of the great square was a house, which he calls L'Audiencia; and in which ten or twelve persons sate every day, to determine any disputes which might arise respecting the sale of goods.

The city was divided into four *quarters*: this division is still preserved, in the limits assigned to the quarters of St. Paul, St. Sebastian, St. John, and St. Mary; and the present streets have, for the most part, the same direction as the old ones. But what gives to this city a peculiar and distinctive character is, that it is entirely on the continent, between the extremities of the two lakes of Tezcuco and Chalco. This has been occasioned by the gradual draining of the great lake, and the consequent drying up of the waters around the city. Hence Mexico is now two miles and half from the banks of the former, and five miles and half from those of the latter.

Adorned with numerous *teocallis*, (or temples,) like so many Mahometan steeples, surrounded with water and embankments, founded on islands covered with verdure, and receiving, hourly, in its streets, thousands of boats, which vivified the lake, the ancient Mexico, according to the accounts of the first conquerors, must have resembled some of the cities of Holland, China, or the Delta of Lower Egypt.

As reconstructed by the Spaniards, it exhibits, at the present day, perhaps a less vivid, though a more august and majestic appearance, than the ancient city. With the exception of Petersburg, Berlin, Philadelphia, and some quarters of Westminster, there does not exist a place of the same extent, which can be compared to the capital of New Spain, for the uniform level of the ground on which it stands, for the regularity and breadth of the streets, and the extent of its public places. The architecture is, for the most part, in a pure style; and many of the edifices are of a very beautiful structure. The exterior of the houses is not loaded with ornaments. Two sorts of hewn stone, give to the Mexican buildings an air of solidity, and sometimes even of magnificence. There are none of those wooden balconies and galleries to be seen, which so much disfigure all the European cities in both the Indies. The balustrades and gates are all of iron, ornamented with bronze; and the houses, instead of roofs, have terraces, like those in Italy, and other southern countries of the old continent.

Mexico has, of late, received many additional embellishments. An edifice, for the School of Mines, which was built at an expence of more than £.120,000 sterling, would adorn the principal places of Paris or London. Two great palaces have been constructed by Mexican artists, pupils of the Academy of Fine Arts. One of these has a beautiful interior, ornamented with columns.

But, notwithstanding the progress of the arts, within the last thirty years, it is much less from the grandeur and beauty of the monuments, than from the breadth and straightness of the streets; and much less from its edifices, than from its uniform regularity, its extent and position, that the capital of New Spain attracts the admiration of Europeans. M. De Humboldt had successively visited, within a very short space of time, Lima, Mexico, Philadelphia, Washington, Paris, Rome, Naples, and the largest cities of Germany; and notwithstanding unavoidable comparisons, of which several might be supposed disadvantageous to the capital of Mexico, there was left on his mind, a recollection of grandeur, which he principally attributed to the majestic character of its situation, and the beauty of the surrounding scenery.

In fact, nothing can present a more rich and varied appearance than the *valley of Mexico*, when, in a fine summer morning, a person ascends one of the towers of the cathedral, or the adjacent hill of Chapoltepec. A beautiful vegetation surrounds this hill. From its summit, the eye wanders over a vast plain of richly-cultivated fields, which extend to the very feet of colossal mountains, that are covered with perpetual snow. The city appears as if washed by the waters of the lake of Tezcuco, whose basin, surrounded by villages and hamlets, brings to mind the most beautiful lakes of the mountains of Switzerland. Large avenues of elms and poplars lead, in every direction, to the capital; and two aqueducts, constructed over arches of great elevation, cross the plain, and exhibit an appearance equally agreeable and interesting.

Mexico is remarkable for its excellent police. Most of the *streets* have broad pavements; and they are clean, and well lighted. Water is, every where, to be had; but it is brackish, like the water of the lake. There are, however, two *aqueducts*, by which the city receives fresh-water, from distant springs. Some remains of the *dikes* or *embankments*, are still to be seen: they, at present, form great paved causeys, across marshy ground; and, as they are considerably elevated, they possess the double advantage, of admitting the passage of carriages, and restraining the overflowings of the lake. This city has six principal *gates*; and is surrounded by a ditch, but is without walls.

The objects which chiefly attract the attention of strangers, are 1. The *Cathedral*, which is partly in the Gothic style of architecture, and has two towers, ornamented with pilasters and statues, of very beautiful symmetry. 2. The *Treasury*, which adjoins to the palace of the viceroys: from this building, since the beginning of the 16th century, more than 270 millions sterling, in gold and silver coin, have been issued. 3. The *Convents*. 4. The *Hospital*, or rather the two united hospitals, of which one maintains six hundred, and the other eight hundred children and old people. 5. The *Acordada*, a fine edifice, of which the prisons are spacious and well aired. 6. The *School of Mines*. 7. The *Botanical Garden*, in one of the courts of the viceroy's palace. 8. The edifices of the *University* and the *Public Library*, which, however, are very unworthy of so great and ancient an establishment. 9. The *Academy of Fine Arts*.

Mexico is the see of an archbishop, and contains twenty-three convents for monks, and fifteen for nuns. Its whole population is estimated at one hundred and forty thousand persons.

On the north-side of the city, near the suburbs, is a *public walk*, which forms a large square, having a basin in the middle, and where eight walks terminate.

The *markets* of Mexico are well supplied with eatables; particularly with roots and fruit. It is an interesting spectacle, which may be enjoyed every morning at sunrise, to see these provisions, and a great quantity of flowers, brought by Indians, in boats, along the canals. Most of the roots are cultivated on what are called *chinampas*, or "floating gardens." These are of two sorts: one moveable, and driven about by the winds, and the other fixed and attached to the shore. The first alone merit the denomination of floating-gardens.

Simple lumps of earth, in lakes or rivers, carried away from the banks, have given rise to the invention of chinampas. The floating-gardens, of which very many were found by the Spaniards, when they first invaded

Mexico, and of which many still exist in the lake of Chalco, were rafts formed of reeds, rushes, roots, and branches of underwood. The Indians cover these light and well connected materials with a black mould, which becomes extremely fertile. The chinampas sometimes contain the cottage of the Indian, who acts as guard for a group of floating gardens. When removed from one side of the banks to the other, they are either towed or are pushed with long poles. Every chinampa forms an oblong square about three hundred feet in length, and eighteen or nineteen feet broad. Narrow ditches, communicating symmetrically between them, separate these squares. The mould fit for cultivation rises about three feet above the surface of the surrounding water. On these chinampas are cultivated beans, peas, pimento, potatoes, artichokes, cauliflowers, and a great variety of other vegetables. Their sides are generally ornamented with flowers, and sometimes with hedges of rose-bushes. The promenade in boats, around the chinampas of the river Istracalco, is one of the most agreeable amusements that can be enjoyed in the environs of Mexico. The vegetation is extremely vigorous, on a soil which is continually refreshed with water.

The *Hill of Chapoltepec*, near Mexico, was chosen by the young viceroy Galvez, as the site of a villa for himself and his successors. The castle has been finished externally, but the apartments were not completed when M. de Humboldt was here. This building cost the king of Spain more than £.62,000 sterling.

With respect to the two great *lakes*, Tezcuco and Chalco, which are situated in the valley of Mexico, one is of fresh water, and the other salt. They are separated by a narrow range of mountains, which rise in the middle of the plain; and their waters mingle together, in a strait between the hills. On both these lakes there are numerous towns and villages, which carry on their commerce with each other in canoes, without touching the continent.

FOOTNOTES:

[3] From this place, Mr. Pike was conducted, through St. Antonio, in a north-westerly direction, to the territories of the United States; and he terminates the account of his travels at *Natchitoches*, on the southern bank of the Red river.

Twenty-first Day's Instruction

MEXICO CONCLUDED.

A Description of some of the most important Places in Mexico.

In an easterly direction from the city of Mexico lies *Tlascala*, a town, which, two hundred years ago, at the time of the Spanish invasion, had a numerous population, and was in a wealthy and flourishing state. The inhabitants of this place were implacable enemies of the Mexicans, and aided the Spaniards in the conquest of their country. It is now, however, little more than a village, containing about three thousand inhabitants. Some parts of the ancient walls still remain, and are composed of alternate strata of brick and clay.

Six leagues south-west from Tlascala, and in the midst of a delightful valley, watered by a river which runs south-west to the Pacific Ocean, stands *Puebla*, the capital of an intendancy, and the see of a bishop. It is a large and regularly built manufacturing town, notorious for the profligacy of its inhabitants.

Cholula, once a sacred Indian town, to which pilgrimages were frequent, but now a mean village, is not far from Puebla. This place is, at present, remarkable only for a curious monument of antiquity, a pyramid which consists of four stages, and is about one hundred and seventy-seven feet in perpendicular height, and one thousand four hundred and twenty-three feet at the base. Its structure appears to consist of alternate strata of bricks and clay. In the midst of this pyramid there is a church, where mass is, every morning, celebrated by an ecclesiastic of Indian extraction, whose residence is on the summit.

Eastward of the intendancy of Puebla is that of *Vera Cruz*. This district is enriched with various natural productions, extremely valuable both in a commercial and economical view. The sugar-cane grows here in great luxuriance: chocolate, tobacco, cotton, sarsaparilla, are all abundant; but the indolence of the inhabitants is so great, and all their wants are so easily supplied, by the natural fertility of the soil, that the country does not produce one half of what, under good management, it might be made to produce. The sugar and cotton plantations are chiefly attended to; but the progress made in these is not great.

The chief city of the province is *Vera Cruz*; a sea-port, the residence of the governor, and the centre of the Spanish West Indian and American commerce. This city is beautifully and regularly built; but on an arid plain, destitute of water, and covered with hills of moving sand, that are formed by the north winds, which blow; with impetuosity, every year, from October till April. These hills are incessantly changing their form and situation: they are from twenty to thirty feet in height; and, by the reflection of the sun's rays upon them, and the high temperature which they acquire during the summer months, they contribute much to increase the suffocating heat of the atmosphere.

The houses in Vera Cruz are chiefly built of wood; for no stone whatever is found in the vicinity of the place. The public edifices are constructed of materials obtained from the bottom of the ocean: the stony habitations of a kind of marine animals called madrepores. The town is of great extent; and is surrounded by a wall, and defended by a kind of citadel, which stands on an adjacent rocky island. The harbour is well protected; but the entrance into it is so narrowed by rocks, that only one ship can pass at a time.

On the annual arrival of the flota, or fleet of merchant-vessels from Old Spain, Vera Cruz is crowded, from all parts of the adjacent country; and a kind of fair is opened, which lasts many weeks. The principal inhabitants are merchants, but very few of them reside wholly in the town; for the heat of the climate, the stagnant water in the vicinity of the place, and the bad quality of the water used for drinking, are the cause of yellow fever and numerous other diseases.

The churches of Vera Cruz are much decorated with silver ornaments. In the dwelling houses, the chief luxury consists of porcelain and other Chinese articles. The whole number of inhabitants is estimated at about thirteen thousand. They are, in general, proud and indolent. The women, few of whom are handsome, live much in retirement.

During the rainy season, the marshes south of the town are haunted by alligators. Sea-fowl of various kinds are here innumerable; and the musquitoes, at certain seasons of the year, are very troublesome. Earthquakes are not unfrequent. The north winds are so tremendous as often to drive vessels on shore: these gales sometimes load the walls with sand; and so much inconvenience is occasioned by them, that, during their continuance, ladies are excused by the priests from going to mass.

The richest merchants of this place have country-houses at *Xalapa*, a town, in a romantic situation, about twenty leagues distant. Here they enjoy a cool and agreeable retreat from the arid climate and noxious exhalations of Vera Cruz. In the vicinity of Xalapa, thick forests of styrax, piper, melastomata, and ferns resembling trees, afford the most delightful promenades imaginable.

The intendancy of Vera Cruz contains, within its limits, two colossal summits; one of which, the *volcano of Orizaba*, is of great height, and has its top inclined towards the south-east, by which the crater is visible to a considerable distance. The other summit, the *Coffre de Perote*, according to M. de Humboldt's measurement, is one thousand three hundred feet higher than the Pic of Tenerife. It serves as a land-mark to vessels approaching Vera Cruz. A thick bed of pumice-stone environs this mountain. Nothing at the summit announces a crater; and the currents of lava observable between some adjacent villages, appear to be the effects of an ancient explosion.

The small *volcano of Tuxtla* is about four leagues from the coast, and near an Indian village, called Saint Jago di Tuxtla. The last eruption of this volcano took place on the 2d of March, 1793; and, during its continuance, the roofs of houses at Oaxaca, Vera Cruz, and Perote, were covered with volcanic ashes. At Perote, fifty-seven leagues distant, the subterraneous noises resembled heavy discharges of artillery.

In the northern part of the intendancy of Vera Cruz, and two leagues from the village of *Papantla*, there is a *pyramidal edifice* of great antiquity. It is in the midst of a forest; and the Indians, for more than two centuries, succeeded in concealing, from the knowledge of the Spaniards, this object of ancient veneration. It was accidentally discovered, by a party of hunters, about thirty years ago. The materials that have been employed in its construction are immense stones cemented with mortar; and it is remarkable for its general symmetry, for the polish of its stones, and the great regularity of their form. Its base is an exact square, each side being eighty-two feet in length. The perpendicular height is about sixty feet. This monument, like all the Mexican teocallis or temples, is composed of several stages. Six are still distinguishable, and a seventh appears to be concealed by the vegetation, with which the sides are covered. A great stair of fifty-seven steps, conducts to the top, where human victims were formerly sacrificed; and, on each side of the great stair, is a small one. The facing of the stories is adorned with hieroglyphics, in which serpents and alligators, carved in relief, are still discernible. Each story contains a great number of square niches, symmetrically distributed.

On the coast of the Pacific Ocean, and at the distance of about three hundred miles south-west from Vera Cruz, stands *Acapulco*, the great western sea-port of Mexico. This place is the principal emporium for the

Indian trade over the Pacific Ocean. The harbour is commodious, capable of containing several hundred ships, and defended by a strong castle. The town itself is mean and ill-built, but extremely populous. Earthquakes are here of such frequent occurrence, that the houses are all very slightly constructed; and the climate, also, is extremely unhealthy. These circumstances occasion most of the principal merchants to reside in the adjacent country, at all times except when business demands their attention in the town.

Several vessels, called "galleons," laden with the precious metals, and with merchandise of other kinds, are every year sent, from this port, to Manila, in the Philippine islands; and others return, laden with the valuable productions of the East Indies. On the arrival of the latter, the town becomes populous and gay; and is then filled with the wealthiest merchants of Mexico and Peru. Such, however, is the general dread of its unhealthiness, that these do not sleep within the walls, but reside chiefly in tents in its vicinity.

At some distance east of Acapulco, in a beautiful and populous valley, stands the town of *Guaxaca* or *Oaxaca*; distinguished by the magnificence of its situation, the temperature and salubrity of its climate, the excellence of its soil, and its general majestic appearance. The streets are wide, straight, and well paved; and the houses are chiefly built of stone. The churches and monasteries are numerous, and richly decorated. On one side of the great square is the town-house, which is constructed with stone of a sea-green colour. The bishop's palace and the cathedral form two other sides of the same square: they are surrounded by arcades, as a shelter against both the sun and the rain. In the suburbs of Guaxaca are gardens, and plantations of cactus or prickly pear-trees, on which great numbers of cochineal insects feed. Guaxaca is not only watered by a beautiful river, but is abundantly supplied, by aqueducts, with pure water from the adjacent mountains. Its population, including Indians, mulattoes, and negroes, amounts to about twenty-four thousand persons.

The *intendancy of Yucatan* forms a peninsula, about a hundred leagues in length, between the bays of Campeachy and Honduras. A ridge of low hills extends along it, from south-west to north-east; and, between this ridge and the *Bay of Campeachy*, the dry and parched soil produces logwood in great abundance and of excellent quality. For nearly five months, during the rainy season, the low grounds are partially inundated: in February the waters are dried up; and, throughout the remainder of the year, there is scarcely any stream to be found. Hence the inhabitants can only be supplied with fresh water by pits and wells. The eastern coast of Yucatan is so shallow and muddy, that large vessels cannot approach within four leagues of the shore. The chief productions of this peninsula are maize, cotton, indigo, and logwood.

The governor resides at a small inland town called *Merida*, situated on an arid plain, and containing about six thousand inhabitants. The principal sea-port is *Campeachy*, near the north-west extremity of the peninsula. This town has a good dock, and a fort which protects both the place and the harbour. The houses are chiefly built of stone. Campeachy has some cotton manufactories, and a trade in wax and salt; but its chief trade is in logwood.

Honduras is an important province, south of Yucatan. Its climate is superior to that of most other parts of America, within the torrid zone. With the exception of a few months in the year, it is refreshed by regular sea-breezes. The periodical rains are here excessively heavy. The dry season is usually comprehended within the months of April, May, and June; and the sun, during this time, is excessively powerful. This province is about three hundred and ninety miles in length, from east to west, and consists of mountains, valleys, and plains, watered by many rivers. Honduras abounds in honey, wax, cotton, corn, fruit, and dyeing woods. It has some gold and silver mines; and its pastures feed great numbers of sheep and cattle. Its vineyards yield grapes twice in the year; but, from indolence and want of cultivation, many parts of it have become desert.

There is a British settlement at a place called *Balize*, near the mouth of a river of the same name. This town is immediately open to the sea; and, though in a low situation, the groups of lofty cocoa-nut trees, and the thickly-interspersed and lively foliage of the tamarind trees, contribute to give a picturesque and pleasing effect to the dwellings of the inhabitants. The number of houses, of all descriptions, is about two hundred; and many of them, particularly such as are the property of the most opulent merchants, are spacious, commodious, and well finished. They are built of wood, and are generally raised eight or ten feet from the ground, on pillars of mahogany. The stores and offices are always on the lower, and the dining and sleeping apartments on the upper story. Every habitation, likewise, has its upper and lower piazzas, which are indispensably necessary in hot climates. Balize stands at the edge of a swamp many miles in extent, which prevents nearly all intercourse with the interior of the country.

The principal articles at present imported from Europe into Honduras, are linens, printed cottons, muslins of the most costly manufacture, negro clothing, broadcloths, hosiery, hats, shoes, boots, earthen and glass wares, silver and plated goods, hardware, and cutlery: salted provisions, from Britain or America, are also in continual demand for the food of the slaves.

Few countries possess greater commercial advantages, in an agricultural view, than this. The productions of the West Indian islands, might all unquestionably be cultivated here, as well as most others which are grown within the tropics. But the cutting of logwood and mahogany is the chief occupation of the British settlers. The banks of the river Balize have long been occupied by mahogany-cutters, even to the distance of two hundred miles from its mouth.

About thirty miles up the Balize, on its banks, are found what are denominated the Indian hills. These are small eminences, which are supposed to have been raised by Indians over their dead; human bones, and fragments of a coarse kind of earthenware, being frequently dug up from them.

Nicaragua is a Spanish province, between Honduras and the isthmus of Darien. It is about eighty leagues in length and fifty in breadth; and consists, for the most part, of high and wooded mountains, some of which are volcanic. The valleys are watered by many streams, but only one of these is of any importance. This is the river *Yare*, which runs, from west to east, through the northern part of the province. The most important productions of Nicaragua are timber, cotton, sugar, honey, and wax. The chief town is *Leon de Nicaragua*, a place of considerable trade, situated near the north-west border of the lake of Nicaragua; and in a sandy plain, at the foot of a volcanic mountain, several leagues from the sea.

From New Spain we must return northward, for the purpose of describing the British dominions of Nova Scotia and Canada.

Twenty-second Day's Instruction

BRITISH AMERICAN DOMINIONS.

NOVA SCOTIA,

Is a province bounded on the east by the *Gulf of St. Lawrence,* on the south by the Atlantic, and on the west by the United States. It is somewhat more than two hundred miles long, and one hundred and seventy miles broad. The southern division is a peninsula of triangular form, having an isthmus not more than thirty miles in breadth. Nova Scotia is divided into counties, and subdivided into townships; and, in the whole, contains somewhat more than fifty thousand inhabitants.

The climate is unhealthy. During a considerable part of the year, the maritime and lower districts are enveloped in fog. The cold of winter is intense, and the heat of summer excessive. The soil is various. In many parts it is thin, barren, gravelly, and covered with forests: in others, especially on the borders of the rivers, it is fertile and agreeable. Some of the tracts yield hemp and flax; but the inhabitants have not hitherto made much progress in agriculture. Nova Scotia has many bays and harbours; but much of the coast is bordered with dangerous rocks. Great numbers of cod-fish are caught in some of the bays, and in many parts of the sea adjacent to the coast.

Halifax, the capital of Nova Scotia, was built about the year 1749. It is now a flourishing town on the sea-coast, and has an excellent harbour, accessible at all seasons of the year, and with depth of water and anchorage sufficient for the largest vessels. The town is about two miles in length, and a quarter of a mile in width; and is laid out in oblong squares, and in streets that run parallel or at right angles to each other. It is defended by forts of timber, and contains about fifteen thousand inhabitants. At its northern extremity is the royal arsenal, which is well built, and amply supplied with naval stores.

CANADA,

Is an extensive but thinly-peopled district, lying between the same parallels of latitude as France and England, but in a climate infinitely more severe. During winter the frost is intense, and the surface of the ground is covered with snow to the depth of several feet. In many parts of the country, however, the summers are hot and pleasant.

The *boundaries* of Canada are, the United States on the south; the Atlantic Ocean, Labrador, and Hudson's Bay, on the east and north; and a wild and undescribed region on the west. This country is divided into two provinces of Upper and Lower Canada: the executive power in each province is vested in a *governor*; and a legislative council and an assembly are appointed for each, having power, with the consent of the governor, to make laws. In the legislative council of Lower Canada, there are fifteen members; and in that of Upper Canada seven; and the appointments are for life. In the assembly of Lower Canada there are fifty members; and in that of Upper Canada sixteen: these are chosen by the freeholders and do not continue in office longer than four years.

Canada was originally discovered by Sebastian Cabot, a navigator sent out by the English about the year 1497; but in the beginning of the seventeenth century, it was colonized by the French, who kept possession of it till the year 1763, when it fell into the hands of the British, to whom it still belongs. The long possession of this country by the French, has occasioned the *French language* to be chiefly spoken: it has also occasioned the prevailing *religion* to be Roman Catholic. The British government permits a toleration of all religions; but by far the greatest number of inhabitants are catholics. The clergy of the church of England, in both provinces, are only twelve in number, including the bishop of Quebec; whereas, those of the church of Rome amount to one hundred and twenty, including a bishop, and three vicars-general.

The whole number of *inhabitants* is considered to be about two hundred thousand, of whom fifty thousand are Indians. "Essentially a Frenchman, (says Mr. Hall,) the Canadian is gay, courteous, and contented. If the rigours of the climate have somewhat chilled the overflowing vivacity derived from his parent stock, he has still a sufficient portion of good spirits and loquacity. To strangers and travellers he is invariably civil; and he seems to value their good word beyond their money. He is considered parsimonious, because all his gains arise from his savings, and he is satisfied with the humblest fare." The Canadians have a great antipathy to the inhabitants of the United States. At this day, many even of the better informed among them believe that the American government is constantly plotting the ruin of Canada.

Whilst Canada was in the hands of the French, the *commerce* of the country was chiefly confined to the fisheries and fur-trade: agriculture was neglected, and extensive tracts of fertile soil lay uncultivated. But the English have both peopled and improved a very considerable portion of territory;

and the trade is now of much importance. The Canadians export to Britain and to different British establishments, wheat and other grain, biscuit, beef, pork, butter, salmon, oil, timber, hemp, and various other articles. In many parts of both Canadas the *soil* is well adapted for the production of grain. Tobacco also thrives well in it; and culinary vegetables arrive at great perfection. The forests produce beech-trees, oaks, elms, ash, pine, sycamore, chesnut, and walnut; and a species of maple-tree, from the juice of which sugar is made, abounds throughout the country.

Many extensive tracts in Canada are covered with lakes and marshes; and the country is intersected by numerous rivers, some of which are navigable to considerable distances. Of the *lakes*, the most important are lake Superior, lake Huron, lake Michigan, lake Ontario, and lake Erie. These are adjacent to the territory of the United States. Lake Winipic is an expanse of water, more than two hundred and fifty miles in length, situated about the 53d degree of north latitude. The largest and noblest *river* in Canada is the St. Lawrence, which flows from lake Ontario, past the two towns of Montreal and Quebec, and falls into the Gulf of St. Lawrence. This river meets the tide four miles from the sea; and to this place it is navigable for large vessels.

A Description of Quebec.

This city, the capital of Canada, stands at the northern extremity of a strip of high land, which follows the course of the river St. Lawrence, as far as the mouth of the Charles. The basis of these heights is a dark slate rock, of which most of the buildings in the town are constructed. *Cape Diamond* terminates the promontory, with a bold precipice towards the river. This rock derives its name from numerous transparent crystals, which are found upon it; and which are so abundant that, after a shower of rain, the ground glitters with them.

The Lower Town of Quebec is built at the foot of the heights; and the Upper Town occupies their crest. The former, snug and dirty, is the abode of persons engaged in trade, and of most of the lower classes: the latter, lofty and cold, is the seat of government, and the principal residence of the military.

With few exceptions, the *houses* in Quebec are built of stone. The roofs of the better sort are covered with sheets of iron or tin, and those of an inferior description, with boards. On the roofs ladders are usually placed, near the garret-windows, for the purpose of the chimney-sweepers ascending, on the outside, to clean the chimneys: for, in this country boys do not go up the chimneys, as in England; but two men, one at the top and the other at the bottom, sweep them, by pulling up and down a bundle of twigs or furze, tied to a rope.

The *streets* of the Lower Town are, for the most part, narrow and irregular. St. Peter's street is the best paved, and the widest of the whole. It contains several good and substantial *houses*, which are chiefly occupied by merchants and traders; but, from the colour of the stone of which the houses are constructed, and of the iron roofs, all the streets of Quebec have a heavy and gloomy appearance.

A street, called *Mountain Street*, which leads to the Upper Town, winds, in a serpentine direction, from the market-place up the hill, and terminates near the Upper Town market-place. This street, in winter, is extremely dangerous. The quantity of snow and ice, which here accumulate in large masses, renders it necessary for the inhabitants to wear outer shoes, that are shod with iron spikes. The boys of Quebec have a favourite amusement, in lying at full length with their breast upon a small kind of sledge, and sliding along the snow, from the top of the hill to the bottom: they glide down with astonishing velocity; yet, with their feet, they can guide or stop themselves, at pleasure.

The *shops* or stores of the traders in the Lower Town, do not exhibit any of that diversified and pleasing appearance which is so remarkable in London. Here the stranger sees nothing but heavy stone buildings, gloomy casements, and iron-cased shutters, painted red. If any show is made at the window, it is with paltry articles of cooking, earthen and hardware: there is, however, a tolerable display of bear-skins, seal-skins, foxes-tails, and buffalo-robes.

The *taverns* in Quebec are numerous; yet a stranger is much surprised to find only two houses which deserve that high-sounding appellation. This arises from the vanity that possesses all our trans-Atlantic brethren, to designate their paltry public-houses or spirit-shops, by the more dignified title of "tavern;" for through the whole of America, every dirty hole, where a few glasses of rum, gin, or whisky, are sold, is so called.

Of the *public buildings* in Quebec, the most important is the government-house, or castle of St. Louis, a large, plain, stone edifice, which forms one side of an open place or square, called the parade. Its front resembles that of a country gentleman's house in England; and the interior contains comfortable family apartments. The furniture is inherited and paid for by the successive owners. Opposite to the government-house stand the English cathedral church, and the court-house, both handsome buildings of modern construction. The other sides of the parade are formed by the Union Hotel, and a row of buildings which form the commencement of St. Louis Street.

The *Upper Town* is by far the most agreeable part of Quebec: its streets are not, indeed, remarkable for width, but many of them are well paved. In the Upper Town the heat, during summer, is not so intense as in the Lower Town; nor, in winter, though the cold is much severer, is it, as a residence, so dreary and uncomfortable.

There are, in Quebec, several catholic *charitable institutions*. Of these, the principal is the "Hotel Dieu," founded in 1637, for the accommodation and relief of poor sick people: it is under the management of a superior and thirty-six nuns. The "General Hospital," which stands at a little distance from the town, is a somewhat similar institution; and is governed by a superior and forty-three nuns. In the admission of patients into each of these establishments, no distinction is made, as to catholics or protestants. The Ursuline convent, founded in 1639, for the education of female children, stands within the city, and has a considerable appearance of wealth. Among the ornaments of the chapel are the skull and bones of a missionary, who had been murdered by the Indians for attempting their conversion.

About two miles from the town is a break in the line of cliffs, which forms a little recess, called *Wolf's Cove*. A steep pathway leads thence to the heights of the plains of Abram. On these plains are still to be seen, in the turf, traces of field-works, which were thrown up by the British army, in the celebrated siege of Quebec; and a stone is pointed out as that on which General Wolf expired.

The *markets* of Quebec are well supplied with every thing that the country affords; and, in general, at a very cheap rate. In the autumn, as soon as the river betwixt the town and the island of Orleans, is frozen over, an abundance of provisions is received from that island. The Canadians, at the commencement of winter, kill the greatest part of their stock, and carry it to market in a frozen state. The inhabitants of the towns supply themselves, at this season, with butcher's meat, poultry, and vegetables, to serve them till spring. These are kept in garrets or cellars; and, so long as they continue frozen, their goodness is preserved. Before they are prepared for the table, they are laid for some hours in cold water, to be thawed. In wintertime, milk is brought to market in large frozen cakes.

Great quantities of maple-sugar are sold, in Quebec, at about half the price of West India sugar. The manufacturing of this article takes place in the spring. The sap or juice, after it has been drawn from the trees, is boiled, and then poured into shallow dishes, where it takes the form of a thick and hard cake. Maple-sugar is very hard; and, when used, is scraped with a knife, as, otherwise, it would be a long time in dissolving.

The fruit of Canada is not remarkable either for excellence or cheapness. Strawberries and raspberries are, however, brought to market in great abundance: they are gathered on the plains, at the back of Quebec, and in the neighbouring woods, where they grow wild, in the utmost luxuriance. Apples and pears are chiefly procured from the vicinity of Montreal. Walnuts and filberts are by no means common; but hickory-nuts and hazel-nuts are to be obtained in all the woods.

The *climate* of Lower Canada is subject to violent extremes of heat and cold. At Quebec, the thermometer, in summer, is sometimes as high as 103 degrees of Fahrenheit's thermometer; and, in winter, is at 36 degrees below 0. The average of summer heat is, in general, from 75 to 80 degrees; and the mean of the cold, in winter, is about 0.

From Christmas to Lady-day the weather is remarkably clear and fine; the sky is of an azure blue colour, and seldom obscured by fogs or clouds; and the frost is not often interrupted by falls of snow or rain. These advantages render a Canadian winter so agreeable, that the inhabitants, from sudden alterations of the weather, are never under the necessity of changing their style of dress, unless it be to discard their greatcoats and fur-caps, which, in consequence of the powerful warmth of the sun, is sometimes necessary. In the early part of the winter there is always much snow.

The spring, summer, and autumn of Canada, are all comprised within the five months of May, June, July, August, and September. The rest of the year may be considered as winter. During the month of October, the weather is sometimes pleasant, but nature has then put on her gloomy mantle; and the chilling blasts, from the north-west, remind the Canadians of the approach of snow and ice. November and April are the two most disagreeable months of the year: in one of these the snow is beginning to fall, and in the other it is going away.

Mr. Hall's *Journey from Quebec to Montreal.*

Mr. Hall was in Canada during the summer of 1816; and, on the 28th of July, he left Quebec, on a journey to Montreal. He deviated somewhat from the usual road, that he might pass by the *Jacques Cartier bridge,* six or seven miles above the ferry. Here the river falls wildly down, betwixt its wooded shores; and, after forming several cascades, foams through a narrow channel, which seems cut out of the solid rock, to receive it. The rock, which constitutes its bed, is formed into regular platforms, descending, by natural steps, to the edge of the torrent. The Jacques Cartier is a river famous for its salmon, which are caught of large size, and in great abundance, below the bridge. At the foot of this bridge stands a little inn, where the angler may have his game cooked for supper, and where he may sleep in the lull of the torrent, below his chamber-window. After quitting this neighbourhood, the scenery of the St. Lawrence becomes flat and uniform. The road follows the direction of the river, sometimes running along the cliff, which once embanked it, and sometimes descending to the water's edge.

From Quebec to Montreal, the country may be considered as one long village. On each shore there is a stripe of land, seldom exceeding a mile in breadth, which is bounded by forests, and thickly studded with farm-houses, white-washed from top to bottom: to these, log-barns and stables are attached, and commonly a neat plot of garden-ground.

Mr. Hall preferred the travelling in Lower Canada to that in every other part of the American continent. You arrive (he says) at the post-house, (as the words *"maison de poste,"* scrawled over the door, give you notice;) "Have you horses, Madame?" *"Oui, Monsieur, tout de suite."* A loud cry of *"Oh! bon homme,"* forwards the intelligence to her husband, at work, perhaps, in an adjacent field. *"Mais, asseyez vous, Monsieur;"* and, if you have patience to do this quietly, for a few minutes, you will see crebillion, papillon, or some other *on* arrive, at a full canter, from pasture, mounted by honest *Jean*, in his blue nightcap, with all his habiliments shaking in the wind. The preliminary of splicing and compounding the broken harness having been adjusted, the whip cracks, and you start to the exhilarating cry of *"marche donc,"* at the rate of six, and often seven miles an hour.

The village of *"Trois Rivieres"* stands at the three mouths of the *River St. Maurice*. It contains an Ursuline convent, which marks it for a place of some note, in a catholic country; but it is still more worthy of distinction, as being the residence of the amiable Abbé de la Colonne, brother to the unfortunate French minister of that name.

Having engaged two experienced boatmen, and a bark canoe, Mr. Hall ascended the St. Maurice, to visit the *falls of Shawinne Gamme*, distant somewhat more than twenty miles. At his return, he left the St. Maurice, and, having been ferried from *Berthier* to *Contrecœur*, he proceeded, *"en caleche,"* with two crebillions, towards *St. Ours*, in the direction of the *Belœil Mountain*, which was seen before him in the misty horizon. The meadows were profusely decorated with orange lilies; and the banks and dingles with the crimson cones of the sumac, and a variety of flowering shrubs. Several brigs and merchants' ships were dropping down with the tide, their crowded sails scarcely swelling in the languid summer breeze.

The Canadian summer, observes Mr. Hall, is hot in proportion to the severity of the winter; and the heat is sufficient to enable the cultivator to raise Indian corn, water-melons, gourds, capsicums, and such vegetables as require a short and intense heat. Hence the country assumes the aspect of a Portuguese summer, by way of appendix to a Russian winter.

Mr. Hall passed through the village of *Belœil*; again crossed the river, and proceeded towards the mountain, which towered, like an immense wall of rock, above the flat surrounding country. Scattered at its base were a few wretched houses, the inhabitants of which subsisted by the produce of their apple-orchards.

The weather was excessively hot; and volumes of smoke, from the casual, or intentional burning of the woods, every where clouded the horizon, and seemed to give additional heat to the glowing landscape.

The basis of the *Montreal Mountain* is freestone; the ascent is consequently less steep, and the surface less broken, than that of Belœil: it is thickly wooded, and, from the river, forms an elegant back-ground to the city.

A Description of Montreal.

When approached from the water, the town of *Montreal*, which is situated on an island in the River St. Lawrence, has a very singular appearance. This is occasioned by the grey stone of the buildings, and their tin-covered roofs; the latter of which emit a strong glare, when the sun shines. The shore is steep, and forms a kind of natural wharf, upon which the vessels discharge their cargoes: hence the shipping which frequent the harbour of Montreal are often anchored close to the shore. Many English vessels visit this place; but the navigation of the St. Lawrence, above Quebec, is so hazardous, that few captains are willing to make the voyage a second time.

The interior of the town of Montreal is extremely gloomy. The *streets* are regularly built, but the buildings are ponderous masses of stone, erected with little taste, and less judgment. Including the garrets, they have seldom more than two stories above the ground-floor. The doors and window-shutters are covered with large sheets of tin, painted red or lead-colour, and corresponding with the gloomy colour of the stone, with which most of the houses have been built; hence a heavy sameness of appearance pervades all the streets.

The only *open places* in the town, are the two markets, and a square, called the Place d'Armes, in which, under the French government, the troops of the garrison are accustomed to parade. The French catholic church occupies the whole east side of the square; and, on the south side, is a tavern, called the Montreal Hotel. Every thing, in this tavern, is neat, cleanly, well conducted, and perfectly agreeable to an Englishman's taste.

Montreal is divided into the *Upper* and *Lower towns*, though these have very little difference in elevation. The principal street of the latter, extends, from north to south, through the whole length of the place. This street contains the wholesale and retail stores of the merchants and traders, the lower market-place, the post-office, the Hotel Dieu, a large tavern, and several smaller ones. It is narrow, but it presents a scene of greater bustle than any other part of the town; and is the chief mart of the trade carried on in Montreal.

Most of the streets are well paved; and the improvements which are going on throughout the town, will, in a few years, render it much more commodious and agreeable than it is at present. The four streets or *suburbs* occupy a considerable space of ground, and the number of inhabitants is computed at twelve thousand. The *religious* and *charitable institutions* of this place, are counterparts to those at Quebec. There are a general hospital, and an Hotel Dieu, for the relief of sick poor. The principal catholic church is rich and handsome. The college or seminary, is a capacious stone building, and has lately been repaired and enlarged. It was originally endowed as a branch of the seminary at Paris; but, since the French Revolution, it has afforded an asylum to several members of the latter, whose learning and talents have been employed in its advancement. Among other *public edifices* must be reckoned the English church, an unfinished building; the old monastery of Franciscan Friars, now converted into barracks; the court-house, and the government-house. The court-house is a neat and spacious building. In front of it, a column has been erected in honour of Lord Nelson, and is crowned with a statue of him. Near the court-house a gaol has been built, upon the site of the old college of Jesuits.

There seems to be a greater spirit of municipal improvement in Montreal than in Quebec. It is also, probably, a richer place; for, being the emporium of the fur-trade, its merchants carry on a considerable traffic with the United States, and particularly with Vermont and New York.

At the back of the town, and behind the court-house, is a *parade*, where the troops are exercised. The ground, along this part, is considerably elevated, and forms a steep bank, several hundred yards in length. Here the inhabitants walk in an evening, and enjoy a beautiful view of the suburbs of St. Lawrence and St. Antoine; and of numerous gardens, orchards, and plantations, adorned with neat, and, in many instances, even handsome villas. Green fields are interspersed amidst this rich variety of objects, which are concentrated in an extensive valley, that gradually rises towards a lofty mountain, about two miles and a half distant; and covered, towards its upper part, with trees and shrubs. It is from this mountain that the town obtained its name of Montreal, or "Royal Mount."

All the principal north-west merchants reside in this town; which is the emporium of their trade, and the grand mart of the commerce carried on between Canada and the United States: they live in a splendid style, and keep expensive tables.

The *markets* of Montreal are plentifully supplied with provisions, which are much cheaper here than in Quebec. Large supplies are brought in, every winter, from the United States; particularly cod-fish, which is packed in ice, and conveyed in sledges from Boston. Two weekly newspapers, called the Gazette and the Canadian Courant, are published here.

At Montreal, the winter is considered to be two months shorter than it is at Quebec; and the heat of summer is more oppressive.

Twenty-third Day's Instruction

NORTH WESTERN TERRITORY.

The Route, from Montreal to Fort Chepewyan, pursued by a company of traders, called the North-west Company.

The requisite number of canoes being purchased, the goods being formed into packages, and the lakes and rivers being free from ice, which they usually are in the beginning of May, the persons employed by the North-west Company set out from *La Chine*, eight miles above Montreal.

Each canoe carries eight or ten men, and a luggage consisting of sixty-five packages of goods, about six hundred weight of biscuit, two hundred weight of pork, and three bushels of peas, for the men's provisions: two oil-cloths to cover the goods, a sail, and an axe, a towing-line, a kettle, and a sponge to bail out the water; together with a quantity of gum, bark, and watape, to repair the canoe. An European, on seeing these slender vessels, thus laden, heaped up, and their sides not more than six inches out of the water, would imagine it impossible that they should perform a long and perilous voyage; but the Canadians are so expert in the management of them, that few accidents happen.

Leaving La Chine, they proceed to *St. Ann's*, within two miles of the western extremity of the island of Montreal. At the rapid of St. Ann, the navigators are obliged to take out part, if not the whole of the lading; and to replace it when they have passed the cataract. The *Lake of the two Mountains*, which they next reach, is about twenty miles long, but not more than three miles wide, and is, nearly surrounded by cultivated fields.

At the end of the lake, the water contracts into the *Utawas river*; which, after a course of fifteen miles, is interrupted by a succession of rapids and cascades for upwards of ten miles: at the foot of these the Canadian Seignories terminate. Here the voyagers are frequently obliged to unload their canoes, and carry the goods upon their backs, or rather suspended in slings from their heads. Each man's ordinary load is two packages, though some of the men carry three. In some places, the ground will not admit of their carrying the whole at once: in this case, they make two trips; that is, the men leave half their lading, land it at the distance required, and then return for that which was left. There are three carrying places; and, near the last of them, the river is a mile and a half wide, and has a regular current, for about sixty miles, to the first *portage de Chaudiere*. The whole body of water is here precipitated, twenty-five feet, down, craggy and excavated rocks, and in a most wild and romantic manner.

Over this portage, it is requisite to carry the canoe and all its lading; but the rock is so steep, that the canoe cannot be taken out of the water by fewer than twelve men, and it is carried by six men.

The next remarkable object which the traders approach, is a lake called *Nepisingui*, about twelve leagues long, and fifteen miles wide, in the widest part. The inhabitants of the country adjacent to this lake, consist of the remainder of a numerous tribe called *Nepisinguis*, of the Algonquin nation.

Out of the lake flows the *Riviere de François*, over rocks of considerable height. This river is very irregular, both as to its breadth and form; and it is so interspersed with islands, that, in its whole course, its banks are seldom visible. Of its various channels, that which is generally followed by the canoes is obstructed by five portages. The distance hence to Lake Huron is about twenty-five leagues. There is scarcely a foot of soil to be seen from one end of the river to the other; for its banks consist entirely of rock.

The coast of *Lake Huron* is similar to this; but it is lower, and backed, at some distance, by high lands. The canoes pass along the northern bank of this lake, into *Lake Superior*, the largest and most magnificent body of fresh water in the world. It is clear, of great depth, and abounds in fish of various kinds. Sturgeon are caught here, and trout, some of which weigh from forty to fifty pounds each. The adjacent country is bleak, rocky, and desolate: it contains no large animals, except a few moose and fallow deer; and the little timber that is to be seen, is extremely stunted in its growth. The inhabitants of the coast of Lake Superior are all of the *Algonquin nation*, who subsist chiefly on fish. They do not, at present, exceed one hundred and fifty families; though, a century ago, the whole adjacent country is said to have been inhabited by them.

Near the north-western shore of Lake Superior, and beneath a hill, three or four hundred feet in height, is a fort, containing several houses, erected for the accommodation of the North-west Company and their clerks. This place is called the *Grande Portage*. The traders, who leave Montreal in the beginning of May, usually arrive here about the middle of June. They are met by men who had spent the winter in the establishments; towards the north, and from whom they receive the furs which had been collected in the course of their winter traffic. Upwards of twelve hundred men are thus assembled, every summer, in this remote wilderness; and live together, for several days, in a comfortable and convivial manner. After their accounts are settled, the furs are embarked for Montreal; and the rest of the men proceed to the different posts and establishments in the Indian country. The canoes which are used from the Grande Portage, upwards, are but half the size of those from Montreal. They are each navigated by four, five, or six men, according to the distance which they have to go.

Having embarked on the river *Au Tourt*; and, having overcome numerous obstacles, in cataracts, and other impediments to their course, the persons proceeding on this voyage, reach a trading establishment, on the north side of the river, in 48 degrees 37 minutes, north latitude. Here they are met by people from the Athabasca country, and exchange lading with them. This place also is the residence of the grand chief of the *Algonquin Indians*; and here the elders of these Indians meet in council, to treat of peace or war.

The Au Tourt is one of the finest rivers in the north-western parts of America. Its banks are covered with a rich soil, and, in many parts, are clothed with groves of oak, maple, and cedar-trees. The southern bank is low, and displays the maple, the white birch, and cedar; with the spruce, the alder, and various kinds of underwood. Its waters abound in fish, particularly in sturgeons. In the low grounds, betwixt Lake Superior and this river, are seen vast quantities of rice, which the natives collect, in the month of August, for their winter stores.

Lake Winipic, which the traders next approach, is the great reservoir of several large rivers. It is bounded, on the north, by banks of black and grey rock; and, on the south, by a low and level country, occasionally interrupted with ridges or banks of limestone, from twenty to forty feet in height, bearing timber, but only of moderate growth. From its peculiar situation, this lake seems calculated to become a grand depôt of traffic. It communicates, in a direct and short channel, with the southern shores of Hudson's Bay, by the rivers Severn and Nelson; and it is connected with the countries at the head of the Mississippi and Missouri, by the Assiniboin and Red rivers. The Indians, who inhabit its banks, are of the Knisteneaux and Algonquin tribes.

Beyond lake Winipic, the canoes have to pass along many rapids, and through several small lakes, called *Cedar lake, Mud lake,* and *Sturgeon lake.* This part of the country is frequented by beavers, and numerous animals, valuable on account of their furs; and the plains are inhabited by buffaloes, wolves, and foxes.

On the banks of the rivers, there are factories for the convenience of trade with the natives; and near each of these are tents of different nations of Indians; some of whom are hunters, and others deal in provisions, wolf, buffalo, and fox-skins.

From the mouth of the *Saskatchiwine river*, the canoes proceed, in a northerly direction, through *Sturgeon lake*, and *Beaver lake*. The banks of the river are high, and clothed with cypress-trees; and the inhabitants of the adjacent districts are chiefly Knisteneaux Indians. This description of country, with some variation, prevails as far as the trading establishment of Fort Chepewyan, on the south-eastern bank of the *Lake of the Hills*.

Fort Chepewyan is the residence of a considerable number of persons, who are employed by the North-west Company. Except during a short time in the spring and autumn, when thousands of wild-fowl frequent the vicinity of the lake, these persons subsist almost wholly on fish. This they eat without the variety of any farinaceous grain for bread, any root, or vegetable; and without even salt to quicken its flavour.

Every year, in the autumn, the Indians meet the traders, at this and other forts, where they barter such furs, or provisions, as they have procured. They are here fitted out, by the traders, with such articles as they may want, after which they proceed to hunt beavers; and they return about the end of March or the beginning of April, when they are again fitted out as before. During the summer, most of these Indians retire to the barren grounds, and live there, with their relations and friends.

Account of the Knisteneaux and Chepewyan Indians.

When, in the year 1777, the Europeans first penetrated into the north-western regions of America, these two tribes of Indians were very numerous; but the small-pox, introduced among them by the strangers, proved so fatal, that, at the end of fifteen years, not more than seventy families were left.

The *Knisteneaux*, though at present few in number, occupy a great extent of country. They are of moderate stature, well-proportioned, and extremely active. Their complexion is of a copper-colour, and their hair black. In some of the tribes, the hair is cut into various forms, according to their fancy; and, by others, it is left in the long and lank flow of nature. These Indians, in general, pluck out their beards. Their eyes are black, keen, and penetrating; and their countenance is open and agreeable. Fond of decoration, they paint their bodies with different colours of red, blue, brown, white, and black.

Their dress is, at once, simple and commodious. It consists of tight leggings or leather-gaiters, which reach nearly to the hip; a strip of cloth or leather, about a foot wide, and five feet long, the ends of which are drawn inward, and hang behind and before, over a belt, tied round the waist for that purpose; a close vest or shirt, reaching down to the former garment, and bound at the waist by a broad strip of parchment, fastened with thongs behind; and a cap for the head, consisting of a piece of fur, or a small skin, with the tail of the animal, as a suspended ornament. A kind of robe is occasionally thrown over the whole of this dress, and serves them to wear by day, and to sleep in at night. These articles, with the addition of shoes and mittens, constitute their chief apparel. The materials vary, according to the season, and consist of dressed moose-skin, beaver-skins, prepared with the fur, or European woollens. The leather is neatly painted, and, in some parts, is fancifully worked with porcupine-quills and moose-deer hair. The shirts and leggings are adorned with fringe and tassels; and the shoes and mittens have somewhat of appropriate decoration, and are worked with a considerable degree of skill and taste. Their head-dresses are composed of the feathers of the swan, the eagle, and other birds. The teeth, horns, and claws of different animals, are also the occasional ornaments of their head and neck.

The female dress is composed of materials similar to those used by the men; but it is of a somewhat different form and arrangement. Several of the women have the skin of their faces tatooed or marked with three perpendicular lines: one from the centre of the chin to the under lip, and one on each side parallel to the corner of the mouth.

The Knisteneaux women are very comely. Their figure is generally well proportioned, and the regularity of their features would be acknowledged even by the civilized nations of Europe.

This people are naturally mild and affable. They are just in their dealings, not only among themselves, but with strangers. They are also generous and hospitable; and good-natured in the extreme, except when under the influence of spirituous liquors. Towards their children they are indulgent to a fault. The father, however, though he assumes no command over them, anxiously instructs them, in all the preparatory qualifications, for war and hunting; while the mother is equally attentive to her daughters, in teaching them every thing that is considered necessary to their character and situation.

The Knisteneaux have frequent feasts; and, at some of these, they offer dogs as sacrifices, and make large offerings of their property. The scene of their most important ceremonies is usually an enclosure on the bank of some river or lake, and in a conspicuous situation. On particular occasions they have private sacrifices in their houses. The ceremony of smoking precedes every affair of importance. When a feast is proposed to be given, the chief sends quills or small pieces of wood, as tokens of invitation, to such persons as he wishes to partake of it. At the appointed time the guests arrive, each bringing with him a dish or platter, and a knife; and they take their seats on each side of the chief. The pipe is then lighted, and the chief makes an equal division of every thing that is provided for the occasion. During the eating the chief sings, and accompanies his song with a tambourine. The guest who has first eaten his share of provision is considered as the most distinguished person. At all these feasts a small quantity of meat or drink is sacrificed, by throwing it into the fire or on the earth, before the guests begin to eat. It is expected that each person should devour the whole food that is allotted to him, how great soever the quantity may be; and those who are unable to do this, endeavour to prevail with their friends to assist them. Care is always taken that the bones are burned, as it would be considered a profanation, if the dogs were to touch them.

The medicinal virtues of many herbs are known to the Knisteneaux; and they apply the roots of plants and the bark of trees in the cure of various diseases. But there is among them a class of men, called conjurers, who monopolize the medical science; and who, blending mystery with their art, do not choose to communicate their knowledge.

Like all their other solemn ceremonials, the funeral rites of the Knisteneaux begin with smoking, and are concluded by a feast. The body is dressed in the best habiliments of the deceased, or his relatives, and is then deposited in a grave lined with branches: some domestic utensils are placed on it, and a kind of canopy is erected over it. During this ceremony, great lamentations are made; and, if the deceased is much regretted, the near relations cut off their hair, pierce the fleshy part of their thighs and arms with arrows, knives, &c. and blacken their faces with charcoal. The whole property belonging to him is destroyed, and the relations take, in exchange for the wearing apparel, any rags that will cover their nakedness.

The *Chepewyans* are a sober, timorous, and vagrant people, and of a disposition so selfish as sometimes to have excited suspicions of their integrity. Their complexion is swarthy; their features are coarse, and their hair is lank, but not always of a black colour; nor have they, universally, the piercing eye, which generally animates the Indian countenance. The women have a more agreeable aspect than the men; but, in consequence of their being accustomed, nine months in the year, to travel on snow-shoes, and to drag heavy sledges, their gait is awkward. They are very submissive to their husbands, who sometimes treat them with great cruelty. The men, in general, extract their beards; though some of them are seen to prefer a bushy beard to a smooth chin. They cut their hair in various forms, or leave it in a long, natural flow, according as caprice or fancy suggests. The women always have their hair of great length, and some of them are very attentive to its arrangement. Both sexes have blue or black marks, or from one to four straight lines on their cheeks or forehead, to distinguish the tribe to which they belong. These marks are either tatooed, or are made by drawing a thread, dipped in colour, beneath the skin.

Few people are more attentive to the comforts of dress than these. In winter they wear the skins of deer or fawns, prepared with the hair on, and rendered as fine and soft as chamois leather. In summer their apparel is of similar skins, but prepared without the hair. A ruff or tippet surrounds the neck; and the skin of the head of a deer forms a curious kind of cap.

Plurality of wives is allowed among the Chepewyans; and the ceremony of marriage is very simple. At a very early period, the girls are betrothed to such persons as the parents consider best able to support them. The desires of the women are never considered; and whenever a separation takes place, which sometimes happens, it depends entirely on the will of the husband.

These Indians are not remarkable for activity as hunters: this is owing to the ease with which they snare deer, and spear fish. They are not addicted to the use of spirituous liquors; and are, on the whole, an extremely peaceful tribe. Their weapons and domestic apparatus, in addition to articles procured from Europeans, are spears, bows and arrows, fishing-nets, and lines made of deer-skin thongs. Their amusements are but few. Their music is so inharmonious, and their dancing so awkward, that they might be supposed to be ashamed of both, as they seldom practise either. They shoot at marks, and play at different games; but they prefer sleeping to any of these: and the greatest part of their time is passed in procuring food, and resting after the toil of obtaining it.

The notion which these people entertain of the creation of the world is a very singular one. They believe that the globe was originally one vast ocean, inhabited by no living creature, except an immense bird, whose eyes were of fire, whose glances were lightning, and the clapping of whose wings was thunder. On the descent of this bird to the ocean, and at the instant of touching it, they say that the earth arose, and remained on the surface of the waters. This omnipotent bird then called forth all the variety of animals from the earth, except the Chepewyans, who were produced from a dog; and to this circumstance they attribute their aversion to dog's-flesh. The tradition proceeds to relate, that the great bird, having finished his work, made an arrow, which was to be preserved with great care, and to remain untouched; but that the Chepewyans were so devoid of understanding, as to carry it away; and this sacrilege so enraged the bird, that he has never since appeared. They believe also, that, in ancient times, their ancestors lived till their feet were worn out with walking, and their throats with eating; and they describe a deluge, in which the waters spread over the whole earth, except the highest mountains, on the tops of which the Chepewyans preserved themselves.

They are superstitious in an extreme; and almost every action of their lives, however trivial, is more or less influenced by some superstitious notion. They believe in a good and evil spirit; and in a future state of rewards and punishments. They assert that the souls of persons deceased pass into another world, where they arrive at a large river, on which they embark, in a stone canoe, and that a gentle current bears them on to an extensive lake, in the centre of which is a beautiful island. Within view of this island they receive that judgment for their conduct during life, which terminates their state. If their good actions predominate, they are landed upon the island, where there is to be no end of their happiness. But if their bad actions prevail, the stone canoe sinks, and leaves them up to their chins in the water, to behold and regret the reward which is enjoyed by the good; and eternally to struggle, but with unavailing endeavours, to reach the bliss from which they are for ever excluded.

Twenty-fourth Day's Instruction

NORTH-WESTERN TERRITORY CONCLUDED.

Fort Chepewyan was, for eight years, the head quarters of Mr. (now Sir Alexander) Mackenzie, who held an official situation under the North-west Company; and who, from this place, made two important and laborious excursions, one northward, to the Frozen Sea; and the other westward, to the Pacific Ocean.

Narrative of a Voyage from Fort Chepewyan, along the Rivers to the north Frozen Ocean.

From Voyages through the Continent of North America, by Alexander Mackenzie.

In the first of his excursions, Mr Mackenzie embarked at *Fort Chepewyan,* about nine o'clock in the morning of the 3d of June, 1789. His vessel was a canoe formed of birch-bark, and his crew consisted of one German and four Canadians, two of whom were attended by their wives. He was also accompanied, in a small canoe, by an Indian chief and his two wives. The men were engaged to serve in the twofold capacity of interpreters and hunters.

Mr. Mackenzie had also with him a canoe which he had equipped for the purpose of trade, and had given in charge to M. Le Roux, one of the Company's clerks. In this canoe was shipped part of his provision, the clothing necessary on the voyage, a requisite assortment of articles of merchandise as presents, to ensure them a friendly reception among the Indians; and such arms and ammunition as were considered necessary for defence, as well as for the use of the hunters.

Crossing the south-western extremity of the *Lake of the Hills,* they entered the *Slave river,* and steered, along that river, in a northerly direction. On the ensuing day they arrived at the foot of a succession of rapids; and, in the course of twelve miles, were obliged five times to unload the canoes, and carry the luggage considerable distances overland. One of the Indian canoes was borne, by the fury of the current, down the last of the cataracts, and was dashed to pieces. The hunters here killed seven geese, four ducks, and a beaver. The progress of the boats was much impeded by ice.

The banks of the river, both above and below the rapids, were covered with wood. This was more particularly the case on the western side, where the land was low, and had a black and rich soil. The eastern banks were somewhat elevated; and the soil was a yellow clay, mixed with gravel. At a little distance from the banks were extensive plains, frequented by numerous herds of buffaloes; and the woods, adjacent to the river, were inhabited by elks and rein-deer. The habitations of beavers were seen in all the small lakes and rivers; and the swamps adjacent to the Slave-river, were sometimes covered with wild-fowl.

In the morning of the 9th the voyagers arrived at the *Great Slave Lake*. Here they experienced a most uncomfortable change in the weather, which became extremely cold. The lake was still frozen; and they were obliged to delay their progress for several days, until they could effect a passage across it. In the mean while they occupied themselves in fishing and hunting, for the purpose of adding to their stock of provisions. They had more or less rain almost every day.

On the 20th the ice had somewhat given way, and they recommenced their voyage, in a north-westerly direction. A few days after this, they landed on the main land, at three lodges of *Red-knife Indians*, so called from the copper knives which they use. M. le Roux purchased, of these Indians, some packs of beaver and marten-skins; and Mr. Mackenzie had several consultations with them concerning the country he was about to traverse; but he could obtain from them no information that was important to the objects of his expedition. He, however, engaged one of them, as a guide, in navigating the bays of the lake.

The musquitoes were now so troublesome as to occasion the voyagers much inconvenience. After having, with considerable difficulty, navigated the northern side of the lake, they entered the mouth of a river, which lay in a westerly direction. On the 2d of July, they perceived, at a distance before them, a high mountain, or rather a cluster of mountains, which stretched southward, as far as the view could reach, and had their tops lost in the clouds. The declivities of these mountains were covered with wood; and they were sprinkled with glistening patches of snow, which, at first, Mr. Mackenzie mistook for white stones.

During their progress the voyagers saw several Indian encampments. The current, in some places, was so rapid as to produce a hissing noise, somewhat like the boiling of a kettle. Though it was now the month of July, the weather was extremely cold. The sun set at seven minutes before ten, and rose at seven minutes before two in the morning.

Having passed several islands, and, not long afterwards having seen, on the northern shore, the smoke of several fires, the voyagers made every exertion to approach the spot; and, as they drew near, they observed a party of Indians, running about in great apparent confusion. Some of them were endeavouring to escape into the woods, and others were hurrying to their canoes. The hunters landed, and, in the Chepewyan language, addressed the few who had not escaped; but, so great was their terror, that they did not appear to understand it. When, however, they found it was impossible to conceal themselves, they made signs to the strangers to keep at a distance. With these the latter complied, and not only unloaded their canoe, but pitched their tents, before the Indians made any attempt to approach them. After considerable difficulty they became reconciled; and, as soon as their fears were dissipated, they called their fugitive companions from the woods.

The inhabitants of this place were five families of *Slave* and *Dog-rib Indians*. They were unacquainted with the use of tobacco and ardent spirits; but were delighted to receive, as presents, knives, beads, awls, rings, fire-steels, flints, and hatchets; and, after a little while, they became so familiar, that it was difficult to keep them out of the tents.

These Indians seemed totally ignorant respecting the distant parts of the river, for they believed its course to be so long that it would occupy the voyagers several years to reach the sea. They also described the intervening regions to be inhabited by monsters of the most horrid shapes and destructive powers. One of them, however, by the bribe of a small kettle, an axe, a knife; and some other articles, was induced to accompany the voyagers as a guide.

They amused the strangers by dancing and singing; but neither the dance nor the song had much variety. The men and women arranged themselves promiscuously in a ring. The former had each a bone-dagger, or a piece of stick, between the fingers of his right hand, which he kept extended above his head, in continual motion; while he held his left in an horizontal direction. They leaped about, and threw themselves into various antic postures, to the measure of their music, bringing their heels close together at every pause. Sometimes the men howled, like wild beasts; and he who continued to howl the longest, appeared to be considered the best performer. The women suffered their arms to hang down, as if they were without the power of motion.

These people are of middle stature, thin, ugly, and ill made, particularly about the legs. Many of them appeared to be in a very unhealthy state, owing, probably, to their filthiness. As far as could be discerned, through the grease and dirt that covered them, they were of fairer complexion than the generality of Indians. The women have two double lines of black or blue colour upon each cheek, from the ear to the nose; and the gristle of the nose is perforated, so as to admit a goose-quill, or a small piece of wood to be passed through it. The clothing of these Indians is made of the dressed skins of the rein or moose-deer. Some of them, says Mr. Mackenzie, were decorated with a neat embroidery of porcupine-quills and hair, coloured red, black, yellow, and white; and they had bracelets for their wrists and arms, made of wood, horn, or bone. Round their head they had a kind of band, embroidered with porcupine quills, and ornamented with the claws of bears and wild-fowl.

Their huts or lodges are very simple. A few poles, supported by forks, and forming a semicircle, with some branches or pieces of bark as a covering, constitute the whole of the architecture. Two of these huts are constructed facing each other, and a fire is made between them. Among the furniture are dishes of wood, bark, or horn; and vessels in which they cook their food, narrow at the top, and wide at the bottom. The latter are formed of roots of the spruce fir-tree, so closely interwoven as to hold water. This people have also small leather bags, to hold their embroidered work, their lines, and fishing-nets. They twist the fibres of willow-bark, and the sinews of rein-deer, into fishing-lines; and they make fishing-hooks of horn, wood, or bone. Their weapons for hunting are bows and arrows, spears, daggers, and clubs. They kindle fire, by striking together a piece of white or yellow pyrites and a flint-stone, over a piece of touchwood.

Their canoes are small, pointed at both ends, flat-bottomed, and covered in the fore part. They are made of the bark of the birch-tree, and of fir-wood; but are so light, that the man whom one of these vessels bears on the water, is able to carry it overland, without any difficulty.

On the 9th of July the voyagers had an interview with a party of Indians, who were more pleasing, both in appearance and manners, than any they had hitherto seen. They were stout, healthy, and clean in their persons; and their utensils and weapons resembled those of the Slave and Dog-rib Indians. They obtained iron, in small pieces, from the Esquimaux. Their garments were bordered with a kind of fringe; and their shirts tapered to a point, from the belt downward. One of the men whom Mr. Mackenzie saw, was clad in a shirt made of the skins of musk-rats. These Indians tie their hair in a very singular manner. That which grows on the temples, or on the fore part of the head, is formed into two queues, which hang down before the ears: and that on the crown of the head, is fashioned, in the same manner, towards the back of the neck, and is tied, with the rest of the hair, at some distance from the head. The women, and indeed some of the men, suffer their hair to hang loose on their shoulders.

Mr. Mackenzie prevailed with one of these Indians to accompany him on his voyage; and this man, who was one of the most intelligent Indians he had seen, stated that it would be requisite to sleep ten nights before they could reach the sea; and that, after three nights, the voyagers would reach a settlement of Esquimaux, with whom his nation had formerly made war.

He accompanied Mr. Mackenzie in a canoe; and two of his companions followed in two other canoes. The latter sung their native songs; and this new guide was so much enlivened by these, that the antics he performed, in keeping time to the singing, excited continual alarm lest he should overset his boat. He afterwards went on board Mr. Mackenzie's canoe, where he began to perform an Esquimaux dance, to the no small alarm of the voyagers.

Lower down the river, Mr. Mackenzie had an interview with a party of Indians called *Quarrellers*. They consisted of about forty men, women, and children, and, at first, seemed inclined to offer resistance; but they were soon pacified by presents, of which blue beads were the most acceptable articles.

These Indians represented the distance, over land, to the northern sea, as not very great; and the distance to the sea, westward, (the Pacific Ocean,) to be still shorter.

The river here flowed between high rocks. Indeed, in this part of the country, the banks were, in general, lofty. In some places they were nearly naked, and in others thickly clad with small trees, particularly fir-trees and birch. The tops of the mountains, towards the north, were covered with snow. The channels of the river were so various, that the voyagers were at a loss which to take. They, however, directed their course chiefly towards the north-west.

In this part of the voyage, Mr. Mackenzie was induced to sit up all night, for the purpose of observing the sun: which, at half-past twelve o'clock, was considerably above the horizon.

At four in the morning he landed at three Indian huts. These were of an oval form, each about fifteen feet long, and ten feet wide; and in the middle, only, they were high enough for a person to stand upright. In one part of each the ground was strewed with willow branches, probably as a bed for the family. The door or entrance was about two feet and a half high, and had a covered way or porch, five feet in length; so that it was necessary to creep on all fours, in order to get into or out of these curious habitations. In the top of each hut there was a hole, about eighteen inches square, which served the threefold purpose of a window, a chimney, and occasionally a door. These edifices were formed of wood, covered with branches and grass. On each side of the huts were a few square holes in the ground, probably contrived for the preservation of the winter stock of provisions.

On the 12th of July, the voyagers had reached what they imagined to be an immense lake; and, shortly after they had retired to rest, at night, the man on watch called them up, to remove the baggage, on account of the sudden rising of the water. Some fish were afterwards caught, about the size of a herring, and resembling a species of fish which abounds in Hudson's Bay. On the ensuing day, Mr. Mackenzie ascended an adjacent hill, and saw much ice; and, towards the north-west, two small islands in the ice. On the 14th, many animals were seen in the water, which, at first, were supposed to be pieces of floating-ice, but which were afterwards ascertained to be whales. Hence it became evident that this apparent lake was a part of the *Northern Ocean*. Mr. Mackenzie sailed upon it, to some distance from the shore, and landed at the eastern extremity of an island, which he called *Whale Island*, and which was about seven leagues in length, but not more than a mile broad. The ebbing and flowing of the tide were here observed. He subsequently landed on another island, where an Indian burying-place was observed. The latitude of the shore of this northern ocean, was ascertained to be 69 degrees 14 minutes, north; and the longitude 135 degrees, west.

Narrative of the Return of Mr. Mackenzie *from
the Frozen Ocean to Fort Chepewyan.*

This gentlemen embarked, on his return, at half-past one o'clock, of the 21st of July, the weather being extremely cold and unpleasant. At ten, the canoes re-entered the river; but the opposing current was so strong, that the men were obliged, for a considerable distance, to tow them along. The land on both sides was elevated, and almost perpendicular. Much rain fell.

Mr. Mackenzie subsequently encamped near an Indian village, the inhabitants of which were at first considerably alarmed. They afterwards, however, became familiar. Some of them, having kindled a fire, laid themselves round it, to sleep; and, notwithstanding the excessive coldness of the climate, they had neither skins nor garments to cover them.

The people of this nation are continually at variance with the Esquimaux, who are said to take every opportunity of attacking them, when not in a state to defend themselves. From their account it appeared that a strong party of Esquimaux occasionally ascended the river, in large canoes, to search for flint-stones, which they used as points for their spears and arrows. These Esquimaux were said to wear their hair short; and to have a hole perforated on each side of their mouth, in a line with the under lip, and to place beads in the holes, by way of ornament. Their weapons were bows, arrows, and spears; but they also used slings, from which they threw stones with great dexterity.

The weather was now fine; and Mr. Mackenzie and his men renewed their voyage on the 27th of July. At seven o'clock they once more reached the rapids. Here they found three families of Indians, from whom they obtained some information respecting the adjacent country, and particularly respecting a river which was stated to run on the opposite side of the mountains, in a westerly direction; and which, from the description given of it, Mr. Mackenzie conjectured to be that called *Cook's River*.

At a subsequent interview, with another party of Indians, a misunderstanding took place, in which the Indians seized one of Mr. Mackenzie's boats, and dragged it on shore. Peace, however, being restored, Mr. Mackenzie endeavoured to obtain some further intelligence concerning the river to the westward. His enquiries, however, were to little purpose. The account given by these Indians was very vague; and their description of the inhabitants of the country adjacent to it, was extremely absurd. These, it was stated, were of gigantic stature, and furnished with wings; which, however, they never employed in flying: that they fed on large birds, which they killed with the greatest ease; though common men would be the certain victims of the voracity of such birds. The Indians also described the people who inhabited the mouth of the river, as possessing the extraordinary power of killing with their eyes; and as each being able to devour a large beaver at a single meal. They added that canoes, or vessels of immense size, visited that place. They did not, however, pretend to relate these particulars from their own observation, but from the report of other Indians; for they had themselves never ventured beyond the first range of mountains, from their own dwellings. It, however, appeared to Mr. Mackenzie that, either the Indians knew more of this country than they chose to communicate, or that his interpreter, who had long been tired of the voyage, gave him purposely a wrong account, in order that he might not be induced to extend his excursions.

As soon as the conference was ended, the Indians began to dance; and, in this pastime, old and young, male and female, continued their exertions, till their strength was exhausted. Their actions were accompanied by various noises, in imitation of the rein-deer, the bear, and the wolf.

When the dancing was ended, Mr. Mackenzie assumed an angry tone, expressed his suspicions that information had been purposely withheld from him; and concluded with a threat, that if they did not give him a more satisfactory account, he would compel one of them to accompany him, for the purpose of pointing out the road to the other river. No sooner did they hear this declaration, than they all, in a moment, became sick; and answered, in a faint tone, that they knew no more than what they had already communicated. Finding it useless to persevere in his enquiries, he ceased them; and having purchased a few beaver-skins, and obtained a plentiful supply of food, he continued his voyage.

On the 1st of August, the weather was clear and cold. This was the first night, for many weeks, that the stars had been visible. Nine days afterwards, they arrived in the vicinity of a range of lofty mountains. Accompanied by a young Indian, Mr. Mackenzie landed, for the purpose of ascending one of them. They passed through a wood, chiefly of spruce-firs, so thick that it was with difficulty they could penetrate it. After they had walked more than an hour, the underwood decreased; and was succeeded by birch and poplar trees, the largest and tallest that Mr. Mackenzie had ever seen. The mountains, which had been concealed, by the woods, from their view, were again visible, but, apparently, at as great a distance as when they were first seen from the river. This was a very mortifying circumstance, for Mr. Mackenzie and his companion had been walking nearly three hours. The Indian expressed great anxiety to return; for his shoes and leggings had been torn to pieces, and he was alarmed at the idea of having to proceed all night, through this trackless country. Mr. Mackenzie was, however, determined to proceed, and to return the next day. As they approached the mountains, the ground became marshy; and they waded, in water and grass, up to their knees, till they came within a mile of them; when, suddenly, Mr. Mackenzie sank, up to his armpits, in mud and water. Having, with considerable difficulty, extricated himself, he found it impossible to proceed any further. To cross this unexpected morass was impracticable; and it extended so far, both to the right and left, that he could not attempt to make the circuit of either extremity. He therefore determined to return; and, about midnight, he again reached the river, excessively fatigued with his fruitless expedition.

In the afternoon of the 13th, the voyagers continued their route, and with very favourable weather. They passed several places, where fires had recently been made; and beyond these, they observed a party of Indians, drawing their canoes on the beach, and endeavouring to escape into the woods. These had been so much terrified, by the appearance of the strangers, and the report of their guns, in shooting wild-geese, that they left, on the beach, several weapons and articles of dress. Mr. Mackenzie directed his men to go into the woods, in search of them, but in vain; for they had fled too rapidly to be overtaken.

The voyagers had, for some time, subsisted chiefly on fish, which they had caught in their nets, and on deer and other game, which the hunters had killed.

On Saturday, the 12th of September, at three o'clock in the afternoon, they again arrived at *Fort Chepewyan*; and thus concluded an arduous voyage, which, in the whole, had occupied the space of one hundred and two days.

The Western Coast of America, from California to Behring's Strait.

On the western coast of North America, and lying between the twenty-second and thirty-second degrees of latitude, is a very singular promontory, near seven hundred miles in length, called *California*. It is at present subject to Spain; and is separated from New Mexico, by the *Gulf of California*, an arm of the sea, which is navigable by vessels of the largest size. The general surface of the country is barren, rugged, overrun with hills, rocks, and sand-banks, and unfit for agriculture. But, in a few places, where the Spanish missionaries have established settlements, the lands are fertile, and singularly productive of maize, barley, and peas. The plains, in the interior, are noted for the production of rock-salt.

The Indians of California are very expert in the use of the bow, and subsist chiefly by hunting and fishing. Their skin is dark, and they paint their bodies, by way of ornament: they also pierce their ears, and wear in them trinkets of various kinds. The wealthiest of them wear cloaks made of sea-otter skins, which cover the loins, and reach below their middle. Others, however, have only a piece of cloth round their waist, and a little cloak, formed of rabbit-skin, which covers their shoulders, and is tied beneath the chin. The huts of these Indians are the most miserable that can be imagined. Their form is circular; and about six feet wide and four feet high. In the construction of them, stakes, eight or ten feet long, are driven into the ground, and are brought together so as to form an arch at the top; and trusses of straw, badly arranged upon these stakes, defend the inhabitants from the wind and rain.

Near the Spanish settlement of *Monterey*, in north latitude 30 degrees 35 minutes, M. de la Perouse, the French navigator, states that the soil is tolerably fertile and productive; and the climate is mild, though foggy. This part of California produces, in abundance, olives, figs, pomegranates, grapes, and peaches; the trees of which have all been planted by the missionaries. Beyond Monterey, the interior of the country is covered with immense forests of pines and other trees.

North of California is *New Albion*, a country so called by Sir Francis Drake, who originally discovered it in the year 1578. It was visited about two hundred years afterwards, by Captain Cook. The country is mountainous; and, during the winter and spring, the mountains are covered with snow. The valleys and the grounds along the sea-coast, are clad with trees, and appear like a vast forest.

Captain Cook sailed northward along the coast of New Albion, and anchored his vessels in an inlet called *Nootka Sound*. The inhabitants of the adjacent country approached his ships, and offered for sale the skins of various animals; garments of different kinds, some of fur, and others formed of the bark of trees. But, of all the articles brought to market, the most extraordinary, were human skulls, and hands not quite stripped of their flesh, some of which had evident marks of having been upon the fire. The articles which the natives took, in exchange for their commodities, were knives, chisels, pieces of iron and tin, nails, looking-glasses, buttons, or any kind of metal. Though the commerce was, in general, carried on with mutual honesty, there were some among these people who were much inclined to theft. And they were extremely dangerous thieves; for, possessing sharp iron instruments, they could cut a hook from a tackle, or any other piece of iron from a rope, the moment that the backs of the English were turned; and the dexterity with which they conducted their operations of this nature, frequently eluded the most cautious vigilance. In the progress of the commerce, they would deal for nothing but metal; and, at length, brass was so eagerly sought for, in preference to iron, that, before the navigators quitted the place, scarcely a bit of brass was left in the ships, except what belonged to the different instruments. Whole suits of clothes were stripped of every button; bureaus were deprived of their furniture; copper-kettles, tin-canisters, candlesticks, and whatever of the like kind could be found, all were seized and carried off.

On Captain Cook's first arrival in this inlet, he had honoured it with the name of *King George's Sound*; but as it was called *Nootka*, by the natives, the latter appellation has since been generally adopted. The climate appeared to be much milder than that on the east coast of America, in the same parallel of latitude. With regard to trees, those of which the woods are chiefly composed, are the Canadian pine and white cypress; of the land animals, the most common were bears, deer, foxes, and wolves. The sea animals, which were seen off the coast, were whales, porpoises, seals, and sea-otters. Birds, in general, were not only rare as to the different species, but few in number.

With respect to the inhabitants, their persons are generally under the common stature; but they are usually full or plump, though without being muscular. From their bringing to sale human skulls and bones, it may be inferred that they treat their enemies with a degree of brutal cruelty. To the navigators, however, they appeared to be a docile, courteous, and good-natured people. The chief employments of the men, were those of fishing, and of killing land or sea animals for the sustenance of themselves and their families; while the women were occupied in manufacturing flaxen or woollen garments, and in other domestic offices.

North of Nootka Sound is *Port St. François*, which was visited by M. de la Perouse. There is, at this place, a deep bay which affords a safe anchorage. During three or four months of the year, vegetation near Port St. François is vigorous. In the interior of the country are forests of stately trees; and mountains of granite rise from the sea, and to such an elevation that their summits are capped with snow. Some of the highest mountains were computed by M. de la Perouse, to be ten thousand feet in perpendicular height.

The inhabitants of this part of America are more robust, and better proportioned, than the Californians. The faces of the women are, however, disfigured by having, through the under lip, a piece of wood, by way of ornament. They paint their body and face, tatoo themselves, and pierce their ears and the cartilage of their nose, for the purpose of placing ornaments in them. Their food consists chiefly of game and fish. Their huts, or cabins, are constructed of rushes, or the branches of trees, and are covered with bark. The weapons of the men are bows, javelins, and daggers. The women are chiefly employed in domestic concerns: their dress consists of a leathern shirt, and a mantle of skins; and their feet are generally naked.

The inhabitants of the country, adjacent to an inlet which Captain Cook named *Prince William's Sound*, appeared to have a strong resemblance to the Esquimaux and Greenlanders. Their canoes, their weapons, and their implements for fishing and hunting, are exactly similar, in materials and construction, to those used in Greenland; and the animals are, in general, similar to those that are found at Nootka. Humming-birds frequently flew about the ships while at anchor. Waterfowl were in considerable abundance: but torsk and holibut were almost the only kinds of fish that were caught. Vegetables were few in number; and the trees were chiefly the Canadian and spruce pine.

North of Prince William's Sound, Captain Cook entered an inlet, which, it was hoped, would be found to communicate either with Baffin's or Hudson's Bay to the east; but, after an examination of it, to the distance of seventy leagues from the sea, it was proved to be a river. It is now called *Cook's River*.

The inhabitants who were seen during the examinations of this river, appeared to resemble those of Prince William's Sound. They essentially differed from those of Nootka Sound, both in their persons and language. The only articles seen among them, which were not their own manufacture, were a few glass beads, the iron points of their spears, and their knives of the same metal. A very beneficial fur-trade, might be carried on with the inhabitants of this vast coast; but, without a practical northern passage, the situation is too remote to render such a trade of any advantage to Great Britain.

A long peninsula, called *Alyaska*, extends, from the mouth of Cook's River, in a westerly direction; and, from its extremity a chain of islands stretches almost to the coast of Asia. The main land was observed, by Captain Cook, to be mountainous; and some of the mountains towered above the clouds. One of them, of conical shape, was discovered to be a volcano: smoke issued from its summit.

Northward of Alyaska is a promontory to which Captain Cook gave the name of *Cape Newenham*. At this place he directed one of his lieutenants to land: this gentleman ascended the highest hill within sight, but from its summit he could not see a tree or shrub of any description. The lower grounds, however, were not destitute of grass and herbage.

At the entrance of *Behring's Strait*, is a point of land which Captain Cook called *Cape Prince of Wales*, and which is remarkable as being the most westerly extremity of America hitherto explored. It is not forty miles distant from the coast of Siberia. From near this place, Captain Cook crossed to the opposite shore of Asia; and he continued to traverse the Frozen Sea, in various directions, and through innumerable difficulties, till, at length, the increase of the ice prevented his further progress northward, and he returned into the Pacific Ocean.

Twenty-fifth Day's Instruction

DAVIS'S STRAIT AND BAFFIN'S BAY.

Several expeditions have, at different times, been fitted out, for the purpose of ascertaining whether there exists a north-west passage, or navigable communication, between the Atlantic and Pacific Oceans. The supposed points of communication are the north-western side of Baffin's Bay, on the east, and Behring's Strait on the west. Within the last four years the attention of the public has been more particularly called to this subject, by the fitting out, and progress, of two successive expeditions into Baffin's Bay. To the commander of each, instructions were given that he should, if possible, effect a passage thence, westward, into the Pacific. The first of these expeditions, under the command of Captain Ross, sailed from England in the month of April, 1818: the other, under Captain Parry, who, in the previous expedition, had accompanied Captain Ross as the second in command, sailed on the 10th of May, 1819. Some of the most interesting adventures which they each experienced, and of the most important discoveries which they effected, will now require our attention.

A Narrative of Captain Ross's *Voyage of Discovery, for the purpose of exploring Baffin's Bay, and enquiring into the probability of a North-west Passage.*

The Isabella and Alexander, commanded by Captain Ross and Lieutenant Parry, passed *Cape Farewell*, the south-eastern extremity of Greenland, on the 26th of May, 1818. The voyagers had previously seen a great number of icebergs, or islands of ice, of various shape and size, and of singular and grotesque figure. The height of one of them was estimated at three hundred and twenty-five feet; and a torrent of water was pouring down its side. On another, to which the ships were, for a while, made fast, a stratum of gravel, and stones of various kinds was observed.

Whilst the vessels were near this iceberg, which was in latitude 68 degrees, 22 minutes, they were visited by some Esquimaux, inhabitants of the adjacent country. From these persons they learnt that it had remained aground since the preceding year; and that there was ice all the way thence to *Disco Island*.

In the evening of the 12th of June, the weather being clear and serene, the sky and the water presented one of the most beautiful scenes that can be imagined. The former, near the horizon, was interspersed with light and fleecy clouds, which decreased gradually in colour and density, according to their height; until, in the zenith, they disappeared entirely, and there the sky assumed a rich cerulean blue. The water, on the other hand, presented a spectacle superbly grand. Let any one fancy himself (says Captain Ross) in the midst of an immense plain, extending further than the eye can penetrate, and filled with masses of ice, which present a greater variety of form than the most fertile imagination can conceive; and as various in size as in shape, from the minutest fragments, to stupendous islands, more than one hundred feet in perpendicular height above the surface of the ocean.

In the afternoon of the 14th of June, being near the Danish settlement, on *Kron Prins Island*, in latitude 63 degrees, 54 minutes, the governor of the settlement came on board the Isabella. This person stated that the weather of the preceding winter had been unusually severe; and that, during his residence of eleven years, in Greenland, the intensity of the cold had gradually continued to increase. The whole population of the island consisted of himself and family, six Danes, and one hundred Esquimaux, whose occupation consisted chiefly in the capture of whales and seals.

The vessels proceeded northward, along the edge of the ice, through a crooked and narrow channel, in the midst of a firm field of ice, and a tremendous ridge of icebergs.

At *Wayat's* or *Hare Island*, the astronomical instruments were landed, and some important errors, both of latitude and longitude, were discovered and corrected. Thirty or forty whale-ships were seen fastened to the icebergs along the shore of this island. The only four-footed animals observed on it were white hares and a fox: the birds were ptarmigans, snipes, snow-buntings, and larks.

Beyond Wayat's Island the ships were surrounded by ice of various and extensive forms; and much skill, ardour, and perseverance, were manifested by the navigators working through the narrow channels and floes. On the 23d, and at the distance of ten miles north of Wayat, they reached *Four Island Point*, where they found several whalers which had been stopped by the ice.

A sort of Danish factory was established at this spot, and some Indian huts were seen; but they were in ruins and apparently deserted. Captain Ross sent to the shore one of his crew, an Esquimaux, named John Sacheuse. This man, who had been resident nearly two years in England, and had acquired some knowledge of the English language, had been taken on board the Isabella as an interpreter.

He found a village, consisting of a few huts, formed of seal-skins, and sufficient for the residence of about fifty persons. Being desirous of obtaining from these persons a sledge and dogs, in exchange for a rifle-musket, he conducted seven of them, in their canoes, to the ship. As soon as the bargain was made, they went on shore, and returned, with the sledge and dogs, in a larger canoe, rowed by five women in a standing posture, and all dressed in deer-skins. These people were highly pleased with the treatment they received; and, having partaken of some refreshment in the cabin, they danced on the deck with the sailors, to the animating strains of a Shetland fiddler. Two of the women were daughters of a Danish resident, by an Esquimaux woman: one of the men was the son of a Dane; and they were all of the colour of Mulattoes. After the dance, coffee was served; and, at eight o'clock, the party returned to land.

The progress of the vessels had hitherto been much impeded by the state of the ice. This, however, now began to separate, and they once more proceeded on their voyage; passing among hundreds of icebergs, of extraordinary colours, and the most fantastical shapes.

In latitude 74 degrees 30 minutes, the Isabella was jammed in by the ice, and sustained a severe pressure; being lifted several feet out of the water, but she did not receive any material injury. On the 31st of July, whales were seen in great numbers; and, the boats being sent in pursuit of them, one was killed: it measured forty-six feet in length, and yielded thirteen tons of blubber.

On the 6th and 7th of August, the two ships were again in great danger from the ice. Whilst they were in the midst of the icebergs, they were driven, by a gale of wind, so forcibly against each other, that their sterns came violently in contact, and crushed to pieces a boat that could not be removed in time; and, had not the vessels themselves been excessively strong, they must have been totally destroyed. Attempts were made to liberate them by sawing through the ice: not long after the commencement of the operation, two immense masses of ice came violently in contact, and one of them, fifty feet in height, suddenly broke. Its elevated part fell back with a terrible crash; and overwhelmed, with its ruins, the very spot which the officers had marked out as a place of safety for the ships. Soon afterwards the ice opened, and they were once more out of danger.

The gale having abated, and the weather, which of late had been snowy, having cleared up, land was seen in latitude 75 degrees 54 minutes; and on the 9th of August, the voyagers beheld, at a distance, upon the ice, some people who seemed to be hallooing to the ships. At first they were supposed to be shipwrecked sailors, whose vessel had perished in the late gale; the ships, therefore, were steered nearer to the ice, and the colours were hoisted. It was, however, now discovered, that they were natives of the country, drawn by dogs on sledges, and with wonderful velocity.

When they had approached near enough to the ships, for Sacheuse to be heard, he hailed them in his own language, and they answered him; but neither party seemed to be intelligible. For some time the strangers remained silent; but, on the ships' tacking, they set up a shout, and wheeled off, with amazing swiftness, towards the land.

On the ensuing day eight sledges were seen to approach the ships. Sacheuse volunteered his services to go on the ice, with presents: this was done in the hope of bringing the people to a parley. They halted at some distance from the ships, and by the edge of a canal or chasm in the ice, which prevented any fear or danger of attack from either party. Sacheuse soon discovered that these Indians spoke a dialect of his own language; and he invited them to approach nearer, but they replied, "No, no, go you away;" and one of them, drawing a knife out of his boot, exclaimed: "Go away; I can kill you." Sacheuse told them that he wished to be their friend; and, as a proof of it, he threw them, across the canal, some strings of beads, and a checked shirt. These were beheld with great distrust, and Sacheuse threw them a knife. They approached with caution, took up the knife, and then shouted and pulled their noses. These actions were imitated by Sacheuse, who, in return, called out, "Heigh-yaw!" pulling his nose, with the same gesture. They then pointed to the shirt, and asked him of what skin it was made; but some time elapsed before they would venture to touch it. After this they pointed to the ships, and eagerly enquired, "What are those great creatures? Do they come from the sun or the moon? Do they give us light by night or by day?" Sacheuse said that they were houses made of wood; but this, they replied, could not be the case, for the creatures were alive: they had been seen to flap their wings. Sacheuse again assured them of the truth of all he had told them, and that he was a man like themselves; then pointing towards the south, he said he came, in those houses, from a distant country in that direction. To this they replied, "No, that cannot be: there is nothing but ice there."

On Sacheuse asking these Indians who they were, they replied that they were men, and that they lived in a country towards which they pointed (in the north:) that they had there plenty of water; and that they had come to the present spot, to catch seals and sea-unicorns.

Sacheuse, wishing to become better acquainted with them, returned to the ship, for a plank, to enable him to cross over the chasm. He crossed it; but, on approaching them, they entreated that he would not touch them, as, in that case, they should certainly die. One of them, however, more courageous than the rest, ventured to touch his hand; then, pulling his own nose, he set up a loud shout, in which he was joined by Sacheuse and the other three.

The whole of the natives, eight in number, now came forward, and were met by the commanders of the vessels, and the other officers; but they were, evidently, in a state of great alarm, until the ceremony of pulling noses had been gone through by both parties, shouting, at the same time, *heigh-yaw*! With this people the pulling of noses is a mode of friendly salutation; and their interjection of "heigh-yaw!" is an expression of surprise and pleasure.

The officers gave to the foremost of the natives a looking-glass and a knife; and presented similar articles to the others, as they came up in succession. On seeing their faces in the glasses, their astonishment appeared extreme. They looked round in silence, for a moment, at each other, and at their visitors, and immediately afterwards set up a general shout: this was succeeded by a loud laugh, expressive of delight and surprise. Having, at length, acquired some degree of confidence, they advanced, and, in return for knives, glasses, and beads, gave their own knives, sea-unicorn's horns, and sea-horse teeth.

On approaching the ship, they halted, and were evidently much terrified; and one of the party, after surveying the Isabella, and examining every part of her with his eyes, thus addressed her, in a loud tone: "Who are you? Where do you come from? Is it from the sun or the moon?" pausing between every question, and pulling his nose with the greatest solemnity. This ceremony was repeated, in succession, by all the rest.

Sacheuse again assured them that the ships were only wooden houses; and he showed them the boat, which had been hauled on the ice, for the purpose of being repaired, explaining to them, that it was a smaller vessel of the same kind. This immediately arrested their attention: they advanced to the boat, and examined her, and the carpenter's tools and the oars, very minutely, each object, in its turn, exciting the most ludicrous ejaculations of surprise. The boat was then ordered to be launched into the sea, with a man in it, and hauled up again; at the sight of this operation there seemed no bounds to their clamour. The cable and the ice-anchor, the latter a heavy piece of iron, shaped like the letter S, excited much interest. They tried in vain to remove it; and they eagerly enquired of what skins the cable was made.

By this time the officers of both the ships had surrounded the Indians; while the bow of the Isabella, which was close to the ice, was crowded with sailors; and a more ludicrous, yet more interesting scene, was, perhaps, never beheld, than that which took place whilst the Indians were viewing the ship. Nor is it possible to convey to the imagination any thing like a just representation of the wild amazement, joy, and fear, by which they were successively agitated. The circumstance, however, which chiefly excited their admiration, was a sailor going aloft; for they kept their eyes intently fixed upon him, till he had reached the summit of the mast. The sails, which hung loose, they supposed to be skins.

After this, they were conducted to the foot of a rope-ladder suspended from the deck of the ship; and the mode of ascending it was shown to them; but a considerable time elapsed before they could be prevailed with to ascend. At length one of them went up, and he was followed by the rest. The wonders with which they were now surrounded, excited additional astonishment.

The knowledge which these Indians had of wood seemed to be confined to some kinds of heath, which had stems not thicker than the finger: hence they knew not what to think of the timber with which the ships were constructed. Not being aware of its weight, two or three of them, successively, seized hold of the spare topmast, and evidently with an intention of carrying it off. The only object on board which they seemed to view with contempt, was a little terrier dog; judging, no doubt, that it was too small for drawing a sledge: but they shrunk back, in terror, from a pig, whose pricked ears, and ferocious countenance, presented a somewhat formidable appearance. This animal happening to grunt, one of them was so much terrified, that he became, from that moment, uneasy, and impatient to get out of the ship. In carrying his purpose into effect, however, he did not lose his propensity to thieving, for he seized hold of, and endeavoured to carry off, the smith's anvil: but, finding it infinitely too heavy for his strength, he laid hold of the large hammer, threw it on the ice; and, following it himself, deliberately laid it on his sledge, and drove off. As this was an article that could not be spared, Captain Ross sent a man from the ship, who pursued the depredator, and, with some difficulty, recovered it.

The officers and men on board were much amused by putting into the hands of these Indians a magnifying mirror. On beholding themselves in it, their grimaces were highly entertaining. They first looked into, and then behind it, in hopes of finding the monster which was exaggerating their hideous gestures. A watch was held to the ear of one of them; and he, supposing it alive, asked if it was good to eat. On being shown the glass of the skylight and binnacle, they touched it, and desired to know what kind of ice it was.

Three of the men who remained on board were handed down into the captain's cabin, and shown the use of the chairs: this, however, they did not comprehend; for they appeared to have no notion of any other seat than the ground. They were shown paper, books, drawings, and various mathematical instruments, but these produced in them only the usual effect of astonishment. On being conducted to the gun-room, and afterwards round the ship, they did not appear to notice any thing particularly, except the wood that had been used in her construction. They stamped upon the deck, as if in surprise at the great quantity of this valuable material which they beheld. By the direction of the officers, Sacheuse enquired of these people, whether their country had as many inhabitants as there were pieces of ice, floating round the ship: they replied, "Many more;" and it was supposed that at least a thousand fragments could be distinguished.

The men were now loaded with presents of various kinds, consisting of articles of clothing, biscuit, and pieces of wood; in addition to which the plank that had been used in crossing the chasm, was given to them. They then departed, promising to return as soon as they had eaten and slept. The parting was attended, on each side, by the ceremony of pulling noses.

It has been remarked that these Indians were in possession of knives; and the iron of which their knives were made, was stated to have been procured from a mountain near the sea-shore. They informed Sacheuse that there was a rock, or great quantity of it; and that they cut off from this rock, with a sharp stone, such pieces as they wanted.

In the course of the three following days, the Isabella changed her station some miles westward. At length she was again moored near the ice; and, shortly afterwards, three of the natives appeared at a distance. Sacheuse, who had been furnished with presents, and sent to speak with them, induced them to drive, on their sledges, close to the vessel. The dogs attached to each sledge were six in number. Each dog had a collar of seal-skin, two inches wide, to which one end of a thong, made of strong hide, and about three yards in length, was fastened: the other end was tied to the front of the sledge: thus the dogs were ranged nearly abreast, each dog drawing by a single trace, and without reins. No sooner did they hear the crack of the driver's whip, than they set off at full speed, while he managed them with the greatest apparent ease, guiding them partly by his voice, and partly by the sound of his whip. One of these men pointed out to Captain Ross his house, which was about three miles distant, and could be discerned with a telescope.

A party of ten natives approached the ship, on the ensuing day. These having with them a seal-skin bag filled with air, they began to kick it at each other and at the strangers: in this play the Englishmen joined, to the great amusement of both parties. The inflated skin was what the men had been using as the buoy to a harpoon, in the killing of a sea-unicorn. They gave to Captain Ross a piece of dried sea-unicorn's flesh, which appeared to have been half roasted. This gentleman had already seen them eat dried flesh; and he now had an opportunity of ascertaining that they did not scruple to eat flesh in any state; for, one of them who had a bag full of marine-birds, took out one and devoured it raw.

The officers, desirous of ascertaining whether these Indians had any amusements of music or dancing, prevailed with two of them to give a specimen of their dancing. One of them began to distort his features and turn up his eyes. He then proceeded to execute, in succession, a variety of strange gestures and attitudes, accompanied by hideous distortions of countenance. His body was generally in a stooping posture; and his hands rested on his knees. After a few minutes, he began to sing; and, in a little while, the second performer, who, hitherto, had been looking on, in silence, began to imitate his comrade. They then sang, in chorus, the word, "*hejaw! hejaw!*" After this had continued, with increasing energy, for several minutes, the tune was suddenly changed to one of shrill notes, in which the words "*weehee! weehee!*" were uttered with great rapidity. They then approached each other, by slipping their feet forward: they grinned, and, in great agitation, advanced until their noses touched, when a loud and savage laugh terminated the extraordinary performance.

While this performance was going on, one of the Indians, seeing that the attention of every person was engaged, seized the opportunity of descending into the state-room, and of purloining Captain Ross's best telescope, a case of razors, and a pair of scissors, which he artfully concealed in his tunic, rejoining the party and the amusements, as if nothing had happened. He did not, however, escape detection, for the ship's steward had witnessed the theft, and, now charging him with it, made him return all the articles he had stolen.

Captain Ross gave the name of *Arctic Highlands* to the country inhabited by these Indians, and that of *Prince Regent's Bay*, to the place where the vessels had anchored. It is situated in the north-east corner of Baffin's Bay, between the latitudes of 76 and 79 degrees north; and is bounded, towards the south, by an immense barrier of mountains covered with ice. The interior of the country presents an irregular group of mountainous land, declining gradually towards the sea, which it reaches in an irregular manner, the cliffs ranging from five hundred to one thousand feet in height. This tract was almost covered with ice, and appeared to be impassable.

On the surface of the land, above the cliffs, a scanty appearance of vegetation, of a yellowish green colour, and, in some places, of a heathy brown, was to be seen; and, at the foot of the cliffs, similar traces of a wretched verdure were also apparent. Among the cliffs were seen deep ravines filled with snow, through which the marks of torrents were perceptible. These cliffs run out, in many places, into capes, and are skirted by islands, which, at this time, were clear of ice, and consequently were washed by the waves. Many species of wild-fowl were seen.

The vegetable productions of this country may be said to consist of heath, moss, and coarse grass. There is nothing like cultivation, nor did it appear that the natives used any kind of vegetable food. The moss is in great abundance: it is six or eight inches in length, and, when dried and immersed in oil or blubber, it serves for a wick, and produces a comfortable fire for cooking and warmth, as well as for light.

The whale-fishery might, undoubtedly, be pursued with great success, in this bay and its vicinity. The whales are here not only large and numerous, but, probably from their having been undisturbed, they are tame, and easy to be approached.

The dress of the Arctic Highlanders, as Captain Ross has denominated the people of this country, consists of three pieces, which are all comprised in the name of *tunic*. The upper piece is made of seal-skin, with the hair outside; and is open near the top, so as to admit the wearer's face. The hood part is neatly trimmed with fox's-skin, and is made to fall back on the shoulders, or to cover the head, as may be required. The next piece of dress, which scarcely reaches to the knee, is made of bear's or dog's skin. The boots are of seal-skin, with the hair inward. In the winter this people have a garment of bear-skin, which they put on as a cloak.

The Arctic Highlanders are of a dirty copper colour. Their stature is about five feet: their bodies are corpulent, and their features much resemble those of the Esquimaux. Their cheeks are full and round. Their lips are thick, their eyes are small, and their hair is black, coarse, long, and lank. These people appear to be filthy in the extreme. The faces, hands, and bodies of such as were seen by the voyagers, were covered with oil and dirt; and they seemed never to have washed themselves since they were born: even their hair was matted with filth.

Some attempts were made to ascertain the religious notions of the Arctic Highlanders, but these seem to have proved unsatisfactory; and, perhaps, from the inability of Sacheuse to question them on such a subject. They had a king, whom they represented to be a strong man, very good, and greatly beloved. His house was described to be of stone, and nearly as large as the ship; and they said that every man paid to him a portion of all which they caught or found. They could not be made to understand what was meant by war, nor did the voyagers see, among them, any warlike weapons. It is peculiarly deserving of remark, that these Indians, who derive much of their subsistence from the water, have no canoes or vessels of any description, in which they can go afloat; nor do they appear to have any names by which boats or canoes are designated. It is true that they have no wood for the construction of floating vessels; but such might, without difficulty, be constructed of bone covered with skins.

On the 16th of August, the ice had become sufficiently open, to permit the passage of the vessels to the northward; and they consequently proceeded on their voyage.

In these high latitudes, a kind of marine birds, called Little Awks (*alca alle*) were observed in countless multitudes, and afforded to the sailors, a grateful supply of fresh food. With three muskets, no fewer than one thousand two hundred and sixty-three of them were killed in one day; and, of this number, ninety-three were brought down by one discharge of the muskets.

When the ships were in latitude 75 degrees 54 minutes, the snow on the face of the cliffs was observed to be stained of a deep crimson colour. Some of this snow being collected in buckets, it was found to resemble, in appearance, raspberry ice-cream: when dissolved, the liquor seemed not unlike muddy port-wine; and the sediment appeared, through a microscope, to be composed of dark-red globules. Some of this sediment was brought to England, and it is generally supposed to have been a vegetable substance, the seed, probably, of some species of fungus; or, perhaps, to have been itself a minute kind of fungus.

On the 18th of August, the ships passed *Cape Dudley Digges*, six miles northward of which a majestic glacier, or mass of ice, was remarked to occupy a space of four miles square, extending one mile into the sea, and rising to the height of at least a hundred feet. On the same day the vessels passed *Wolstenholme* and *Whale Sounds*.

About midnight of the 19th, *Sir Thomas Smith's Sound* was distinctly seen. Captain Ross considered the bottom of this sound to have been eighteen leagues distant; but its entrance, he says, was completely blocked up by ice. On the 21st, the ships stood over to explore an opening, supposed to have been that called *Alderman Jones's Sound*; but Captain Ross says that the ice and fog prevented a near approach.

The night of the 24th of August was remarkable for having been the first on which the sun had been observed to set, since the 7th of June. The land was now seen to take a southerly direction; and the ships proceeded along it, as near as they could conveniently approach for the floating masses of ice.

On the 30th they entered a wide opening in the land, the *Sir James Lancaster's Sound* of Baffin. On each side of this opening was a chain of high mountains. The sea was perfectly free from ice, and the vessels proceeded on a westward course for several leagues. The weather had, for some time, been hazy; but, on its clearing up, Captain Ross states that a range of mountains about twenty-four miles distant, were seen to occupy the centre of the inlet. To these he gave the name of *Croker Mountains*, and, imagining that no passage existed through them, he returned into the open sea, and, not long afterwards, sailed for England.

Twenty-sixth Day's Instruction

DAVIS'S STRAIT AND BAFFIN'S BAY CONCLUDED.

The accounts that had been given by Captain Ross, particularly respecting the apparent mountains, named by him *Croker Mountains*, across Sir James Lancaster's Sound, not proving either conclusive or satisfactory, the Lords of the Admiralty ordered two ships, the Hecla and Griper, to be prepared for a further voyage of discovery in Baffin's Bay. The command of these vessels, as already stated, was given to Captain Parry, who, in the previous expedition, had been second in command under Captain Ross. It was one important part of his instructions, that he should advance to the northward, as far as the opening into Lancaster's Sound; that he should explore the bottom of that Sound, and, if possible, pass through it to Behring's Strait. The number of men in both the vessels was ninety-four; and many of them were those who had accompanied Captain Ross.

Narrative of Captain Parry's *Voyage for the Discovery of a North-West Passage from the Atlantic to the Pacific Ocean.*

Captain Parry arrived at the entrance into *Lancaster's Sound*, on the 30th of July, 1819; and, this day, saw no fewer than eighty-two whales. Some of the officers and men landed at *Possession Bay*, and recognized many objects which they had seen there, when with Captain Ross. The tracks of human feet were observed upon the banks of a stream. These at first excited much surprise; but, on examination, they were discovered to have been made by the shoes of some of the same party, eleven months before.

In sailing, westward, up the Sound, Captain Parry says that it is more easy to imagine than to describe the almost breathless anxiety which was visible in every countenance, as the breeze, which had hitherto impelled the vessels, increased to a fresh gale. The mast-heads were crowded by the officers and men looking out; and an unconcerned observer, if, on such an occasion, any could be unconcerned, would have been amused by the eagerness with which the various reports from those stations were received.

After the vessels had proceeded a considerable distance, they passed some bold headlands, and high mountains. They also passed an inlet, to which Captain Parry gave the name of *Croker's Bay*, and which he is of opinion may, hereafter, be found a passage from Lancaster's Sound into the Northern Sea. They were thence carried along briskly for three days. On the 4th of August, there was, from the mast-head, an exclamation of "land!" and that sound, which, on ordinary occasions, is of all others the most joyful to a seaman's ears, was, on this, the signal for disappointment and mortification. The land, however, proved to be an island.

The vessels continued their progress, and several bays, capes, and headlands, were successively discovered. On the 22d there was a clear and extensive view to the northward; the water was free from ice, and the voyagers now felt that they had entered the Polar Sea. The magnificent opening through which their passage had been effected, from Baffin's Bay, to a channel dignified with the name of *Wellington*, was called, by Captain Parry, *Barron's Straits*.

In latitude 75 degrees 3 minutes, and longitude 103 degrees 44 minutes, an island was discovered; and Captain Sabine, with two other officers, landed on it. They found, in four different places, the remains of Esquimaux habitations. These were from seven to ten feet in diameter; and to each was attached a circle four or five feet in diameter, which had probably been the fire-place. The whole encampment appeared to have been deserted for several years; but recent footsteps of rein-deer and musk-oxen were seen in many places.

The circumstances under which the voyagers were now sailing were, perhaps, such as had never occurred since the early days of navigation. There was land towards the north; ice, it was supposed, was towards the south; the compasses by which the vessels had been steered, now varied so much, that they had become useless; and all the surrounding objects were obscured by a dense fog: consequently, there was now no other mode of regulating the course of the ships, than by trusting to the steadiness of the wind.

On the 2d of September a star was seen; the first that had been visible for more than two months. Two days afterwards, at a quarter past nine in the evening, the ships, in latitude 74 degrees 44 minutes, crossed the meridian of 110 degrees from Greenwich, by which they became entitled to £.5000; a reward offered by the British government to the first vessels which should cross that longitude, to the north of America. In order to commemorate the event, a lofty headland that they had just passed, was called *Bounty Cape*. On the following day the ships, for the first time since they had quitted the English coast, dropped anchor in a roadstead, which was called the *Bay of the Hecla and Griper*; and the crews landed on the largest of a group of islands, which Captain Parry named *Melville Island*. The ensigns and pendants were hoisted, as soon as the vessels had anchored; and it excited, in the voyagers, no ordinary sensations of pleasure, to see the British flag waving, for the first time, in regions, which, hitherto, had been considered beyond the limits of the habitable world.

The wind now became unfavourable to their progress; and a rapid accumulation of the ice, exposed the vessels to the greatest danger, and the crews to incessant fatigue. For several days they were unable to proceed further than along the coast of the island. This was the more mortifying, as Captain Parry had looked forward to the month of September, as the period, of all others, favourable to the rapid prosecution of his voyage. To add to his anxiety, a party of seamen, who had been sent on shore, to hunt deer, lost their way, and, for three nights, were exposed to the inclemency of the weather. The most distressing apprehensions were entertained respecting the fate of these men; nor, were they finally recovered, without considerable danger to those who were sent in search of them, and who, had their recovery been delayed one day longer, must themselves have perished. In gratitude for this preservation, the nearest headland was named *Cape Providence*.

The increasing dangers and difficulties attendant on continuing the navigation westward, prevented the vessels from proceeding further than to some distance along the coast of Melville Island. And, at length, Captain Parry, finding that no hope could be entertained, during the present season, of penetrating beyond this island, he was induced to return to Hecla and Griper Bay, for the purpose of passing there the winter.

It was now, however, requisite to cut a canal through the ice, which, since their departure, had extended a considerable distance into the sea; and to draw the ships up it into the harbour. In this operation, two parallel lines were cut, distant from each other, little more than the breadth of the ships; and the ice was divided into square pieces, which were subdivided diagonally, and were either floated out of the canal, or sunk beneath the adjacent ice. The labour of cutting this canal may be imagined, when it is stated that the length was more than four thousand yards, and that the average thickness of the ice was seven inches. At three o'clock of September the 26th, the third day spent in this operation, the vessels reached their winter quarters; an event which was hailed with three hearty cheers, by the united ships' crews. The group of islands which had been discovered, were called the *North Georgian Islands*.

As the ships had now attained that station where, in all probability, they were destined to remain for eight or nine months, every precaution was taken for their security, and for the preservation of the various stores which they contained. A regular system also was adopted, for the maintenance of good order, cleanliness, and the health of the crews, during the approaching long, dark, and dreary winter. All the masts, except the lower ones, were dismantled; and the boats, spars, ropes, and sails, were removed on shore, in order to give as much room as possible on the deck. The ropes and sails were all hard frozen, and it was requisite to keep them in that state, till the return of spring. A housing of planks, covered with wadding-tilt, such as is used for stage-waggons, was formed upon the deck of each of the vessels; and thus constituted a comfortable shelter from the snow and the wind.

The crews were in excellent health, and every care was taken to preserve it. Regulations were made, in the allowances both of bread and meat: as a preservative against scurvy, the men were allowed a quantity of vinegar with their meat, and they, every day, took a portion of lime-juice and sugar. The next care was for the minds of the men, the health of which Captain Parry wisely considered to have no small influence on that of the body. This excellent officer, anxious for their amusement during the long and tedious interval of winter, proposed, that a play should occasionally be got up on board the Hecla. He considered this to be the readiest means of preserving, among the crews, that cheerfulness and good-humour which had hitherto subsisted. The proposal was readily seconded by the officers of both ships: Lieutenant Beechey was consequently elected stage-manager, and the first performance was fixed for the 5th of November. In order still further to promote good-humour, and to furnish amusing occupation, a weekly newspaper was set on foot, called the "North Georgia Gazette, and Winter Chronicle," of which Captain Sabine undertook to be the editor, under a promise that it should be supported by original contributions from the officers of the two ships.

On the 4th of November the sun sank beneath the horizon, not to appear again above it for the space of ninety-six days. On the 5th the theatre was opened, with the farce of "Miss in her Teens;" and Captain Parry found so much benefit accrue to his men, from the amusement which this kind of spectacle afforded them, and with the occupation of fitting up the theatre and taking it down again, that the dramatic representations were continued through the whole winter, and were performed and witnessed with equal pleasure, even when the cold upon the stage was intense.

The sinking of the sun below the horizon, for so long a period, seemed to occasion a painful sensation to the animals, inhabitants of the island, as well as to the human beings who had sought a temporary asylum on it: for, from that time, the wolves began to approach the ships, as if drawn thither by a melancholy sympathy; and they often howled, most piteously, for many successive hours. They, however, seldom appeared in greater numbers than two or three together; and it was somewhat extraordinary, that although the crews of both vessels were, for many weeks, intent on killing or catching some of them, they never could succeed. Only one bear was seen during the whole winter: it was of the white kind, and had tracked Captain Sabine's servant quite to the ships; but, being there saluted by a volley of balls, it ran off and escaped.

The circumstances under which the crews of these vessels were situated, being such as had never before occurred, it cannot be uninteresting to know in what manner they passed their time during three months of nearly total darkness, and in the midst of a severe winter.

The officers and quarter-masters were divided into four watches, which were regularly kept, as at sea; while the remainder of the ship's company were allowed to enjoy their night's rest undisturbed. The hands were turned up at a quarter before six in the morning; and both the decks were well rubbed with stones and warm sand, before eight o'clock, at which time both officers and men went to breakfast. Three quarters of an hour being allowed, after breakfast, for the men to prepare themselves for muster, they were all assembled on the deck at a quarter past nine; and a strict inspection took place, as to their personal cleanliness, and the good condition, as well as sufficient warmth, of their clothing. The reports of the officers having been made to Captain Parry, the men were then allowed to walk about, or, more usually, to run round the upper deck; whilst he went down to examine the state of the deck below, accompanied by Lieutenant Beechey and Mr. Edwards the surgeon.

The state of this deck may be said, indeed, to have constituted the chief source of anxiety; and, at this period, to have occupied by far the greatest share of attention. Whenever any dampness appeared, or, what more frequently happened, any accumulation of ice had taken place during the preceding night, the necessary means were immediately adopted for removing it: in the former case, usually by rubbing the wood with cloths, and then directing hot air to the place; and, in the latter, by scraping off the ice, so as to prevent its wetting the deck, by any accidental increase of temperature. In this respect the bed-places were peculiarly troublesome; the inner partition, or that next the ship's side, being, almost invariably, covered with more or less dampness or ice, according to the temperature of the deck during the preceding night.

All the requisite examinations being finished, the men, when the weather would permit, were sent out to walk on shore till noon; but, when the day was too inclement to admit of this exercise, they were ordered to run round and round the deck, keeping step to the tune of an organ, or to a song of their own singing. A few of the men did not, at first, quite like this systematic mode of taking exercise; but, when they found that no plea, except that of illness, was admitted as an excuse, they not only willingly and cheerfully complied, but they made it the occasion of much humour and frolic among themselves.

The officers, who dined at two o'clock, were also in the habit of occupying one or two hours, of the middle of the day, in rambling on shore, even in the darkest period; except when a fresh wind or a heavy snow-drift confined them within the housing of the ships. It may well be imagined, that, at this period, there was but little to be met with in their walks on shore, which could either amuse or interest them. The necessity of not exceeding the limited distance of one or two miles, lest a snow-drift, which often arose very suddenly, should prevent their return, added considerably to the dull and tedious monotony which, day after day, presented itself. Towards the south was the sea, covered with one unbroken surface of ice, uniform in its dazzling whiteness, except that, in some parts, a few hummocks were seen thrown up somewhat above the general level. Nor did the land offer much greater variety: it was covered with snow, except here and there a brown patch of bare ground in some exposed situations, where the wind had not allowed the snow to remain. When viewed from the summit of the neighbouring hills, on one of those calm, clear days, which not unfrequently occurred during the winter, the scene was such as to induce contemplations, that had, perhaps, more of melancholy than of any other feeling. Not an object was to be seen on which the eye could long rest with pleasure, unless when directed to the spot where the ships lay. The smoke which there issued from the several fires, affording a certain indication of the presence of man, gave a partial cheerfulness to this part of the prospect; and the sound of voices, which, during the cold weather, could be heard at a much greater distance than usual, served, now and then, to break the silence which reigned around,—a silence far different from that peaceable composure which characterizes the landscape of a cultivated country: it was the death-like stillness of the most dreary desolation, the total absence of animated existence.

The weather became intensely severe; and, during the latter part of November, and the first half of December, Captain Parry's journal presents little more than observations on it; and oh the meteoric appearances and fantastic illusions of light and colour, with which the voyagers were often amused. At one time, the moon appeared to be curiously deformed by refraction; the lower edges of it seeming to be indented with deep notches, and afterwards to be cut off square at the bottom; whilst a single ray or column of light, of the same diameter as the moon, was observed to descend from it to the top of a hill. At another time, several transparent clouds were seen to emit, upward, columns of light, resembling the aurora borealis. The aurora borealis itself appears to have been seldom witnessed, in the splendour with which it occasionally illuminates even the northern parts of Scotland; still it was both frequent and vivid enough to give variety and beauty to the long nights which the voyagers had to endure.

The new year was ushered in by weather comparatively mild; but it soon regained its former severity. Captain Parry and his crews did not, however, experience those effects from the cold, even when 49 degrees below 0, which preceding voyagers have stated; such as a dreadful sensation on the lungs, when the air is inhaled at a very low temperature; or the vapour with which an inhabited room is charged, condensing into a shower of snow, immediately on the opening of a door or window. What they did observe was this: on the opening of the doors, at the top and bottom of the hatch-way ladders, the vapour was condensed, by the sudden admission of the cold air, into a visible form, exactly resembling a very thick smoke. This apparent smoke settled on the pannels of the doors and on the bulk-heads, and immediately froze, by which the latter were covered with a thick coating of ice, which it was necessary frequently to scrape off.

The extreme severity of the cold, which was sometimes prevalent, may be imagined from the following fact:—A house, erected on the shore, for scientific purposes, caught fire; and a servant of Captain Sabine, in his endeavours to extinguish it, exposed his hands, in the first instance, to the operation of considerable heat; and he afterwards, for some time, remained without gloves, in the open air. When taken on board the ship, his hands presented a strange appearance. They were perfectly hard, inflexible, and colourless; possessing a degree of translucency, and exhibiting more the external character of pieces of sculptured marble, than of animated matter. They were immediately plunged into the cold bath, where they were continued more than two hours, before their flexibility could be restored. The abstraction of heat had been so great, that the water, in contact with the fingers, congealed upon them, even half an hour after they had been immersed. During the cold application, the man suffered acute pain, by which he became so faint and exhausted, that it was requisite to put him to bed. In less than three hours, an inflammation came on, which extended high up the arm; and, soon afterwards, each hand, from the wrist downward, was enclosed in a kind of bladder, containing nearly a pint of viscid serous fluid. There were, however, three fingers of one hand, and two of the other, in which this vesication did not form. These fingers continued cold and insensible, nor could the circulation in them be restored; and, eventually, the amputation of them became necessary.

The distance at which sounds were heard in the open air, during the continuance of intense cold, seems almost incredible. Captain Parry says that his people were distinctly heard, conversing in a common tone of voice, at the distance of a mile; and that he heard a man singing to himself, at even a still greater distance. Another circumstance occurred, scarcely less curious than this: the smell of smoke was so strong, two miles leeward of the ships, that it impeded the breathing. This shows to what a distance the smoke was carried horizontally, owing to the difficulty with which it rises, at a very low temperature of the atmosphere.

In the severest weather, the officers sometimes amused themselves by freezing quicksilver, and beating it out on an anvil, so great was the severity of the cold; yet, not the slightest inconvenience was suffered, from exposure to the open air, by persons well clothed, so long as the weather was perfectly calm; but, in walking against even a very light wind, a smarting sensation was experienced all over the face, accompanied by a pain in the middle of the forehead, which soon became severe.

As a specimen of the average proportion of ice formed in the harbour, it is stated that, where the depth of the water was twenty-five feet, the ice was found to be six feet and a half thick; and the snow on the surface was eight inches deep.

Towards the end of January, some of the port-holes of one of the vessels were opened, in order to admit the carpenters and armorers to repair the main-top-sail-yard. On the 3d of February the sun was seen from the main-top of the Hecla, for the first time since the 11th of November. By the 7th, there was sufficient day-light, from eight o'clock till four, to enable the men to perform, with facility, any work on the outside of the ships.

On the 15th, Captain Parry was induced, by the cheering presence of the sun, for several hours above the horizon, to open the dead-lights, or shutters, of his stern-windows, in order to admit the day-light, after a privation of it, for four months, in that part of the ship. The baize curtains, which had been nailed close to the windows, in the beginning of the winter, were, however, so firmly frozen to them, that it was necessary to cut them away; and twelve large buckets full of ice or frozen vapour, were taken from between the double sashes, before they could be got clear. This premature uncovering of the windows, however, caused such a change in the temperature of the Hecla, that, for several weeks afterwards, those on board were sensible of a more intense degree of cold, than they had felt during all the preceding part of the winter.

The months of March and April seem to have passed tediously on, in watching the state of the weather. The crew of the Griper became somewhat sickly, in consequence of the extreme moisture, which it was found impossible to exclude from their bed-places. In May, Captain Parry laid out a small garden, planting it with radishes, onions, mustard, and cress; but the experiment failed, though some common ship-peas, planted by the men, throve extremely well.

On the 12th of May, some ptarmigans were seen. These were hailed as a sure omen of returning summer. Several of the men went out on shooting excursions; and, being exposed, for several hours, to the glare of the sun and snow, became affected with that painful inflammation in the eyes, called "snow-blindness." As a preventive of this complaint, a piece of black crape was given to each man, to be worn as a kind of short veil, attached to the hat. This was found to be sufficiently efficacious. But a more convenient mode was adopted by some of the officers: they took out the glasses from spectacles, and substituted black or green crape in their place.

In the beginning of May, the men cut the ice round the Hecla. This was done by means of axes and saws, and with astonishing labour; for the ice was still more than six feet thick. On the 17th, the operation was completed, and the ships were once more afloat.

Captain Parry and Captain Sabine, accompanied by ten other persons, officers and men, set off, on the 1st of June, to make a tour through the island. They took with them tents, fuel, and provisions; and carried their luggage in a small, light cart, to which the sailors occasionally fastened their blankets, by way of sails. They travelled by night, as well to have the benefit which any warmth of the sun might give during their hours of rest, as to avoid the glare of its light upon the snow. The vegetable productions which they observed, were chiefly the dwarf willow, sorrel, poppy, saxifrage, and ranunculus. The animals were mice, deer, a musk ox, a pair of swallows, ducks, geese, plovers, and ptarmigans; with some of which they occasionally varied their fare. The tracks, both of deer and musk oxen, were numerous; and one deer followed the party for some time, and gambolled round them, at a distance of only thirty yards. The soil of the island was, in general, barren; but, in some places, it was rich, and abounded with the finest moss. On one part of the beach, the travellers found a point of land eighty feet above the sea: this they named *Point Nias*, after one of the officers of the party; and they had the patience to raise on it, as a memorial of their exertions, a monument of ice, of conical form, twelve feet broad at the base, and as many in height. They enclosed within the mass, in a tin cylinder, an account of the party who had erected it, with a few silver and copper English coins; and Mr. Fisher, the assistant surgeon, constructed it with a solidity which may make it last, for many years, as a land-mark; for it is visible at the distance of several miles, both by sea and land. In one place, within a hundred yards of the sea, the remains of six Esquimaux huts were discovered. After a fortnight's absence, the party returned to the ships.

The approach of summer now began to be apparent, from the state of vegetation on the island; and, during the warm weather, a great quantity of sorrel was daily gathered. The hunting parties also brought in an abundance of animal food. The total quantity obtained, during the continuance of the vessels at Melville island, was 3 musk oxen, 68 hares, 53 geese, 59 ducks, and 144 ptarmigans; affording, in the whole, 3766 pounds of meat.

On the 22d of June, the men were delighted to observe that the ice had begun to be in motion; and, on the 16th of July, the snow had entirely disappeared, except along the sides of caverns, and in other hollows, where it had formed considerable drifts. The appearance of the land was, consequently, much the same as it had been when the ships first reached the island. The walks which the men were now enabled to take, and the luxurious living afforded by the hunting-parties, together with the abundant supply of sorrel, which was always at command, were the means of completely eradicating the scurvy; and the whole of the ships' companies were now in as good health, and certainly in as good spirits, as when the expedition left England.

After having made an accurate survey of Winter Harbour, where the vessels had been frozen up nearly eleven months, Captain Parry resolved to quit it. Accordingly, on the 1st of August, the vessels weighed anchor, and stood out to sea. Towards the west, the direction in which they were proceeding, the sea, at first, presented a very flattering appearance, being more clear of ice than it had been a month later in the preceding year, and presenting a fine navigable channel, two miles and a half in width, which, from the mast-head, appeared to continue as far as the eye could reach.

They had not, however, proceeded many leagues westward of their winter quarters, when the wind blew directly against them, and their course was further opposed by a strong current, which set towards the east. To these difficulties, great danger was soon added, from the drifting and pressure of the ice, which threatened the Griper, in particular, with total destruction. They penetrated to the longitude of 113 degrees 48 minutes, being the westernmost meridian hitherto reached, in the Polar Sea, to the north of America. But they had made so little progress, and were in such incessant danger; and the officers had so little hope of being able to effect any further discoveries of importance, during the present season, that Captain Parry at length determined to return.

On a consultation with his officers, respecting the best course to be pursued, it was resolved that, in their voyage homeward, they should run along the edge of the ice, with the intention of availing themselves of any opening that might lead towards the coast of America. It was not till the 26th, that the ships got clear of *Cape Providence*; but, after that, they had an open channel, and sailed before the wind, with such rapidity, and so little interruption, that, in six days, they cleared *Sir James Lancaster's Sound*, and were once more in *Baffin's Bay*. They now stood along the western shore of this bay, which they found indented with several deep bays or inlets.

On the 3d of September, they passed some icebergs, which were a hundred and fifty or two hundred feet above the surface of the water; and, soon afterwards, in an inlet, which Captain Ross had named the *River Clyde*, the voyagers saw four canoes, each of which contained an *Esquimaux*. These approached the ships; and the men, at their own desire, were taken on board. Three of them were young, and the fourth about sixty years of age. They appeared to be much pleased; and expressed their delight by jumping, and by loud and repeated ejaculations. Although there was no interpreter, they bartered several articles, in a manner that showed they were no strangers to traffic.

Some of the officers landed, and went to visit two Esquimaux tents, which were situated within a low point of land, that formed the eastern side of the entrance to a considerable branch of the inlet. The inhabitants, men, women, and children, on beholding them, came running out, with loud and continued shouting. Two of the women had infants slung, in a kind of bag, at their back, much in the same manner as gypsies are accustomed to carry their children. There were seven other children, from twelve to three years of age, besides two infants in arms.

The officers purchased whatever things these people had to dispose of, and, in exchange for them, gave knives, axes, brass kettles, needles, and other articles; and then added such presents as they considered might be further serviceable to them. Though they appeared anxious to possess whatever the visitors had to give they did not exhibit any disposition to pilfer. And, in some of the bargains, particularly for a sledge and a dog, the articles, though previously paid for, were all punctually delivered.

In stature these Indians, like the Esquimaux in general, are much below the usual standard. The height of the men is from four feet and a half to five feet and a half, and of the women about four feet ten inches. Their faces, in the younger individuals, are round and plump: their skin is smooth, and their complexion not very dark: their teeth are very white, and their eyes small; their nose is small, and their hair black, straight, and glossy. All the women, except one, had their faces tatooed; and two of them had their hands tatooed also. The children were, in general, good-looking; and one of them, a boy about twelve years of age, was a remarkably fine, and even handsome lad.

The dress of the men consists of a seal-skin jacket, with a hood, which is occasionally drawn over the head. The breeches are also, generally, of seal-skin; and the boots, which are formed so as to meet the breeches, are of the same material. In the dress of the women, the drawers cover the middle part of the body, from the hips to one-third down the thighs; the rest of which, as far as the knees, is naked. The children are all remarkably well clad; their dress, both in the males and females, being, in every respect, similar to that of the men.

The tents which constitute the summer habitations of these Esquimaux, are principally supported by a pole of whalebone, about fourteen feet high. This pole stands perpendicularly, and has four or five feet of it projecting above the skins which form the roof and sides. The length of the tent is about seventeen feet, and the breadth from seven to nine; and the bed occupies nearly one-third of the whole apartment. The covering of the tent is fastened to the ground by curved pieces of bone.

Captain Parry, after taking leave of these his new acquaintance, directed his course towards England; and arrived in the river Thames about the middle of November.

With regard to the probable existence and accomplishment of a north-west passage into the Pacific Ocean, this indefatigable and accomplished officer remarks, that, as to the existence of such a passage, he does not entertain a doubt; but that he is not sanguine as to its ever being accomplished. The difficulties that are presented by the increasing breadth and thickness of the ice to the westward, after passing Barrow's Strait, added to the excessive severity of the climate, and the shortness of the season in which the Polar Sea can be navigated; these are circumstances which render almost hopeless any attempt to pass from the Atlantic westward. Captain Parry seems inclined to think that there is more probability of being able to effect the passage, by sailing from Behring's Strait, eastward, than from Baffin's Bay towards the west. But, in this case, it would be an impracticable passage for British ships. The great length of the voyage, the impossibility of taking out a sufficiency of provisions and fuel, and the severe trial to which the health of the crews would be subjected, by suddenly passing from the heat of the torrid zone, into the intense cold of a long winter, seem to render hopeless all our efforts to effect the voyage in this direction.

Twenty-seventh Day's Instruction

LABRADOR AND GREENLAND.

On the south-western side of Davis's Strait is the wild, extensive, and uncivilized country of *Labrador*. Its coast was first discovered by the Portuguese navigators; but the frigidity of its climate is such, that no settlements of any importance have ever been fixed upon its shores. Even the extent of the country has been but imperfectly ascertained; for all the knowledge we have hitherto obtained respecting it, relates only to the coast. The inland territory remains yet unexplored.

Captain George Cartwright resided on the coast of Labrador, at different intervals, for sixteen years. He states that the face of the country, as far as he could discover it, was mountainous and desolate; and that some of the mountains were of considerable elevation. The soil, in some parts of the southern coast, appears, at first sight, to be fertile and covered with verdure; but, on examination, it is found to be poor, and the verdure is that of coarse plants, which would not serve as food for horses, cattle, or sheep. Some attempts have been made to cultivate this coast, but the depredations of bears and wolves have proved a formidable impediment; and such is the severity of the climate, that cattle must be housed for nine months in the year.

The whole eastern coast of Labrador exhibits a very barren appearance: the mountains rise abruptly from the sea, and are composed of rocks, that are thinly covered with peat earth. This produces only stunted spruce trees, and a few plants; but the adjacent sea, and the various rivers and lakes, abound with fish, fowl, and amphibious animals. Springs are rare, and fresh water is chiefly supplied by melted snow. In the various bays of this coast, there are numerous islands, on which eider-ducks, and multitudes of other sea-fowl breed. On some of the larger islands there are deer, foxes, and hares. The fruits of Labrador consist chiefly of currants, raspberries, cranberries, whortle-berries, apples, and pears. Among the mineral productions is a kind of felspar, which, when polished, exhibits a display of brilliant and beautiful colours.

The climate of this country, though severe, is healthy. There is little appearance of summer till about the middle of July; and, in September, winter indicates its approach. During summer the heat is sometimes unpleasant; and the cold of winter is of long duration, and generally intense. In Labrador, as in all other countries of northern climates, the quadrupeds are clothed with a longer and thicker fur during winter, than in summer; and many of the birds have a softer down, and feathers of a closer texture, than those of milder countries. Some of the animals also assume a white clothing at the commencement of winter.

The native inhabitants of Labrador are *mountaineers* and Esquimaux, between whom there subsists an invincible aversion. The former, who inhabit the interior districts towards the north, are of dark colour, and robust constitution, though their limbs are small. They subsist chiefly on rein-deer, which they are very dexterous in killing: they also kill foxes, martens, and beavers. As these people live a wandering life, they never build houses; but they construct a kind of tents, and cover them with branches of trees, and with deer-skins. Their summer dress consists of skins freed from the hair; and their winter-dress is formed of beaver and deer-skins, with the hair on. During the summer they traverse the country, in canoes, along the rivers and lakes. These canoes are covered with the bark of the birch-tree; and, although they are so light as to be easily carried, some of them are large enough to contain a whole family, together with the materials of their traffic. In winter the mountaineers of Labrador pass over the snow, by means of what are called snow-shoes.

These mountaineers are esteemed an industrious people. They bear fatigue with almost incredible resolution and patience; and will often travel two successive days without food. They, every year, come to the Canada merchants, who have seal-fisheries on the southern coast, and bargain their furs, in exchange for blanketing, fire-arms, and ammunition; and they are immoderately fond of spirits. Some of them profess to be Roman Catholics; but their whole religion seems to consist in reciting a few prayers, and in counting their beads.

It is customary with these Indians, to destroy such persons among them as become aged and decrepit. This practice they endeavour to vindicate from their mode of life: for they assert that those who are unable to procure the necessaries requisite for their existence, ought not live merely to consume them.

The *Esquimaux*, who inhabit the northern parts of the country, are a race similar to the Greenlanders. They have a deep tawny or rather copper-coloured complexion; and are inferior in size to the generality of Europeans.

Their faces are flat, and their noses short. Their hair is black and coarse; and their hands and feet are remarkably small. Their dress, like that of the mountaineers, is entirely of skins; and consists of a sort of hooded shirt, of breeches, stockings, and boots. The dress of the different sexes is similar, except that the women wear large boots, and have their upper garment ornamented with a kind of tail. In their boots they occasionally place their children; but the youngest child is always carried at the back of its mother, in the hood of her jacket. The women ornament their heads with large strings of beads, which they fasten to the hair above their ears.

The weapons of these Esquimaux are darts, bows, and arrows; and their food consists chiefly of the flesh of seals, deer, and birds; and of fish. Some of their canoes are near twenty feet in length, and not more than two feet wide. They each contain only one person; are formed of a frame-work, covered with skins; and are so extremely light, that they are easily overset. Notwithstanding this, and the circumstance that few of the Esquimaux are able to swim, these people are able to navigate them, in safety, without a compass, and even in the thickest fogs. When the ground is covered with snow, they traverse the country in sledges, drawn by dogs.

During winter, they live in houses, or rather in a kind of cavern, which they sink in the earth; and, during summer, they occupy tents, made circular with poles, and covered with skins. Their only beverage is water. The men are extremely indolent; and all the laborious occupations, except that of procuring food, are performed by the women. They sew with the sinews of deer; and much of their needlework is very neat. The Esquimaux cannot reckon, numerically, beyond six; and their compound numbers reach no further than 21: all beyond this are called a multitude.

The principal articles of export, obtained from the coast of Labrador, are cod-fish, salmon, oil, whalebone, and furs of various kinds.

NEWFOUNDLAND.

Near the south-eastern extremity of Labrador is the island of *Newfoundland*; which, at present, constitutes an important station, for the British cod-fisheries. It is of triangular form, and about three hundred miles in circuit; and, though it lies between the same parallels of latitude as the south of France, its climate is very severe. In winter the rivers are frozen to the thickness of several feet; and, during this season, the earth is covered with snow, and the cold is so intense that the power of vegetation is destroyed. The coasts abound in creeks, roads, and harbours; and the interior of the island is full of steep rocks, woody hills, and sandy valleys; and of plains, interspersed with rocks, lakes, and marshes. A very small portion of it is at present cultivated; for neither the soil nor the climate is favourable to productions necessary to the support of human life. *St. John's*, the chief town of the island, is a mean and ill-built place, with narrow and dirty streets. It is situated on the south-eastern part of the coast, and has a considerable harbour.

This island formerly belonged to the French; but, in 1713, it was ceded to the English, to whom it still belongs. Its chief importance is derived from its vicinity to an immense bank, beneath the surface of the ocean, which is frequented by myriads of cod-fish. On this bank there are annually employed more than two thousand fishing-vessels; and four hundred merchant-ships, in conveying the fish to different parts of the world. All the fish are caught by lines; and they are conveyed to the shores of Newfoundland, to be salted and dried, or otherwise prepared for exportation. The Newfoundland fishery usually commences about the middle of May, and continues till the end of September.

GREENLAND,

Is an extensive peninsula, or, as some geographers believe, an immense island, lying north of the 60th degree of latitude, and between the 48th and 70th degrees of west longitude. It is said to have been originally discovered, as early as the tenth century, by a party of exiled Icelanders, who gave to it the name of "Greenland," from its exhibiting a much greater appearance of verdure than Iceland. *Cape Farewell*, its southernmost point, is a small island divided from the shore by a narrow inlet.

The interior of the country is dreary and mountainous; and some of the mountains are so lofty, that they are visible to the distance of more than forty leagues. They are covered with perpetual snow; and ice and snow, like the glaciers of Switzerland, fill the elevated plains, and even many of the valleys. The lowlands, adjacent to the sea-coast, are clothed with verdure during the summer season. The coast is indented with many bays and creeks, which extend far into the land; but many parts of it are altogether inaccessible by shipping, on account of the enormous masses of floating ice, which abound in the extreme northern seas.

Christian Missionaries were settled in this country, by the Danes, many centuries ago; and they formed churches and monasteries in different parts, through an extent of country nearly two hundred miles in length. From authentic records it appears that Greenland was anciently divided into two districts, the westernmost of which contained four parishes and one hundred villages; and the other, twelve parishes, one hundred and twenty villages, the see of a bishop, and two monasteries. The present inhabitants of the western districts are, however, separated from those of the east by impassable deserts and mountains.

This country is subject to Denmark; and the parts of it that are chiefly visited by Danes and Norwegians, lie between the 64th and 68th degrees of north latitude; and, to this distance, the climate is said not to be very severe. At one time there was a Danish factory as far north as the 73d degree; but, beyond the 68th degree of latitude, the cold in winter is, in general, so intense, that even the rocks burst by the expansive power of the frost. Thunder and lightning seldom occur in Greenland; but the aurora borealis is frequently visible, particularly in the spring of the year; and is often so bright and vivid, as to afford sufficient light for a person to read by it.

Some of the southern parts of Greenland are fertile; but, in general, the soil resembles that of other mountainous countries; the hills being barren, and the valleys and low grounds being rich and fruitful. The principal quadrupeds of this country are rein-deer, dogs resembling wolves, Arctic foxes, and white or polar bears. The walrus and several kinds of seals frequent the shores. Eagles and other birds of prey are numerous. Whales and porpesses abound along the coasts; and the adjacent sea and bays yield an abundance of holibut, turbot, cod, haddocks, and other fish.

The inhabitants of Greenland are supposed to have had their origin from the Esquimaux of Labrador, for they nearly resemble that people. They are short, and somewhat corpulent; and have broad faces, flat noses, thick lips, black hair, and a yellowish tawny complexion. The keenness of the wind and the glare of the snow, render them subject to painful disorders in the eyes: they are also afflicted with many diseases, which tend to render them short lived. They are a quiet, orderly, and good-humoured people; but of a cold, phlegmatic, and indolent disposition. They never wash themselves with water, but lick their hands, and then rub their faces with them; in the same manner as a cat washes herself with her paws. In most of their habits they are extremely filthy.

When animal food can be procured, they prefer it to any other; but, in times of scarcity, they are sometimes compelled to subsist on sea-weeds, and on roots dressed in train-oil and fat. The intestines of animals, and offals of various kinds, are accounted by them as dainties.

Their clothes are chiefly made of the skins of rein-deer and seals. The men wear their hair short; and commonly hanging down from the crown of the head on every side. The women, on the contrary, seldom cut their hair.

The Greenlanders all speak the same language, though different dialects prevail in different parts of the country; and so numerous are the words of their language, that, like the Chinese, they are said to have a proper word for every object or art that requires distinction.

These people have no traditions respecting the memorable actions of their ancestors; further than that, many winters ago, some Norwegian settlers were slain by the population of the adjacent country, who unanimously rose in arms against them. Among other strange notions entertained by the Greenlanders, they imagine that rain is occasioned by the overflowing of reservoirs in the heavens; and they assert that, if the banks of these reservoirs should burst, the sky would fall down. The medical practice in this country is confined to a set of men who have the appellation of "Angekoks," or conjurers.

When a Greenlander is at the point of death, his friends and relatives array him in his best clothes and boots. They silently bewail him for an hour, after which they prepare for his interment. The body, having been sewed up in his best seal or deer-skin, is laid in the burying-place, covered with a skin, and with green sods; and, over these, with heaps of stones, to defend it from the attack of predaceous animals. Near the place of interment, the survivors deposit the weapons of the deceased, and the tools he daily used. With the women are deposited their knives and sewing implements. The intention in so doing is, that the person departed may not be without employment in the next world.

The Greenlanders are said to worship the sun, and to offer sacrifices to an imaginary evil spirit, that he may not prevent their success in hunting and fishing. They have a confused notion respecting the immortality of the soul, and the existence of a future state; and they believe that the spirits of deceased persons sometimes appear on the earth, and hold communication with the "Angekoks," or conjurers, to whom peculiar privileges and honours belong.

The traffic that is carried on among the Greenlanders is simple and concise, and is wholly conducted by exchange or barter. These people very rarely cheat or take undue advantage of one another; and it is considered infamous to be guilty of theft. But they are said to glory in over-reaching or robbing an European; as they consider this a proof of superior talent and ingenuity.

Wherever a great assembly or rendezvous of Greenlanders takes place, as at a dancing-match or any grand festival, there are always some persons who expose their wares to view, and who publicly announce what goods they want in exchange for them. The chief articles of traffic, with Europeans, are fox and seal-skins, whale and seal-oil, whalebone, and the horns of narwhals. For these, they receive, in exchange, iron points for their spears, knives, saws, gimlets, chisels, needles, chests, boxes, clothing, and utensils of various kinds.

The chief festival of the Greenlanders is that which they call the sun-feast; but this is merely held for the purpose of dancing and other amusements, and not for any religious acts or ceremonies. It is held about the commencement of the new-year, and for the purpose of rejoicing at the return of the sun, and the renewal of weather for hunting and fishing. At this feast they assemble, in various parts of the country, and in large parties. After gorging themselves with food, they rise up to play and to dance. Their only musical instrument is a drum; and the sound of this they accompany with songs, in honour of seal-catching, and exploits in hunting. The Greenlanders do not, on these occasions, intoxicate themselves with ardent spirits, like some of the American Indians; for their only beverage is water. There are other dancing-meetings held in the course of the year; but these are all conducted in a similar manner. The Greenlanders occupy much of their time in hunting and fishing. On shore they hunt rein-deer and other animals; and at sea they pursue whales, seals, and walruses: they also catch great quantities of fish and sea-fowl. Their canoes are formed of thin boards, fastened together by the sinews of animals, and covered with a dressed seal-skin, both above and below; so that only a circular hole is left in the middle, large enough to admit the body of one man. Into this hole he thrusts himself, up to the waist; after which he fastens the skin so tight round his body, that no water can enter. Thus secured, and armed with a paddle, which is broad at both ends, he ventures out to sea, even in the most stormy weather; and, if he be unfortunate enough to have his canoe overset, he can easily raise himself by means of his paddle. Besides this description of canoes, the Greenlanders have boats so large that they will contain fifty persons, with all their tackle, baggage, and provisions. These carry a mast and a triangular sail; the latter of which is made of the membranes and entrails of seals. The management of the larger boats is always given to women; who also perform the whole drudgery of the household, even to the building and repairing of the dwellings.

During winter, the Greenlanders live in houses, and, during the summer, in tents. The houses are constructed of stones, with layers of earth and sods between them; and the rafters are covered with bushes and turf. The entrance is through a hole in the roof, which serves also as a chimney. The walls are hung with skins, fastened on by pegs, made of the bones of seals. These huts are divided, by skins, into several apartments, according to the number of families which inhabit them; and the inhabitants sleep on skins, upon the ground. The huts are well warmed with fires; and are lighted by lamps, filled with train oil, and furnished with moss instead of a wick. These lamps burn so bright as to give considerable heat as well as warmth.

At the outside of the dwelling-house are separate buildings, for store-houses, in which the inhabitants lay up their stock of provisions, train oil, and other useful articles. Near the store-houses they arrange their boats, with the bottoms upward; and they hang beneath these their hunting and fishing-tackle, and their skins. The summer-tents of the Greenlanders are of a conical form, and are constructed of poles, covered, both inside and out, with skins.

The seas in the vicinity of Greenland are, every year, frequented by both European and American vessels, employed in the whale-fishery. Such of these as enter Davis's Strait, generally resort to Disco Bay; and a few have penetrated even still further north than this. It is stated that, in the year 1754, a whaler, under the command of a Captain Wilson, was conducted, on the eastern side of Greenland, as far north as to the 83d degree of latitude: the sea was clear of ice, as far as the commander of this ship could descry; but as he did not meet with any whales, and began to apprehend some danger from proceeding onward, he returned; and, in the same year, another whale-fisher sailed as far north as to 84½ degrees. These are the highest northern latitudes which any vessels have hitherto reached.